D1692700

The Sociable City

THE ARTS AND INTELLECTUAL LIFE
IN MODERN AMERICA

Casey Nelson Blake, Series Editor

Volumes in the series explore questions at the intersection of the history of expressive culture and the history of ideas in modern America. The series is meant as a bold intervention in two fields of cultural inquiry. It challenges scholars in American studies and cultural studies to move beyond sociological categories of analysis to consider the ideas that have informed and given form to artistic expression—whether architecture and the visual arts or music, dance, theater, and literature. The series also expands the domain of intellectual history by examining how artistic works, and aesthetic experience more generally, participate in the discussion of truth and value, civic purpose, and personal meaning that have engaged scholars since the late nineteenth century.

Advisory Board: Steven Conn, Lynn Garafola, Charles McGovern, Angela L. Miller, Penny M. Von Eschen, David M. Scobey, and Richard Cándida Smith.

THE SOCIABLE CITY

An American Intellectual Tradition

Jamin Creed Rowan

PENN

UNIVERSITY OF PENNSYLVANIA PRESS

PHILADELPHIA

Copyright © 2017 University of Pennsylvania Press

All rights reserved. Except for brief quotations used for purposes of review or scholarly citation, none of this book may be reproduced in any form by any means without written permission from the publisher.

Published by
University of Pennsylvania Press
Philadelphia, Pennsylvania 19104-4112
www.upenn.edu/pennpress

Printed in the United States of America on acid-free paper
1 3 5 7 9 10 8 6 4 2

Library of Congress Cataloging-in-Publication Data

Names: Rowan, Jamin Creed, author.
Title: The sociable city: an American intellectual tradition / Jamin Creed Rowan.
Other titles: Arts and intellectual life in modern America.
Description: 1st edition. | Philadelphia : University of Pennsylvania Press, [2017] | Series: The arts and intellectual life in modern America | Includes bibliographical references and index.
Identifiers: LCCN 2016050508 | ISBN 9780812249293 (hardcover: alk. paper)
Subjects: LCSH: City planning—Social aspects—United States—History—19th century. | City planning—Social aspects—United States—History—20th century. | Urban ecology (Sociology)—United States—History—19th century. | Urban ecology (Sociology)—United States—History—20th century. | City and own life—United States—Psychological aspects—History—19th century. | City and town life—United States—Psychological aspects—History—20th century. | Public spaces—Social aspects—United States—History—19th century. | Public spaces—Social aspects—United States—History—20th century.
Classification: LCC HT167 .R69 2017 | DDC 307.1/216097309034—dc23
LC record available at https://lccn.loc.gov/2016050508

CONTENTS

Introduction. Finding Fellow-Feeling in the City	1
Chapter 1. The Settlement Movement's Push for Public Sympathy	15
Chapter 2. New Deal Urbanism and the Contraction of Sympathy	42
Chapter 3. Literary Urbanists and the Interwar Development of Urban Sociability	75
Chapter 4. The Ecology of Sociability in the Postwar City	98
Chapter 5. Jane Jacobs and the Consolidation of Urban Sociability	124
Conclusion. The Future of Urban Sociability	154
Notes	161
Index	187
Acknowledgments	193

The Sociable City

INTRODUCTION

Finding Fellow-Feeling in the City

On February 25, 1870, Frederick Law Olmsted addressed the American Social Science Association at Boston's Lowell Institute. As a result of his leadership in the design, construction, and ongoing operation of New York City's Central Park during the late 1850s and throughout the 1860s, Olmsted had become one of the nation's most vocal interpreters of urban life. Although he would eventually try to persuade his Bostonian listeners of the civic value of building their own version of Central Park, he began his speech by telling them what they, no doubt, already knew—that the processes of urbanization that had radically reshaped their city would continue to transform the nation's landscape. Unlike many of his fellow urbanists, Olmsted was only mildly troubled by the "amount of disease and misery and of vice and crime" to be found in cities, assured that "modern Science" would quickly fix these problems. He expressed much more concern for the city's corrosive effects on the social interactions among its inhabitants. In what may be one of the earliest and most genteel descriptions of road rage, Olmsted explained that when he and those gathered to hear him walked "through the denser part of a town, to merely avoid collision with those we meet and pass upon the sidewalks, we have constantly to watch, to foresee, and to guard against their movements." Such navigational wariness demanded of urban pedestrians a careful "consideration of [others'] intentions, a calculation of their strength and weakness, which is not so much for their benefit as our own." On the city's streets and sidewalks, Olmsted fretted, "our minds are thus brought into close dealings with other minds without any friendly flowing toward them, but rather a drawing from them." The city's built environment encouraged those who moved through it to regard each other "in a hard if not always hardening way." Olmsted despairingly informed those gathered at the Lowell Institute that the mentally and emotionally "restraining and confining conditions" of the city he had just described compelled city dwellers like themselves to "look closely upon others without sympathy."[1]

Olmsted was simply telling his audience what many had already been saying, and would continue to say, about urban life—that the city dramatically changes the way individuals interact with and feel toward one another. In expressing their deep concerns about the ability of city dwellers to connect with one another in emotionally and socially satisfying ways, Olmsted contributed to an increasingly robust antiurbanist discourse that would pervade American culture for years to come. Antiurbanism in the United States has always had at its core the accusation that city life inevitably entails what Steven Conn describes as the "loss of intimate social relations" and "nurturing communities." Although the language with which antiurbanists have accused the modern city of being incompatible with socially and emotionally legitimate relationships has evolved over time, this discourse has tended to revolve around the assumption that city dwellers could not develop fellow-feelings for one another. Olmsted was neither the first nor the last observer of city life to suggest that the interactions and affiliations among those who encountered one another in the city's public spaces were emotionally hollow and socially insignificant.[2]

Like many other nineteenth-century urbanists, Olmsted articulated his particular misgivings about the social side effects of urban life through the language and logic of sympathy. By the mid-nineteenth century, the concept of sympathy had become for most Americans the social ideal against which they evaluated nearly every type of interaction and relationship. Closely informed by the writings of Scottish moral philosophers such as Adam Smith, Archibald Alison, and Hugh Blair, the U.S. culture of sympathy had taken shape since colonial times in a wide variety of political, religious, educational, and cultural settings. To invoke the concept of sympathy during this time period was to draw on a wide range of cultural sources and intellectual traditions, but perhaps none of these influenced the formation of sentimental culture in the United States more powerfully than Smith's foundational explication of sympathy in *The Theory of Moral Sentiments* (1759). Smith famously characterized sympathy as the imaginative process through which an individual acquires a "fellow-feeling" for another being. Because "we have no immediate experience of what other men feel," Smith explained, "we can form no idea of the manner in which they are affected, but by conceiving what we ourselves should feel in the like situation." Through the use of their "imagination," individuals "enter as it were" into another's body and, in so doing, "become in some measure the same person with him, and thence form some idea of his sensations, and even feel something which, though weaker in degree, is not altogether unlike them." While Smith was quick to admit that the most one could hope to achieve through an "imaginary change of situation" is a feeling "analogous" to that experienced by the object of one's sympathy, not an exact replica, he nevertheless suggested that the emotional connection between individuals generated through this "extremely imperfect" and emotionally imprecise process qualified as "fellow-feeling."[3]

Since the publication of Smith's seminal account of sympathy's affective operations, the term has been used to signify both the process by which individuals acquire a fellow-feeling for others and the emotional product of that process. Teasing apart the sympathetic process from its affective outcome helps clarify the complexion of the particular paradigms through which Olmsted and other nineteenth-century urbanists appraised urban life. These urban intellectuals worried that the early industrial city—with its influx of migrants and immigrants, the cultural instability and economic volatility that attended this in-migration, and its still relatively compact urban form—fundamentally interfered with the sympathetic process by discouraging urbanites from imagining themselves in the situations of those around them. Olmsted, in particular, worried that the built environment that molded Boston's public realm in 1870—an environment that was still shaped primarily by the need of residents to reach their daily destinations on foot—prevented those it sheltered from inhabiting the sympathetic imagination.[4] Given the perpetually crowded sidewalks on which urbanites most frequently encountered one another in public, they were more likely to "guard against" the "movements" of other pedestrians than form some idea of their sensations; instead of engaging "with other minds" in a way that would extend a "friendly flowing toward them," city dwellers would inwardly experience a "hardening" of their feelings for their fellow urbanites. Furthermore, Olmsted reasoned that, even if pedestrians wanted to imagine themselves in another's situation, they would have difficulty doing so because they typically had "no experience of anything in common" with those they encountered on the city's overcrowded sidewalks. In short, Olmsted argued that the early industrial city undermined the ability of its inhabitants to make the sympathetic leap across the increasingly wide social, economic, and cultural chasms that separated them from one another.[5]

If nineteenth-century urbanists were concerned about the opportunities for individuals to participate in the sympathetic process while navigating the early industrial city's public sphere, they were perhaps even more anxious about the ability of city residents to acquire the specific brand of fellow-feelings privileged by their culture—affections that might, according to Elizabeth Barnes, be said to fall under the category of "familial feeling."[6] For many of Olmsted's contemporaries, a fellow-feeling could only qualify as a sympathetic feeling if it were qualitatively similar to the emotions that one might have for a family member or close friend: love, intimacy, brotherhood, sisterhood. Many nineteenth-century writers insisted that sympathetic emotions would enable individuals to experience social relationships as if they were familial ones. But in place of the familial feelings on which Olmsted and others felt strong social relationships and healthy communities should be built, Olmsted perceived that urbanites felt "vigilance, wariness, and activity" toward those they encountered on the city's streets.[7] His distress that individuals who encountered one another in the early industrial city's public spaces would inevitably "look closely upon others without sympathy" echoes the concerns shared by many of his fellow urbanists about the inability of those inhabiting the industrial city to acquire familial feelings for one another. City observers would continue to rest their cases against urban life on the claim that sympathy was hard to come by in the city.

Like many urbanists who would follow Olmsted, his diagnosis of the city's social shortcomings drove him to modify its built environment. His particular understanding of the process by which individuals acquire fellow-feelings and his expectations of the relational forms that those affections ought to assume motivated him to create public urban spaces in which city dwellers would be more likely to attain fellow-feelings for one another than they were on walking the city's congested streets. Olmsted responded to what he perceived to be the impossibility of experiencing sympathy in the city by designing and constructing urban parks. He intended his parks to "completely shut out the city" and, in so doing, to provide their users with spaces where "they may stroll for an hour, seeing, hearing, and feeling nothing of the bustle and jar of the streets." By providing urbanites with a "broad, open space of clean greensward" in which they could walk without having to "guard against" others' movements and smaller nooks into which they could "bivouac at frequent intervals ... without discommoding one another," Olmsted's parks gave urbanites opportunities to participate in the sympathetic process and establish familial feelings for one another.[8] Although his parks operated within the public realm, Olmsted designed them to behave almost as if they were private domestic spaces that allowed city dwellers to place themselves in another's situation. Unlike the smaller parks and public squares that punctuated the antebellum city and that provided places for what Mary P. Ryan describes as "informal, casual, largely unplanned social interaction," Olmsted's great parks promised users a more carefully managed and intimate social experience.[9] Olmsted explained to the American Social Science Association that he intended his parks to reproduce the social atmosphere of the home by giving "play to faculties such as may be dormant in business or on the promenade"—faculties and feelings that facilitated the "close relation of family life, the association of children, of mothers, of lovers, of those who may be lovers." He wanted to create public spaces that would "stimulate and keep alive the more tender sympathies." The scores of urban parks Olmsted designed throughout the country expressed his powerful desires to help city dwellers achieve the intimate and tender relationships that he and his culture valued most.[10]

Olmsted's evaluation of the interactions among urbanites in the city's public spaces and his subsequent efforts to reshape the city's built environment model a pattern of thinking about and acting within the city that other urban intellectuals would pursue in the coming years—a pattern that this book will trace over the course of the century following Olmsted's speech to the American Social Science Association. In Olmsted's wake, a long line of religious leaders, novelists, playwrights, journalists, social scientists, community activists, municipal and federal politicians, city planners, and others worried in their own particular ways about the ability of city dwellers to attain fellow-feelings for one another. While subsequent urbanists were equally invested in the affective quality of the interactions and relationships among urbanites in the city's public spaces, they had very different understandings of the city's role in frustrating or facilitating meaningful social relations among its inhabitants. Like Olmsted, many of the urban intellectuals who followed him wanted city dwellers to experience fellow-feelings for one another. But some of them thought quite differently about the processes by which those fellow-feelings could be realized and the particular interpersonal emotions that best signified those feelings. That is to say, not all urbanists thought that city dwellers ought to feel toward one another the same way that relatives and close friends felt about each other, nor did they sense that the ability of urbanites to obtain fellow-feelings for each other depended on their ability to imagine themselves in the situations of others.

This book, in fact, is primarily interested in the efforts of late nineteenth- and twentieth-century urbanists to call attention to and legitimize the

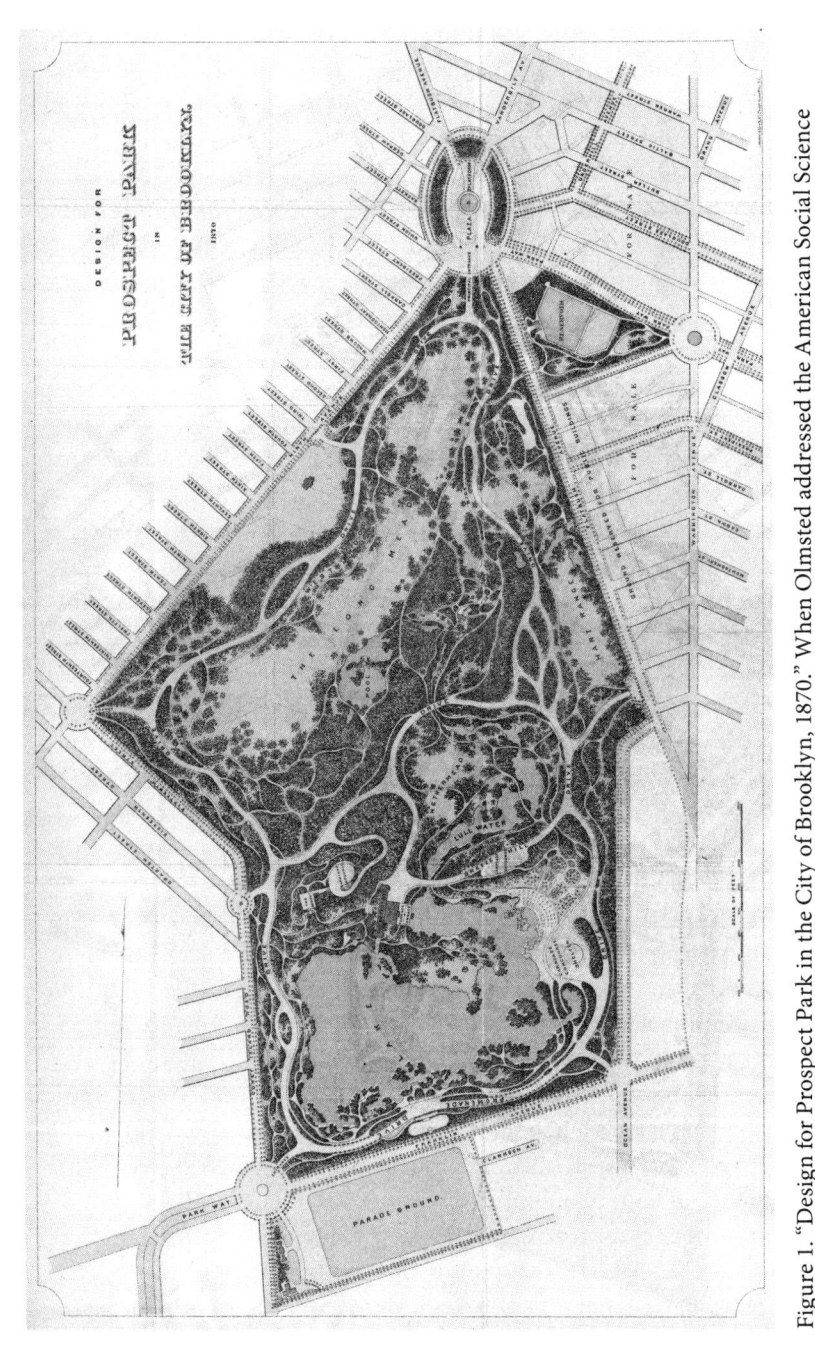

Figure 1. "Design for Prospect Park in the City of Brooklyn, 1870." When Olmsted addressed the American Social Science Association at Boston's Lowell Institute in 1870, he and Calvert Vaux had recently designed Prospect Park. The park had opened to the public in 1867 and would remain under construction until 1873. Prospect Park contains many of the classic design elements Olmsted deployed to shut out the city and restore sympathy to urban relationships.

fellow-feelings and relationships that city dwellers cultivated in the very streets from which Olmsted sought to remove them. Because their culture had emphasized the desirability of private, intimate relationships for so long, urbanists struggled to find ways to capture and validate the less intimate, more casual interactions and fellow-feelings that physically and emotionally connected urbanites to one another. "Intimacy," Richard Sennett observes, has operated in our culture's imagination as a type of "tyranny" in that it has created a "belief in one standard of truth to measure the complexities of social reality."[11] The urban intellectuals that appear in the pages that follow bumped up against and grappled with intimacy's conceptual tyranny in their attempts to diversify the standards with which the public might assign value to the multiplicity of relational forms and affections that inevitably arise among urbanites within the city's public spaces. As the U.S. city's physical and social landscapes evolved over the course of the late nineteenth and twentieth centuries, urban intellectuals developed new vocabularies, narratives, and representational forms through which they might acknowledge the social and emotional value of a wide variety of interactions among city dwellers.

The Sociable City sets out to map the evolution of an urbanist discourse that initially remained tethered to the concept of sympathy but that shifted over the course of the first half of the twentieth century to revolve around the idea of sociability. The pages that follow track the evolution of a structure of sympathetic fellow-feeling and emergence of a structure of sociable fellow-feeling in U.S. urbanist discourse. If, as Raymond Williams has written, a "structure of feeling" refers to the "elements of social and material (physical or natural) experience" within which "meanings and values . . . are actively lived and felt," this book examines the work of urban intellectuals who drew attention to the new ways in which city dwellers were navigating the shifting social and material elements of the late nineteenth- and twentieth-century U.S. city in order to experience fellow-feelings with those around them.[12] Of course, the structures of sympathetic fellow-feeling Olmsted and other nineteenth-century urbanists embraced shifted and persisted well into the twentieth century and the urbanist discourses that embraced sympathy as the ideal form of fellow-feeling continued to shape the city's built environment. But structures of sociable fellow-feeling became increasingly visible in twentieth-century urbanist discourse as observers of city life sought to make sense of the new social and material experiences available within the rapidly changing U.S. city. As urbanists confronted the inadequacy of the language and logic of sympathy to capture the significance of the many different forms of affiliation forged among city dwellers, they developed new patterns for talking about and assessing the social value of those affiliations.

As U.S. urbanists established a different set of expectations about what kinds of interdependencies among city dwellers mattered, they approached the expansion and redevelopment of the city's built environment in very different ways than did Olmsted and those like him who valued intimate relationships. These urbanists sought to modify the city in order to better facilitate sociable interactions among city dwellers in public spaces and therefore to cultivate a very different set of fellow-feelings than the tender, familial fellow-feelings that Olmsted had placed at the center of his approach to urban landscape design. The structure of sociable fellow-feeling that emerged and gained currency within twentieth-century urbanist discourse inspired city makers both to preserve particular elements of the industrial cityscape and to construct new urban infrastructure. Those who privileged sociable relationships in their vision of urban life strove to create a very different kind of built environment than did those who felt that intimate relationships were the only relationships worth promoting. Intimacy tends to require private spaces, whereas sociability tends to flourish in public and semi-public spaces. While understanding the ways in which structures of sympathetic and sociable fellow-feeling shaped the physical structure of cities does not explain everything about the development and redevelopment of the U.S. cityscape, this understanding does allow us to make more sense of why city planners, developers, and politicians have endorsed certain urban forms and designs above others.

The Sociable City attempts to trace the effect of the mental and physical work carried out by a variety of urbanists on the U.S. culture's urban imaginary and the landscapes that this imaginary has produced. It provides an intellectual and cultural history of the efforts of urbanists to assess the affective quality of the interactions among city dwellers in public spaces and of the ways in which those assessments have shaped the U.S. city's built environment. At the heart of this project, then, is the claim that our society's decisions about what kinds of interpersonal affections matter most have determined the kinds of cities that we have created. This assertion is a slightly more refined version of Jane Jacobs's pronouncement in *The Death and Life of Great American Cities* that "private investment shapes cities, but social ideas (and laws) shape private investment. First comes the image of what we want, then the machinery is adapted to turn out that image."[13] This book investigates the history of what we have wanted urban relationships to look like and considers how those desires have shaped the cities in which we live. It carries out this investigation primarily by turning to source materials that tend to be overlooked by those who have made it their business to write about the history of urban life and thought: memoirs, plays, novels, literary journalism, and museum exhibits. Contrary to Morton and Lucia White's insistence that it would be "extremely difficult to cull ... a large anthology of poetry or social philosophy in celebration of American urban life," this book contends that there is an expansive body of literary, cultural, and philosophical work dedicated to exploring and advocating the social configurations made possible by the city.[14] Many of the urbanists that populate this book strove to legitimize the interactions and relationships among city dwellers that have been seen for far too long as socially and emotionally illegitimate.

The intellectual and cultural history that I construct in the pages that follow maps a transition within the tradition of U.S. urbanism from outlooks that privileged sympathetic structures of fellow-feeling to those that prioritized sociable structures of fellow-feeling. During the late nineteenth and early twentieth centuries, urbanists would, as the first two chapters demonstrate, continue to draw on and modify the language and logic of sympathy in their efforts to assess the wide variety of associations into which city dwellers entered. I pick up this history with the turn-of-the-century U.S. settlement movement. Settlement workers such as Jane Addams, who had chosen to live in the industrial city's densest immigrant neighborhoods, called attention to the need for the city dweller to "make new channels through which his sympathy may flow." Unlike Olmsted, Addams and other settlement figures such as Lillian Wald, Mary Kingsbury Simkhovitch, and W. E. B. Du Bois argued that urbanites could experience fellow-feelings for one another within the industrial city's congested neighborhoods. While settlement workers sought to expand the range of affections that might be considered to adequately connect city dwellers to one another—Addams saw what she called "cosmopolitan affection" as distinct from and more desirable than the familial feelings valued in nineteenth-century sentimental culture—they still favored face-to-face interactions as the source from which valid fellow-feelings might spring.[15] Although friend, neighbor, and citizen (rather than brother and sister) functioned as the relational forms that best captured the types of fellow-feelings promoted within settlement discourse, settlement workers sought to create spaces that would, like Olmsted's parks, allow city dwellers to come into close contact with one another in a somewhat domesticated environment. The urban house served not only as the literal center of settlement work—the place where settlement workers lived communally and from which they carried out many of their community-improvement activities and sociological studies—but also as the movement's spatial ideal. The cafés, kindergartens, theaters, and other public and semi-public spaces that settlement workers created in urban neighborhoods were extensions (sometimes literally so) of the settlement home and were designed to provide a place in which urbanites could cultivate friendships with one another.

As settlement leaders and other early twentieth-century thinkers continued to expand the concept of sympathy in order to accommodate the social and affective dynamics of a variety of relationships, other urban intellectuals pursued an urbanist discourse of sympathy that accentuated the singular importance of relationships founded on emotional intimacy. Nowhere was this strain of urban sympathy more visible than in the public housing movement of the 1920s and '30s. Despite the encouragement of public housing advocates such as Catherine Bauer to consider the needs of society more broadly, many social scientists, city planners, politicians, and other urbanists responded to the social ills facing the early twentieth-century city—overcrowding, decaying infrastructure, and unaffordable urban housing—by stressing the need to provide spaces in which city dwellers could maintain the close familial relationships that these social ills appeared to threaten. Many public housing proponents contended not only that better, more affordable housing would improve relationships within families but also that these new structures would create the physical environment in which unrelated urbanites might acquire familial feelings for each other. As the Federal Theatre Project's production of Arthur Arent's *One-Third of a Nation* (1938) made clear, the passage of the U.S. Housing Act of 1937—which created the political mechanisms through which cities received federal funds for slum clearance and low-income housing construction—signaled the codification in federal policy and, subsequently, in the city's built environment of a relatively narrow and conventional understanding of fellow-feelings.[16] Despite the efforts of some settlement workers, social scientists, and public housing activists to use the language and logic of sympathy to account for a range of fellow-feelings that connected city dwellers to one another, New Deal political ideologies and cultural narratives calcified the conceptual possibilities of sympathy in such a way that an urbanist discourse that revolved around sympathy became nearly incapable of signifying and privileging anything other than emotionally intimate relationships. In its codified and calcified form, the urbanist discourse of sympathy facilitated an approach to urban redevelopment that sacrificed local streets, small commercial establishments, community gathering places, and other public spaces for the construction of housing projects, large commercial developments, public works, and highways—an approach that was primarily invested in the development of private spaces and that would sustain the nation's urban renewal agenda for decades to come.

While the deep intellectual and cultural traditions that supported an urbanist discourse of sympathy continued to inform conversations about the nature of affiliations among city dwellers, urban intellectuals in the middle decades of the twentieth century began to develop what I have chosen to call a discourse of sociability. Aware of the increasing inability of an urbanist discourse based on sympathy to account for and validate interactions among urbanites in public spaces that did not necessarily engender intimacy but that nevertheless generated fellow-feelings, urbanists cultivated alternative ways of thinking and talking about the broad spectrum of social processes and emotions that might activate and signify fellow-feelings. The final three chapters of this book trace the emergence of this discourse of sociability. The fellow-feelings that the urbanists who contributed to this discourse made visible and valuable belonged to the public domain's affective orbit rather than the private sphere's emotional loop. Perhaps no other group of urban intellectuals more single-mindedly developed the discourse of urban sociability than the first wave of city journalists at the *New Yorker*—journalists such as E. B. White, Meyer Berger, Joseph Mitchell, and A. J. Liebling. Compared to the intense interpersonal emotions commonly associated with sympathy, the types of fellow-feelings that *New Yorker* reporters claimed connected city dwellers to one another in the public realm were relatively mild and modest. The urban intellectuals who operated within the discursive framework of sociability called attention to the ways the emotional impulse to appreciate, cooperate with, protect, or simply recognize another human being were capable of linking urbanites to one another in emotionally meaningful and socially satisfying ways—even when those affections did not result in brotherhood, sisterhood, or friendship. The urbanist discourse of sociability that these writers began to develop at the *New Yorker* clarified and gave credibility to the affective processes entailed in what Iris Marion Young describes as the "being together of strangers."[17]

Although the discourse of sociability emerged in the pages of the *New Yorker* and in urban tenement novels such as Betty Smith's *A Tree Grows in*

Brooklyn (1943) during the interwar period, its distinct approach to making sense of urban relationships found its clearest rationale in the relatively young science of ecology.[18] In the postwar years, many urban intellectuals turned to the evolving discipline of ecology to extend the public's understanding of the affective dimensions and relational possibilities of the interrelationships among city dwellers. Ecologically minded urbanists tapped into mid-century ecology's new cache of scientific data and social terminology to call attention to the types of cooperative relationships among city dwellers about which *New Yorker* journalists and tenement novelists had written. The ecological discourse that these urbanists drew on—a discourse popularized by individuals such as Rachel Carson and institutions such as the American Museum of Natural History—further illuminated and validated the kinds of interdependencies among urbanites who were not necessarily familiar with one another but who shared the same urban environment. New ecological research that emerged during the interwar and postwar periods also pushed urban intellectuals to recognize that the breadth and depth of the interdependencies that connected city dwellers to one another were far more extensive than city journalists, tenement novelists, and others had realized. Mid-century urbanists who took up ecological habits of thinking saw new kinds of interrelations among urbanites—especially among those who did not physically or socially interact with one another in, but who still shared, the city's public realm. Ecological urbanists were quick to point out that, while individuals might attain fellow-feelings for those with whom they shared the city through face-to-face interactions, they might just as easily feel sociable toward those with whom they had never personally interacted. They suggested that the kind of "being together of strangers" capable of producing fellow-feelings did not necessarily require the physical and temporal co-presence of strangers.

This ecologically inflected discourse of sociability offered community activists, city planners, and politicians an image of the city that helped them challenge the ways in which urban renewal projects were remaking the city's built environment and disrupting its social orders. Rather than demand the creation of alternative spaces or the construction of better private ones, the discourse of sociability called for the preservation of the public spaces within which the interdependencies among urbanites had been established and continued to operate. To tear down a building or remove a street to make room for a civic center or highway, ecological urbanists argued, was to upset a multitude of fragile relationships in impossible-to-anticipate ways and thus to throw the city's delicate social ecosystem out of balance. Those who valued the city's informal and often invisible social networks insisted that preserving and creating a physically diverse built environment would be critical if the city were to sustain the somewhat less emotionally intense fellow-feelings capable of binding an increasingly diverse population of city dwellers to one another. Perhaps no urbanist articulated the discourse of sociability and its spatial implications more precisely or persuasively than Jane Jacobs, one of the twentieth century's most important city planners and urban writers. Jacobs synthesized and elaborated the discourse of urban sociability, giving the somewhat discrete attempts of previous urbanists to characterize urban affiliations as emotionally and socially significant the sensibility of a cultural formation. I argue that the publication of *The Death and Life of Great American Cities* signaled the consolidation and popularization of an urbanist discourse of sociability.

The intellectual and cultural history that this book provides illuminates a more nuanced and enriched vocabulary for understanding the nature of social interactions within the history of U.S. urban thought. For too long, urbanists and historians have filtered their appraisals of the quality of social interactions among urbanites through inadequate urban types or oversimplified categories. For many, the figure of the *flâneur* has provided the primary critical angle into discussions about the affective dimensions of social exchanges among city dwellers in public spaces. The *flâneur* views other urbanites as commodities to be consumed rather than as individuals to whom he has emotional or ethical obligations.[19] Early twentieth-century urban sociology reduced the multiplicity of relational forms into which city dwellers might enter to two categories: primary and secondary relationships. Sociology's dyadic approach to urban sociality, along with its assessments of primary (superior) and secondary (inferior) relationships, persisted in urbanist thought for much of the twentieth century.[20] More recently, urbanists have been too eager to measure the value of affiliations among urban strangers exclusively in terms of the degree to which those affiliations create a sense of community or togetherness among city dwellers. But, as Ash Amin reminds us, the contemporary "turn towards the interpersonal as the measure of community offers an overly restrictive account" of the "phenomenology" of urban relationships.[21]

By calling attention to the sophisticated modes of thinking about urban sociality in our past, we are in a position not only to understand better why we have built and managed cities in the ways we have but also to imagine an urban future that will more effectively preserve and facilitate the kinds of interpersonal associations and social networks that city dwellers will need for their lives to be as manageable, equitable, and fulfilling as possible. AbdouMaliq Simone persuasively and urgently points out the irony in the fact that the "very dimension that characterizes the city—its capacities to continuously reshape the ways in which people, places, materials, ideas, and affect are intersected—is often the very thing that is left out of the larger analytical picture." The failure of those responsible for planning and operating cities to consider carefully the "city's capacity to provoke relations of all kinds" as they look toward its future development and governance is, according to Simone, unacceptable; the "possibilities of ways of being in the city" with others must remain, he insists, "front and center in our collective considerations of urban life."[22] This book is an attempt to move a historically and conceptually rich conversation about urban fellow-feelings closer to the center of how we understand our urban past and the growing discussion about our planet's urban future. By exposing how our decisions about what interpersonal affections matter most have shaped other decisions about what kinds of cities we build, we will be more open to acknowledging the validity of the new types of social arrangements that will inevitably continue to arise in cities and more willing to modify the built environment to make room for them.

CHAPTER 1

The Settlement Movement's Push for Public Sympathy

When Jane Addams and Ellen Gates Starr moved to the Nineteenth Ward of Chicago in 1889 and founded the Hull-House Settlement, they encountered a very different kind of city from the one Frederick Law Olmsted had responded to just twenty years earlier. The arrival of hundreds of thousands of Southern blacks, Italians, Jews, and other immigrants, along with significant economic transformations and technological advancements, had radically altered the city's social landscape and built environment. Addams described the consequences of these explosive changes to the U.S. city after having lived in Chicago's West Side for a few years. She was quick to point out the wear and tear on the city's infrastructure caused by dramatic population growth, noting that the "streets are inexpressibly dirty, the number of schools inadequate, factory legislation unenforced, the street-lighting bad, the paving miserable and altogether lacking in the alleys and smaller streets, and the stables defy all laws of sanitation." Addams also drew her readers' attention to the fundamental shifts in how people lived and made a living in the city. Many of her West Side neighbors resided in the wooden homes that were "originally built for one family and are now occupied by several," while others lived in the type of "brick tenement buildings" that had been springing up in the city since the late 1870s. Most of the city's new residents worked in the factories and sweatshops that had recently taken root in the outskirts of Chicago, especially its southern and western edges. Because of these physical and social changes within the city, Addams noted, many of the neighborhood's "older and richer inhabitants seem anxious to move away as rapidly as they can afford it"—a move made possible by new modes of mass transit that allowed these upper-class urbanites to live in new suburban communities and affordably commute downtown.[1]

The most concerning byproduct of the urban transformations Addams described was an intensified spatial stratification and subsequent emotional disconnection among city dwellers. In what would become a foundational document of the settlement movement, "A New Impulse to an Old Gospel," Addams explained in 1892 that the city's entire "social organism" had "broken down" into distinct classes and races, and that this breakdown was most visible in the "large districts of our great cities."[2] Segregation had always been part of city life, but new lines of class and ethnic separation had emerged in the Gilded Age city. This new style of segregation was manufactured not only by emerging residential patterns initiated by a changing industrial geography and new forms of mass transit, but also by significant spatial transformations during the previous two decades that channeled urbanites away from public and toward private spaces. The late nineteenth-century city—with its apartment houses, large department stores, and houses of public amusement—became a place in which individuals could circumvent more easily than they could before the city's civic spaces.[3] Addams was quick to point out that cities such as Chicago also began to sidestep working-class neighborhoods such as the Nineteenth Ward and its inhabitants. She observed that the "club-houses, libraries, galleries, and semi-public conveniences for social life" were located just a few too many "blocks away" for her neighbors to access them and thus to interact with many of their fellow Chicagoans.[4]

Unlike Olmsted, who worried that the early industrial city's claustrophobic scale negated the possibility of fellow-feeling by forcing urbanites to encounter one another in tight spaces, Addams agonized over the ways in which the industrial city "deadens the sympathies" of its inhabitants by spatially separating them from one another. Despite her society's supposed commitment to advancing democracy in the political realm—its willingness to "give the franchise to the immigrant from a sense of justice"—she found the blatant "lack of democracy in social affairs" very disturbing. She lamented the fact that city dwellers "live for the moment side by side" but do so "without knowledge of each other, without fellowship."[5] The established citizens in Chicago's West Side, she observed, felt no obligation to invite any of the recently arrived Italian, German, Bohemian, Russian, Polish, or Greek immigrants to their homes to forge fellow-feelings with them. W. E. B. Du Bois observed an even more pronounced lack of fellowship among black and white city dwellers while living in the College Settlement of Philadelphia in the mid-1890s. While conducting sociological research among the thousands of black residents living in Philadelphia's Seventh Ward, he learned firsthand that the segregation of urban blacks was "more conspicuous" and "more patent to the eye" than the segregation experienced by "Jews, Italians, and even Americans." Black Philadelphians constituted a "large group of people—perhaps forty-five thousand, a city within a city—who do not form an integral part of the large social group." Black urbanites fell outside what Du Bois would describe in *The Souls of Black Folk* (1903) as the "pale of sympathy," by which he meant the bonds of a familial fellow-feeling that so easily united white citizens.[6]

Addams, Starr, Du Bois, and their settlement colleagues in Chicago, Philadelphia, New York, Boston, and other U.S. cities hoped that settlement houses might provide the kind of semi-public space that could, to borrow Addams's phrase, "socialize their democracy" by keeping sympathies alive among city dwellers.[7] But when settlement intellectuals talked about "sympathy," they often intended to signify a different set of affective processes and relational forms than their sentimental predecessors had signaled through their use of the term. Participants in the Progressive Era settlement movement stretched the urban discourse of sympathy beyond the boundaries established by Olmsted and other nineteenth-century urbanists to account for and validate fellow-feelings among city dwellers that did not fit neatly within the categories of affection and sociality typically associated with the domestic realm. Addams argued that her increasingly urban society must be willing to rethink the social ideals that had arisen and taken root in much less urban times and places. And by expanding the discourse of sympathy to legitimize some of the interpersonal feelings and relationships experienced by urbanites, Addams and other settlement intellectuals encouraged the city dweller to "make new channels through which his sympathy may flow." The settlement discourse of urban sympathy both acknowledged and promoted "sympathy in a larger measure and of a quality better adapted to the contemporaneous situation"—a type of fellow-feeling Addams characterized as "cosmopolitan affection."[8] Du Bois and other settlement writers joined Addams in extending the nineteenth-century urban discourse of sympathy. In advocating for "public sympathy" among Philadelphia's black and white residents, Du Bois hoped both to make visible and to instigate interracial urban relationships that produced more emotionally satisfying, socially just, and economically rewarding relationships than those that grew out of the "mere altruistic interest in an alien people."⁹

Like the urban discourse of sympathy that preceded it, settlement sympathy suggested that the cultivation of fellow-feeling among individuals depended on face-to-face interactions. Although settlement leaders sought to enlarge the range of affections that might be considered to connect city dwellers to one another, they still privileged personal contact as the source of socially and emotionally legitimate relationships. The belief in the value of frequent interactions with one's neighbors served as perhaps the principal tenet of the settlement movement's social philosophy. By moving to the city's dense immigrant neighborhoods and living "side by side with their neighbors"—those whom the industrial city had physically and emotionally segregated from them—settlement residents would, Addams believed, "grow into a sense of relationship and mutual interests" with their neighbors.[10] While settlement workers occasionally experienced these social bonds as familial bonds, they tended to characterize their relationships with their neighbors in terms of friendship and citizenship. It is true that settlement residents visited their neighbors in their homes, but they more often encountered one another in the city's public and semi-public spaces. Settlement workers claimed that city dwellers could solidify their fellow-feelings for other urbanites as friends through their sociological investigations of urban life. As they worked to situate themselves and their neighbors in the context of the larger historical, economic, political, and cultural forces that shaped the lives and identities of city dwellers, settlement residents felt that urbanites could carve out more distinctly public avenues along which their sympathy for one another might travel. The settlement movement's discourse of sympathy, then, both called attention to the legitimacy of relationships formed in the city's public and semi-public spaces and sought to enhance the ability of city dwellers to experience a sense of connection to one another by providing them with new social and intellectual strategies.

The settlement movement's account of the kinds of interpersonal feelings and relationships that mattered most inspired settlement workers to modify the industrial city's built environment in order to facilitate the processes of a more distinctly urban sympathy and the kinds of fellow-feelings that these processes produced. Unlike Olmsted, settlement residents did not seek to remove city dwellers as far from the city as possible, but instead attempted to create much smaller scale public and semi-public spaces in the city's dense immigrant neighborhoods. Their most recognizable and significant spatial innovation was the settlement house itself. According to Addams, the decision to establish Hull-House Settlement grew out of the "belief that the mere foothold of a house, easily accessible, ample in space, hospitable and tolerant in spirit, situated in the midst of the large foreign colonies which so easily isolate themselves in American cities, would be in itself a serviceable thing for Chicago."[11] Originally built as a private home by a wealthy Chicagoan, its spaces were modified by Addams and Starr so that it would function as a welcoming space—the type of semi-public space Addams claimed was hard to find in Chicago's Nineteenth Ward. While the settlement house performed at times as a domestic space for its residents, they and their neighbors more often experienced it as a public one. Its dining room hosted drawing classes, while its parlor supported kindergarten classes and its bedrooms accommodated neighborhood labor meetings. But the settlement house was just one of the many spatial innovations that settlement workers brought to the industrial city. The Hull-House campus, for instance, eventually included an additional thirteen buildings, which housed a gymnasium, coffeehouse, playground, museum, and branch of the city's public library. Not all settlement houses were as spatially expansive and diverse as Hull-House, but it was not unique in its ability to morph private spaces into public ones and to expand beyond the boundaries of the house itself to provide spaces in which the city's increasingly diverse inhabitants could come into direct contact with one another and acquire the kinds of fellow-feelings for one another that settlement residents felt would create a more democratic society.[12]

Despite the settlement movement's efforts to stretch the urbanist discourse of sympathy to legitimate the interpersonal affections and relational forms that urbanites experienced in the city's public and semi-public spaces, its insistence on the value of direct contact and the friendships that they sustained failed to reckon adequately with the structures of economic and political power that shaped the industrial city and the lives of those it sheltered. When Du Bois addressed a group of settlement workers, volunteers, and neighbors at Brooklyn's Lincoln Settlement in 1910, he claimed to know of "no more effective way to work for the social uplift, not simply of the Negro people but the city of Brooklyn and the state of New York and indeed of the United States, than through efficient aid to an institution like the Lincoln Settlement." His faith in the ability of public sympathy to move black urbanites beyond the line of discrimination that prevented them from realizing their social, economic, and cultural aspirations clearly underestimated the persistence of discrimination throughout the twentieth century.[13] The type of personal contact privileged and promoted within settlement discourse as the source of fellow-feeling became increasingly difficult to experience in cities that, over the course of the twentieth century, found new ways to segregate black and other marginalized urbanites from privileged metropolitan residents. Du Bois and other settlement intellectuals also underestimated, as they would soon find out, the tendency of an urban discourse of sympathy to backslide conceptually toward the types of emotional intimacies that the language and logic of sympathy had conjured for much of the eighteenth and nineteenth centuries—the familial feelings that bound individuals together in relationships that approximated those forged within the domestic sphere. Sympathy thus proved to be less capable than settlement residents had initially hoped of doing the social, cultural, and material work they wanted it to do.

"New Channels" of Sympathy

As settlement writers worked toward establishing their movement's own distinct discourse of sympathy, they often drew on the domestic rhetoric that had enveloped the concept in the nineteenth century. Settlement residents were especially attracted to the notion of a universal brotherhood. Writing for the *College Settlement News* in 1896, Isabel Eaton explained that everything the settlement movement "stands for can be put into one word, Brotherhood." By projecting the affective quality of domestic relationships onto the public relationships forged within the city, settlement workers hoped to overcome what Clarence Meily described in *Charities and the Commons* in 1905 as the "horizontal stratification of the sympathetic impulse" fostered by the city's industrial geography.[14] When put into practice, the kinship model of sympathy would bring settlement residents into relationships of equality with the urban poor. In relating to their neighbors as if they were siblings, settlement workers hoped to overcome the vast social and physical distance that paternalistic charity work had perpetuated. One settlement resident explained that being involved in a settlement's clubs, which brought together settlement workers and their neighbors on a regular basis, inevitably led her to the realization that the "people amongst whom she works are of one blood with her."[15] The early settlement movement's parlance of brotherhood also tapped into the rhetorical resources of what Addams referred to in 1892 as a "certain *renaissance* going forward in Christianity." The Social

Gospel movement's conviction of the spiritual nature of the interrelationships among members of the human family gave the language of brotherhood in settlement writing an even sharper edge with which to cut through the social and economic inequalities among urbanites.[16] To the extent that brotherhood continued to operate within settlement literature as way to explain the nature of the relationships that connected urbanites to one another, a relatively conventional discourse of sympathy persisted within this Progressive Era movement.

Not all settlement residents, though, felt that the concept of brotherhood—and the domestic and Christian style of sympathy it signaled—adequately expressed the settlement movement's investment in a less intimate but equally valuable style of urban sociality. Brotherhood may have characterized the type of democratic equality that settlement workers aspired to achieve in their relationships with their neighbors, but it also implied an interpersonal intimacy that some felt they could not or did not want to sustain. Brotherhood, as a relational model, did not fully account for the affective variability of the social interactions that settlement workers experienced as they navigated the city. Vida Scudder, one of the movement's most eloquent spokeswomen, recalled that many of the earliest settlement volunteers had reasoned that "since bad air, over-crowding, and hard manual labor were obviously the lot of great numbers of our brethren," settlement residents should also "accept these things" as their "lot" in life. After living at Boston's Dennison House for several years, however, Scudder admitted that thinking of the urban poor as "brethren" was a little too "sentimental" and a bit misguided. As she came to see it, the initial desire of settlement volunteers to achieve a complete "self-identification with the life and conditions of the poor"—to become one blood with them—had, by the turn of the century, "shrunk to a vanishing point."[17] As the movement matured, many settlement residents had enough experience to realize that this conventional sympathetic rhetoric did not sufficiently capture the nature of their relationships with their neighbors. Scudder may have overstated the degree to which the concept of brotherhood diminished as a structure of fellow-feeling that informed the behavior and affections of settlement residents, but she and many others became increasingly convinced that this sentimental discourse of sympathy too often overlooked the social inequalities that settlement workers had to acknowledge and negotiate in their encounters with city dwellers. Settlement workers realized that capturing the type of affections that grew out of their interactions with others in the industrial city could only be described with a vocabulary capable of communicating much more than social and emotional solidarity.

When Addams wrote about "longing for a wider union than that of family or class" in the *Atlantic Monthly* in 1899, a decade after she had settled at Hull-House with Starr, she was longing to experience not just a union that included individuals whose lives fell outside the boundaries of her own family and class but also a new affect—one that would be qualitatively different than that which held families and classes together. Addams and other settlement writers expressed dissatisfaction with the type of urban philanthropy that utilized the language and logic of charity to articulate the union between the classes. The problem with speaking about urban relationships in terms of charity, Addams reasoned, was that it established an "unconscious division of the world into the philanthropists and those to be helped." Addams insisted that the industrial city, with its crowded and diverse immigrant and working-class neighborhoods, had created the physical and social conditions within which an "affection" that was "large and real enough" to leave behind social distinctions had already begun to emerge. She pointed readers to urban neighborhoods like Chicago's Nineteenth Ward where, because the "economic condition of all" was equally "precarious," the "outflow of sympathy and material assistance" could readily traverse family, ethnic, and cultural boundaries. Addams would later describe the larger affections that allowed her immigrant neighbors to achieve a wider union as a "cosmopolitan affection."[18] It was this cosmopolitan affection that she and others hoped a settlement discourse of sympathy could legitimize by making its operations in the lives of urbanites more visible.

Du Bois developed perhaps an even more precise articulation of the type of binding affection that Addams and other settlement writers had been trying to express during the settlement movement's first decade. In his landmark settlement study of Philadelphia's Seventh Ward, *The Philadelphia Negro* (1899), Du Bois described a "public sympathy" capable of connecting white Philadelphians to their black neighbors. For Du Bois, public sympathy captured an affective process and fellow-feeling that connected city dwellers to one another as they interfaced with one another's public identities. More specifically, he suggested that, as urbanites approached one another through the identities they performed in the public world of work, rather than the racial identities socially constructed for them, they were connected to each other through a public sympathy that ensured each participant in the relationship opportunities to take up various positions within the city's economic, social, cultural, and political grid. The city dweller who operated under the affective structure of "charitable interest" might "contribute handsomely to relieve Negroes in poverty and distress" while simultaneously refusing to "let a Negro work in his store or mill," thus compromising their philanthropic intentions. But those who pursued the fellow-feelings Du Bois referred to as public sympathy entered into relationships in which both individuals viewed one another as "fellow-laborers" in the city's industrial economy.[19]

Du Bois and other settlement writers increasingly relied on a new set of terms to differentiate cosmopolitan affection and public sympathy from the type of sympathy signified by the terminology of brotherhood. John P. Gavit, a resident at Chicago Commons, made it clear near the end of the nineteenth century that settlement workers were "not so much teachers, preachers or benefactors as friends, neighbors, fellow-citizens, fellow-sufferers, [and] fellow-men."[20] Among the words Gavit used to distinguish the types of urban relationships forged by settlement residents from those fashioned by philanthropists, missionaries, and charitable agents, *friend* became the most frequently invoked by both residents and their neighbors. The president of the Woman's Club at Chicago Commons, a recent immigrant to the neighborhood, recalled that, when she and her neighbors first arrived in Chicago, they found themselves "shut up in our homes, as if they were jails." When they visited the settlement house, they felt that they were "among friends, friends that were interested in us and in our daily lives. Its doors were open to us at any and all times, with a sympathizing friend always ready to listen to us."[21] The type of sympathy she experienced at Chicago Commons was qualitatively different from what she experienced in her home, and she used *friend* to signal this difference. The term accounted for relationships that were less intimate and private than those among family members. *Friend* was capacious enough to indicate a wide range of relationships formed within the public sphere. The terms that follow *friend* in Gavit's list—*neighbor, citizen,* and *fellow-men*—offer just a brief glimpse of the affective scope signified by this word. *Friend* could be used to describe a relationship that involved relatively intimate feelings, such as those expressed by the president of the Chicago Commons Woman's Club, just as accurately as it could be used to denote relationships that entailed the less intimate, but no less valid, emotional attachments between citizens. Regardless of the affective register on which a friendship between settlement residents and their urban neighbors operated, the concept of *friend* captured both the mutuality and continuity of the kinds of urban relationships that settlement workers advocated.

The "Rectifying Influence" of Personal Contact and Social Science

The urbanist discourse of sympathy that settlement intellectuals refined during the Progressive Era emphasized two particular avenues through which city dwellers connected emotionally with one another. First, settlement intellectuals stressed that public sympathy grew out of frequent personal contact among urbanites. Settlement residents avowed that mixing with urbanites in public and semi-public spaces was essential to the development of cosmopolitan fellow-feelings. Second, settlement writers argued that a social scientific understanding of urban processes and lives played a critical role in facilitating public sympathy among city dwellers. Their writings showcased the ways that approaching interpersonal interactions with a sociological understanding of the larger structures within which all urbanites lived and worked generated emotionally and socially valuable relationships. Although city dwellers might pursue a number of other social practices in their efforts to acquire a cosmopolitan affection for their neighbors, Addams, Du Bois, and other leading settlement intellectuals championed personal contact and sociological research as significant elements of a more distinctly urban style of sympathy.

One of the basic premises of the settlement movement was that the best way to attain fellow-feelings for another individual was to place oneself, quite literally, as close to another's physical situation as possible. The insistence on the social value of continual personal contact among urbanites instigated the movement's commitment to the idea and act of settling. By choosing to settle permanently (or semipermanently) in working-class industrial neighborhoods, settlement residents committed themselves to repeatedly negotiating their cultural, political, and personal values with individuals from other classes and cultures. Samuel A. Barnett, one of the British intellectuals credited with launching the settlement movement in London's East End in the 1880s, explained that, as settlement residents "daily walk through mean streets," "feel the depression of the smoke-laden air," "see what is the work and what are the pleasures of the people," "go to local meetings," "meet for casual talks," and "hear of the wrongs, of the sorrows, of the anger, and of the ignorance which are in the minds of workmen," they learn to "look at life from another standpoint." Walking, feeling, seeing, and talking with other urbanites would not necessarily lead settlement residents to experience "any change of opinion," Barnett reasoned, but the resulting "sympathy makes them express the old opinion in a different spirit."[22] Alternatively, this affective process might lead settlement residents to change their opinion but not necessarily take up the exact opinion of their neighbors. Seeing the world from "another standpoint" might not always mean adopting another's exact point of view. For settlement intellectuals, sympathizing with another individual did not require city dwellers to overcome all personal and cultural differences to arrive at an identical and shared emotion; instead, it required them to stand close enough to one another so that their repeated contact could lead them to modify their own ideas or feelings in some way. Experiencing this internal transformation and recognizing this change as the result of having come into direct contact with another human being—of having *settled* with that person—generated fellow-feelings for others. The kind of fellowship that Barnett described, according to Addams, exerted a "rectifying influence" on its participants that gave them the "power of recognizing good" in one another.[23] This act of recognition is what settlement writers often referred to as sympathy.

Du Bois's account of his life in Philadelphia's Seventh Ward illuminates the affective and relational nuances that often accompanied the type of personal contact privileged within settlement discourse. Shortly after moving to Philadelphia with his new bride in August 1896 and settling in a room above a cafeteria run by the College Settlement of Philadelphia, Du Bois immersed himself in the daily life of the neighborhood. At the settlement house, he taught American history to neighborhood boys on Wednesday evenings, regularly lectured at local meetings, attended the lectures of others, and helped organize and run neighborhood clubs. In addition to being deeply involved in the work of the settlement house, Du Bois became fully invested in the life of the Seventh Ward's black community, frequenting formal and informal gatherings at the neighborhood's churches, schools, businesses, and other institutions. On top of these activities, Du Bois "visited and talked with 5,000 persons" in the Seventh Ward "personally and not by proxy" while conducting sociological research. These one-on-one visits and conversations were not without a degree of social awkwardness and discomfort. He later recalled that the "colored people of Philadelphia received me with no open arms" and often "set me to groping"—experiences that led him to conclude he "did not know so much as I might about my own people."[24]

Interacting directly with his neighbors day after day forced Du Bois to acknowledge the inability of conventional cultural narratives to connect him emotionally to those he had been confident he knew and to search for an alternative narrative through which he could experience fellow-feelings for them. Realizing that he could not identify with those he had assumed were his own people, he discovered the inadequacies of his culture's myth of consanguinity. The "groping" that followed the failure of a standard sympathetic paradigm to connect him to his neighbors prompted him to take up an alternative one. Du Bois recounted that, during the "ten minutes to an hour" he spent in each home, conversation often veered off the official questionnaire into "general discussions" about the "condition of the Negroes, which were instructive."[25] Much of the enlightening information that emerged during these conversations could not be recorded on the official sociological schedules, but Du Bois nevertheless stored this new knowledge in his memory and wrote it out as memoranda so that it would inform his future interactions with his neighbors and shape the narrative of his study. Through the process of living among and talking with thousands of black urbanites, Du Bois claimed to have learned "far more from Philadelphia Negroes than I had taught them concerning the Negro Problem."[26] In his retelling, personal contact with his neighbors had exerted the kind of rectifying influence on his ideas and emotions that other settlement intellectuals had described as an essential part of the sympathetic process. Only after settling both physically and socially with other black Philadelphians did Du Bois claim to have attained a sense of fellow-feeling for them.

Settlement writing was not the only turn-of-the-century genre to articulate the social value and satisfaction of cross-cultural contact in the industrial city. Its similarities to these other urban discourses illuminate the ways in which interactions among individuals from different classes or cultures might generate a rectifying influence that disciplined rather than liberated the urban poor. The urban realism of writers such as William Dean Howells, Theodore Dreiser, Upton Sinclair, Jack London, and Edith Wharton often featured narratives that hinged on cross-class contact among characters and that ultimately functioned to reify social hierarchies. And the broader practices of slumming to which urban realism sometimes contributed tended to hide the ways perceptions of class, racial, and sexual difference were changing during this period by inscribing them into the city's built environment. Historians of the settlement movement have been quick to call attention to the ways in which settlement residents and their rhetoric of cross-class and cross-cultural contact often served the same purposes as these other urban discourses—to impose some degree of control on the city's migrant and immigrant communities. While reading settlement studies and memoirs such as Du Bois's *Philadelphia Negro* and Addams's *Twenty Years at Hull-House*, it is easy to see how the promotion and practice of a form of sociality intended to bring about social equality and political transformation may have instead (or perhaps simultaneously) subjected the urban poor to what scholar Christopher Castiglia calls a "sympathetic discipline."[27]

Settlement residents were often aware of the thin line they walked between "doing good 'to' people rather than 'with' them," as Addams put it, which is why they imported into their discourse of sympathy the discipline of sociology. According to settlement writers, public sympathy was a more likely relational outcome when city dwellers understood one another's lives within larger sociological and historical contexts. Although personal interactions with other urbanites helped remind the upper-class city dweller, according to Addams, "how incorrigibly bourgeois her standards" were and how dangerous it would be to "insist" that others take up the "conventions of her own class," settlement discourse incorporated the language and logic of the social sciences to expose more fully and rectify the social standards and class conventions that infused every urban interaction with some dimension of inequality or injustice. Addams once quipped that people "sometimes say that our charity is too scientific"; but she insisted that it would be "much more correct in our estimate if we said that it is not scientific enough."[28] Herman F. Hegner, a resident at Chicago Commons in the 1890s, initially perceived the saloonkeeper in his settlement's neighborhood to be the "agent of immorality and crime" and wanted "nothing to do with him." However, after gathering a "fuller knowledge of facts" about saloonkeepers through social scientific research, Hegner and his settlement colleagues "modified [their] ideas of the ethics" of the saloonkeeper and were thus able to nourish a fellow-feeling for him.[29] Hegner had originally situated the saloonkeeper in a nineteenth-century Protestant narrative that defined him as a moral failure, but sociological research allowed Hegner to liberate this urban figure from that narrative and place him instead in a broader reality that he and the saloonkeeper shared—one shaped by the industrial city's larger economic, political, and cultural forces. Sociological research put urbanites in a position to encounter one another on more common social and material ground than they might have otherwise encountered one another.

The settlement movement's sociological studies became particularly important channels through which urbanites could expand the discourse of sympathy to account for the increasingly large number of black city dwellers with whom they shared the industrial city. Between 1880 and 1910, the black population in Chicago increased almost sevenfold, more than tripled in Manhattan, and nearly tripled in Philadelphia (making it home to the largest black community in the United States). As black citizens sought opportunities in the nation's growing cities in the wake of Emancipation and Reconstruction, their fellow urbanites struggled to know how to interact and connect with their new neighbors. Early settlement residents found it difficult to make room for black migrants under the canopy of public sympathy. They tended to shy away from establishing settlement houses in black urban neighborhoods, which made it difficult to be in personal contact with black urbanites. Furthermore, settlement workers often failed to use sociology to gain an understanding of the larger structural conditions underpinning the black urban community; for instance, none of the essays in *Hull-House Maps and Papers* (1895), one of the earliest and most important sociological studies completed by early settlement workers, addresses the lives of black Chicagoans in any substantial way. When settlement workers did make an effort to understand the condition of urban blacks, they often attributed the social and economic problems their black neighbors faced to the system of slavery—an explanation that was more humane than those offered by popular theories of racial determinism, but not attentive enough to the conditions of the industrial city.[30]

Du Bois attempted to address this racial flaw in settlement discourse by drawing on and adjusting its sociological narrative strategies. Social science could, he felt, make the settlement movement's "cosmopolitan humanitarianism" more cosmopolitan. Like Addams, Du Bois claimed that most efforts to improve the lives of city dwellers were not scientific enough. He informed the students of Atlanta University's sociological club in 1897 that, when people understood the "value and meaning of statistics" gathered by the urban sociologist, they would be able to replace "sentiment and theory" with scientific facts as the foundation of a more effective and compassionate style of sociality.[31] City dwellers could only feel right toward and do right with their black neighbors by understanding the larger forces that restricted their opportunities and informed their choices. To understand the "real condition" of Philadelphia's black inhabitants, Du Bois explained in *The Philadelphia Negro*, one had to situate their urban lives in the context of a reality that had been shaped by both the "physical environment of [the] city" and the "far mightier social environment—the surrounding world of custom, wish, whim, and thought."[32]

To help readers grasp this urban reality, Du Bois thoroughly plotted in words, graphs, diagrams, and maps the built environment and social landscape of Philadelphia's Seventh Ward—a neighborhood that ran between South and Lombard Streets from Seventh to Twenty-Fifth Streets. Du Bois went through great pains to document the physical conditions of the tightly packed row houses, lodging houses, and tenements that sheltered the Seventh Ward's 15,000 black residents. A large number of the families who resided in the Seventh Ward rented single bedrooms and had limited access to a common kitchen. Only 13.7 percent of these families had access to bathrooms and water closets—and many of those who did had to share the use of that bathroom with at least one other family. Du Bois estimated that "over 20 per cent and possibly 30 per cent of the Negro families of this ward lack some of the very elementary accommodations necessary to health and decency," even though they paid "comparatively high rents." Despite the Seventh Ward's inadequate housing conditions, black city dwellers made their way to the neighborhood for its proximity to employment and its dynamic social life. Black life had, for several decades, been centered in the Seventh Ward's churches, secret and beneficial societies, loan associations, political clubs, unions, and schools.[33]

When Du Bois hit the streets of the city's Seventh Ward with a valise full of blank sociological schedules on which to record the data that would form the foundation of *The Philadelphia Negro*, he had to expand the footprint of the settlement movement's sociological structure of inquiry to allow the customs, wishes, whims, and thoughts of the city's black residents to inform his urban narrative. He did this, in part, by modifying the questions settlement workers typically asked of their neighbors while gathering information for their sociological studies. Because of discrimination's elusive nature and the settlement movement's focus on collecting empirical data, settlement workers often overlooked the role social prejudices played in the lives of their subjects. Du Bois altered the questions on the standard schedule in an attempt to capture the "somewhat indefinite term" of prejudice and translate it into "something tangible."[34] The settlement workers who

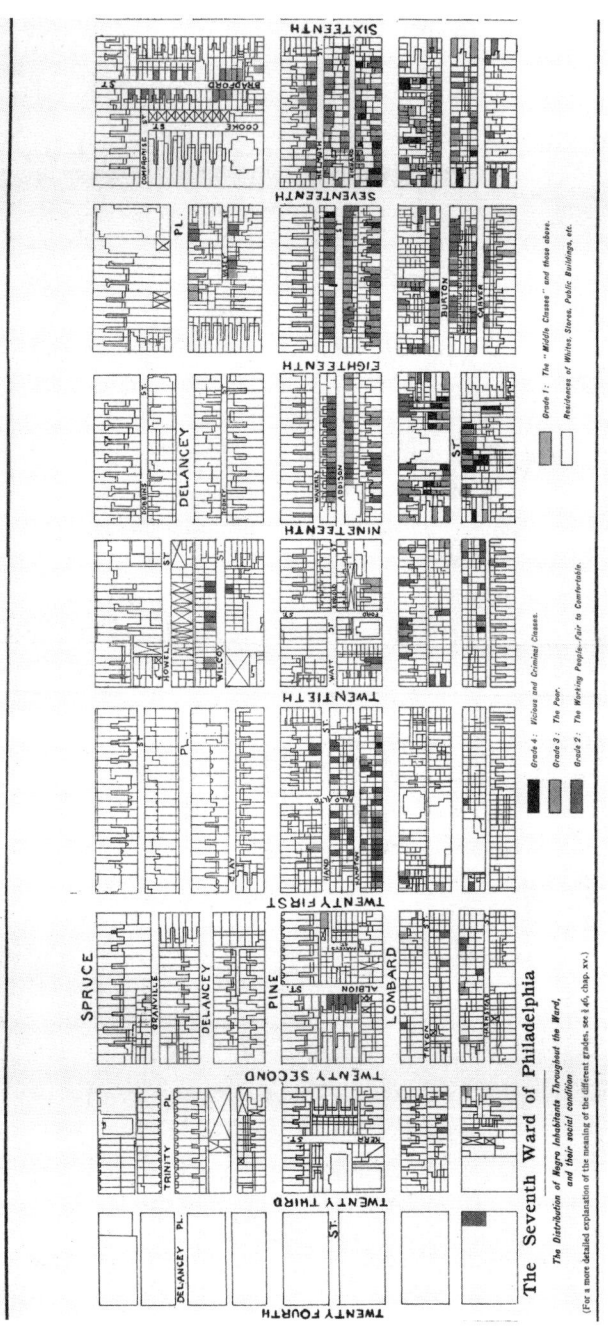

Figure 2. A section of the map of Philadelphia's Seventh Ward that documents Du Bois's sociological findings about the distribution and socioeconomic condition of the ward's black residents. From W. E. B. Du Bois, *The Philadelphia Negro: A Social Study* (Philadelphia: University of Philadelphia Press, 1899). University of Pennsylvania Archives and Records Center, Publications of the University of Pennsylvania.

gathered sociological data for the studies published in *Hull-House Maps and Papers* asked their subjects the following sequence of questions: "Weeks employed at any other profession, trade, or occupation during the year?" and "Name of such other profession, trade, or occupation?"[35] Such questions assumed that those being interviewed had little difficulty finding employment and did not encourage subjects to talk about the challenges they might have encountered in their search for work. Du Bois adjusted these and other questions to allow black urbanites the opportunity to talk about the ways in which prejudice had impeded their ability to secure employment and shelter.[36] Rather than inquiring matter-of-factly how many weeks his neighbors had been employed, he asked questions such as: "Have you had any difficulty in getting work?" and "Have you had any difficulty in renting houses?"[37] By slightly altering the questions that appeared on the standard sociological schedule, Du Bois began to build a more nuanced picture of the "real condition" in which his Seventh Ward neighbors operated—a picture that enabled him to deepen and rectify the fellow-feelings he had acquired through his one-on-one conversations with them.

Du Bois translated the sociological data he acquired through his rigorous survey of Philadelphia's Seventh Ward into a narrative that staged an encounter between readers and the neighborhood's black residents in the larger context of their urban conditions. Settlement writers often tried to recreate for their readers the affect produced through daily urban contact by inundating them with brief, successive, and jarring vignettes of individual city dwellers. Encountering one urbanite after another that could not be understood through the culture's standard explanatory narratives forced readers to become aware, at the very least, of the inadequacies of their own habits of feeling. Throughout *The Philadelphia Negro*, Du Bois reanimated the boiled-down sociological data found in the maps, charts, and tables he included in his study by providing brief, consecutive snapshots of individual urbanites: "C—is a shoemaker; he tried to get work in some of the large department stores. They 'had no place' for him"; "G—is an iron puddler, who belonged to a Pittsburg union. Here he was not recognized as a union man and could not get work except as a stevedore"; "H—was a cooper, but could get no work after repeated trials, and is now a common laborer."[38] In describing the interactions of these anonymous individuals with the gatekeepers of the city's industrial economy, Du Bois drew attention to the personal level on which racism's economic consequences were felt while simultaneously pointing out the structural nature of racism in Philadelphia. The problem was not the individual employers who refused black urbanites work, per se, but the greater "social environment" in which these interactions occurred. As readers encountered Philadelphia's black citizens in the context of the city's physical and social environment, Du Bois hoped that their public sympathy for individuals like C—, G—, and H—would express itself in working alongside them to widen the "narrow opportunities afforded Negroes for earning a decent living" and expand other realms in which they could exercise their own agency. Only when there existed a "social sympathy" and "proper co-operation" between both races, Du Bois reasoned, could Philadelphia "successfully cope with many phases of the Negro problems."[39]

Du Bois saw his use of settlement sociology in *The Philadelphia Negro* as an extension of the structure of interracial friendship constructed by the Pennsylvania Abolition Society (PAS), the country's first abolitionist organization. Unlike the Massachusetts Abolition Society, which tended to rely on sentimental narratives to generate interracial fellow-feeling, the PAS hoped to cultivate within citizens what it described as a "feeling mind" by gathering and disseminating factual information about the nation's black inhabitants. When, for instance, a group of Pennsylvanians mounted a movement to disenfranchise the state's black citizens at the 1838 constitutional convention, the PAS of Philadelphia responded by appointing a committee to gather "such statistical and other information as will show the present condition of the colored population of this city and districts." This PAS committee calculated the social value of Philadelphia's black residents by examining them from a "pecuniary point of view" and considering the integral role they played in the local economy. Based on the information gathered during its house-to-house survey of the city, the committee found that, although "some portion of them may live in idleness," a much more significant "proportion of them are usefully and industriously employed." The PAS sought to undermine the "false estimate which still prevails amongst the mass of our citizens, as to the value of the colored people as a component part of the community."[40] Rather than engender fellow-feelings among white Philadelphians for their black neighbors by primarily portraying the latter as fellow mothers and fathers, the PAS encouraged city dwellers to think of their neighbors as "fellow-laborers in the Society." Members of the PAS conceived of themselves as "fast friends" with their black neighbors, literally working alongside them in the public world of work rather than as philanthropists bestowing gifts from afar.[41] The PAS wanted to route the intellectual and emotional response to its statistical findings away from private affect and toward a more public form of interpersonal feeling—toward the very kind of public sympathy that Du Bois described in *Philadelphia Negro*.

When rank-and-file settlement residents talked about their experiences while living and working in settlement houses, they echoed the urbanist discourse of sympathy established by more prominent settlement voices. When the Church Social Union surveyed dozens of ordinary settlement workers, asking if their "attitude toward social and industrial questions" had changed during their settlement residence, one worker responded that she "saw so much and heard so much that was entirely new" that her "feeling toward the poor has changed from pity to a sense of honest comradeship." Another resident answered that she had "gained a more sympathetic knowledge of the laboring-man in general, and of trades unions in particular." Although neither resident talked in explicit terms about how she came to acquire a new sense of fellow-feeling for her urban neighbors, their answers suggest that their altered sympathy for those in their community had been fed principally by two channels: daily contact and sociological research. Seeing and hearing the urban poor regularly transformed the first respondent's affective connection to them from "pity" to "comradeship." And the second respondent's use of the phrase "sympathetic knowledge" implies that her fellow-feeling for the "laboring-man" had been cultivated through sociological data. Both had acquired what another respondent described as a "new sympathy with workingmen as a class, a new discontent with our present industrial system."[42] It would be easy to interpret the "new sympathy" that this resident claimed to have obtained simply as additional fellow-feelings—a quantitative increase in sympathy. But it might be more accurate to think of this "new sympathy" as a distinctly different range of affections than those that the resident had experienced prior to her engagement in settlement work.

Building Places of Exchange

The settlement movement's commitment to a particular style of sympathy inspired its participants to remake the industrial city's landscape. They worked to create spaces in the industrial city that, as Addams explained, "clothed in brick and mortar and made visible to the world that which we were trying to do." Settlement residents joined a throng of other urbanists at the turn of the century in redeveloping and regulating the industrial city's built environment in attempts to improve the quality of urban life.[43] As the

White City at the Chicago Columbian Exposition of 1893 and Daniel H. Burnham and Edward H. Bennett's 1909 *Plan of Chicago* demonstrated, many of these progressive urbanists sought to reshape the industrial city on a monumental scale—they reimagined the entire organization of the city and developed the building techniques and political strategies in order to transform it. While settlement residents played an important role in securing the zoning regulations, tenement codes, and sanitation laws that made the large-scale transformation of urban space possible, they were perhaps even more invested in constructing the smaller-scale and more localized spaces in which urbanites could directly engage with one another and participate together in the production and dissemination of sociological knowledge. Settlement residents were deeply committed to creating spaces that gave city dwellers access to what one of Hull-House's young residents called a "place of exchange."[44]

Although settlement workers believed that urbanites could experience some measure of public sympathy for one another on the industrial city's congested streets and in its run-down tenement neighborhoods, they shared Olmsted's conviction that its inhabitants were more likely to achieve fellow-feelings for one another when interacting in spaces at some remove from the city's purely public places. But if Olmsted's particular understanding of the sympathetic process inspired him to design urban spaces that "completely shut out the city" and removed urbanites from the "bustle and jar of the streets," the discourse of sympathy that settlement intellectuals had cultivated motivated them to create spaces that harnessed rather than repelled the social energy that coursed through the industrial city's streets.[45] Settlement residents wanted to create places in which they and their neighbors could actualize and, to some degree, manage the cross-class and cross-cultural social opportunities made possible by the new demographics of the industrial city—opportunities that the city's built environment had increasingly foreclosed. To facilitate the type of sympathetic exchanges among city dwellers that pulsed at the heart of the settlement movement's urban vision, residents worked with their neighbors to cobble together spaces out of the industrial city's built environment that blurred the boundaries between public and private. They strove to infuse their neighborhoods with "semi-public" locales that were, in Addams's words, "easily accessible" to those who bustled and jarred against one another on the city's streets.[46]

No place better illuminates the complexion of the semi-public spaces that settlement residents assembled at the turn of the century than the settlement house itself. Given the nature of the settlement enterprise, the settlement house continued to serve many of the private functions of the traditional home—its residents had to sleep, eat, and bathe there. But settlement residents learned not only how to transform what had originally served as private space within the nineteenth-century home into public space but also how to continually shift the functionality of those spaces between private and public. That is to say, a single room in the settlement home might function as a private space in the morning and as a public space in the evening.[47] The activation of the public identity of conventionally private spaces such as dining rooms, kitchens, bedrooms, or stairways was frequently instigated by residents' desires to provide themselves and their neighbors with opportunities to participate in the social processes that would generate a cosmopolitan affection among them. Dorothea Moore recalled that, in the evening, the Hull-House dining room served as a "meeting ground" between residents and neighbors where the "generalizations of the over young are discouraged with kindness and qualifying facts" and where more experienced individuals could be "induced to reconsider and admit another fact of the great truth." As the "free play of the individual" at the dinner table met with the "friction" and "juice of humor" provided by urbanites of different ages, classes, and cultures, city dwellers together expanded what Moore called the "social consciousness of the living house."[48] The enclosed space of the dining room put urbanites in a position to experience the rectifying influence fabricated through close-range personal contact and the exchange of sociological facts. As residents, older immigrants, scholars, factory workers, and children participated in the continuous feedback loop of interacting with one another, reconsidering opinions, and qualifying assertions, they acquired fellow-feelings for one another because of, not in spite of, the friction their interactions produced.

When settlement residents saw opportunities to provide additional meeting grounds that would appeal to different cross-sections of the city's inhabitants, they often expanded beyond the walls of the house itself. But their core spatial strategy of constructing places in which urbanites could engage in direct personal exchanges remained constant. Over the course of Hull-House's two-decade expansion, the settlement complex dedicated portions of its city-block footprint to a coffeehouse, dining hall, art gallery, and auditorium so that city dwellers could continue to have access to places of exchange. Other segments of the settlement's expanded facilities provided meeting grounds for the rapidly growing number of social clubs hosted by

Figure 3. Hull-House Dining Room. JAMC 0000 0162 1007, University of Illinois at Chicago Library, Special Collections.

the settlement. Clubs such as the Working People's Social Science Club and Hull-House Woman's Club initially met in the drawing room, parlor, and bedrooms of Hull-House but later relocated to spaces in adjacent buildings that replicated in slightly enlarged dimensions the spatial and social dynamics of the original settlement home. The semi-public spaces in which the settlement's social clubs met invited city dwellers to enter into what Addams characterizes as "friendly relations" with one another. In these spaces, urbanites came in "contact, many of them for the first time, with the industrial and social problems challenging the moral resources of our contemporary life." As club members encountered new understandings of the industrial city's problems through lectures and discussions at their club meetings, Addams claimed that they were "led from a sense of isolation to one of civic responsibility." Engaging in the production and dissemination of sociological information helped members of a club know how best to express "sympathy and kindliness at the same time in concrete form." The small, semi-public spaces of the settlement put city dwellers in a position to extend the movement's brand of sociality beyond its physical boundaries by helping them imagine themselves not only as friends to one another but as citizens of a much larger world. The many different places of exchange crammed together within the settlement cultivated "citizens who are conversant with adverse social conditions" and who, along with similarly informed urbanites in other cities, "may in time remove the reproach of social neglect and indifference which has so long rested upon the citizens of the new world."[49] Addams and other settlement intellectuals argued that the movement's spatial innovations had the potential to transform not only the industrial city's social landscape but also the larger modern world of which it was a part.

The spatial logic of the mature settlement complex's layout underscored the model of relationality that the settlement movement's discourse of sympathy privileged. Although the settlement's spaces became slightly less flexible as its different services, activities, and organizations acquired their own discrete locations, settlement residents continued to use single spaces for multiple purposes and to repurpose spaces that had been earmarked for uses that were no longer necessary. The settlement movement's mixed-use and improvisational approach to urban space frustrated architects such as Allen B. Pond, who designed the Hull-House complex and five additional settlements. He found it irritating that Hull-House was an "aggregation of partially related units" rather than a "logical organism." In his desire for an architecture that was "made up of parts having special functions but still interrelated and severally interdependent," Pond articulated the reasoning of single-use zoning that was emerging in the early 1900s and that would exert a stranglehold on city planning for much of the remainder of the twentieth century. While he lamented that Hull-House had "grown'by a long series of wholly unforeseeable accretions," the ways in which the settlement house layered multiple uses on single spaces and placed its many activities and services in close proximity to one another echoed in physical form the settlement's social philosophy of contact and friction.[50] But, even more important, the settlement's accretive style of urbanism perpetuated and extended the fellow-feelings that may have originated within a particular club or at a specific lecture beyond the spatial confines of that club. The settlement's mixture and overlap of uses within its finite number of rooms drew urbanites into and through its various spaces, where they would have opportunities to follow-up on their initial encounters with one another and pursue both more personal and cerebral relationships. In many ways, the comprehensive spatial logic and organization of settlements such as Hull-House helped city dwellers learn how to extend the fellow-feelings they forged within the discrete spaces that accommodated a club meeting or a meal to the urbanites they would encounter outside those specific spaces.

Du Bois expressed the same kind of confidence in the settlement movement's spatial strategies to solve the city's social problems—particularly its racial problems—that Addams and other settlement intellectuals had expressed. Although Du Bois would not live in a settlement again after leaving Philadelphia in 1897, he continued to draw on the movement's discourse of sympathy and its spatial techniques in offering solutions to race relations. While discussing the "means of bettering the condition of the Negroes" of New York City at a small, mixed-race conference at Mount Olivet Baptist Church on January 4, 1903, Du Bois proposed the "establishment of a kind of social settlement for Negroes."[51] He envisioned a settlement house that would serve as a "clearing house for the local race problem, acting as a directory and adviser in matters of almsgiving, education, religion, and work." By establishing a "physical center for movements affecting the betterment of the Negro, for the gathering of careful information concerning his needs and condition, and for furthering effective cooperation among all established agencies which seek his good," this settlement would create a space in which an "adjustment between the life of the segregated Negro group and that of the larger city" could be worked out. The successful implementation of these social services and the urban Negro's social "adjustment," though, ultimately hinged on the type of personal contact that the settlement house was designed to initiate. Du Bois counseled the meeting's participants that "personal friendship" is ultimately the "main-spring of social help" and the means by which the proposed settlement would be best able to "help the weak and unfortunate" and "find enlarged opportunity for Negroes of ability and desert."[52] These interracial friendships and the public sympathy upon which they were built would, Du Bois professed, lead to increased social and economic opportunities for the black city dweller.

Although the group that gathered at Mount Olivet opted not to act on Du Bois's suggestion to build a settlement house for New York's black community, other individuals active in the city's settlement scene heard of his proposal and attempted to translate his ideas into social practice and physical form. After learning about Du Bois's recommendation from Mary Kingsbury Simkhovitch, founder of Greenwich House in Greenwich Village, Mary White Ovington wrote him in the fall of 1904 to inform him that she hoped to undertake the "work first spoken of in those resolutions" by doing "some work among the Negroes."⁵³ Using *The Philadelphia Negro* as her guide and frequently consulting its author—who, in her estimation, knew the "situation in the city pretty well" and was very familiar with "settlements and their forms of work"—Ovington commenced her own settlement work with an exhausting research routine. By early 1905, she began to visualize the social and physical forms that would best materialize and perpetuate the types of interracial relationships that would lead to individual and collective growth. Ovington did not aspire to meet all the needs Du Bois had enumerated at Mount Olivet, but she did agree with him that the work had to be "carried on by colored and white alike": "Every month I feel that the two races must work together in any philanthropic work in the city. It must be isolation that creates much of the difficulty in the South, and why should we try to produce unnecessary difficulties for ourselves in the North?"⁵⁴

Recognizing that the public would disapprove of lodging white and black settlement workers together in a single domestic space, Ovington sought an alternative to the standard settlement house model. Rather than occupy a Victorian mansion as if it were a "big boarding house," Ovington hoped to "get a model tenement built in one of the crowded Negro quarters, preferably the Sixties, and to have room in it for settlement work." She envisioned that she and her fellow black and white settlement workers would occupy separate self-contained flats in the tenement and that together they would conduct settlement work among the building's tenants and neighbors in the tenement's basement. She planned to have the partition between the front two rooms of her three-room apartment removed to allow more space for settlement workers and neighbors to congregate.⁵⁵ Ovington persuaded philanthropist Henry Phipps to build a model tenement, but he insisted that she not carry out settlement work there. After several delays in construction, Ovington moved into the Tuskegee Apartments at 233 West Sixty-Third Street in the predominantly black San Juan Hill neighborhood in February 1908. She lived there for eight months and did what little settlement work she could, allowing children and mothers to use her rooms during the day and hosting conversations among black and white men and women about the city's and nation's racial problems during the evenings.⁵⁶ When the social barriers to the kind of interracial contact on which her vision of settlement work rested proved too great to allow her fully to actualize that vision, Ovington left the Tuskegee Apartments to establish the Lincoln Settlement House in one of Brooklyn's black neighborhoods with Dr. Verina Morton Jones, an accomplished middle-class black woman. Although Lincoln

Settlement served as an important place of exchange for its black neighbors, it did not provide the opportunities for interracial social exchange that had been so important to Ovington and Du Bois. The real condition of the industrial city—its physical and social environments—made it very difficult for black and white urbanites to participate in the processes of public sympathy that would lead to the friendships that Du Bois claimed were capable of solving many of the city's social problems.

Ovington's failure to establish Du Bois's vision of an interracial settlement house calls attention to some of the blind spots and inadequacies of the settlement movement's discourse of sympathy. Its confidence in the ability of personal contact to generate fellow-feeling rested, to some degree, on a naïveté about the possibility of bringing urbanites into personal contact with one another. Settlement intellectuals could not have anticipated that the political and economic forces that would drive patterns of urban growth throughout the twentieth century would only make it increasingly difficult to experience the kind of cross-class and interracial exchanges on which the sympathetic process they described depended. Intense suburbanization, the restructuring of the urban core, and the unequal distribution of home loans would harden the color line that separated urban blacks from other urbanites and suburbanites. But settlement residents seemed unaware, on some level, of the ways in which the real conditions of the industrial city interfered with the sympathetic process in which they had become so invested. They occasionally underestimated the power of the physical and social environments of their own cities to prevent urbanites from interacting with one another on terms that would allow them to obtain the kinds of fellow-feelings privileged in settlement discourse. The settlement movement's passionate investment in personal contact as the foundation of valuable urban relationships also failed to account adequately for the dramatic growth of the urban population that was already well underway in the Progressive Era. At a certain point, the industrial city's demographics did not match up with the settlement's discourse of urban sympathy. Although many settlements would continue operating for decades, their small semi-public spaces lacked the ability to bring a considerable fraction of an increasingly large number of city dwellers into direct contact with one another. As city populations grew, the settlement movement's discourse of sympathy provided a less and less satisfying account of the many different ways urbanites experienced being in the city with and attaining fellow-feelings for others.

The ability of an urbanist discourse of sympathy to make sense of the wide range of social experiences and relational forms among city dwellers would only become more insufficient as sympathy once again became a term used primarily to signify the kinds of emotional intimacies that Olmsted and others had privileged. Despite the efforts of settlement intellectuals to stretch the language and logic of sympathy beyond its nineteenth-century boundaries in order to legitimate the relationships formed among urbanites in public and semi-public spaces, the conceptual work performed by the term retracted over the course of the first few decades of the twentieth century. New Deal urbanists reclaimed sympathy from the settlement movement to pursue a discourse of sympathy that accentuated the singular importance of relationships founded on emotional intimacy. New Deal political ideologies and cultural narratives calcified the conceptual possibilities of sympathy in such a way that an urbanist discourse that revolved around sympathy became nearly incapable of signifying and privileging anything other than emotionally intimate fellow-feelings and relationships. Settlement residents may have carved new channels through which sympathy could flow among urbanites in public and semi-public spaces, but many of those channels collapsed in the 1930s, forcing urbanists to turn elsewhere to discover a discourse that could more satisfactorily account for and validate interactions among urbanites in public spaces that did not necessarily engender intimacy but that nevertheless generated fellow-feelings.

CHAPTER 2

New Deal Urbanism and the Contraction of Sympathy

In 1941, the Henry Street Settlement produced a play titled *A Dutchman's Farm* at its Neighborhood Playhouse on New York's Lower East Side. Put on, as settlement leader Helen Hall recalled, by one hundred and fifty of the settlement's neighbors, "from dramatic groups to mothers' and fathers' clubs," the production staged the history of housing on the Lower East Side in an effort to persuade its audience of the need for federally and state-funded slum clearance and public housing programs.[1] In the play's climactic scene, six mothers from the Lower East Side travel to Washington, D.C., to appear before a Senate committee and voice support for public housing legislation. As the spokeswoman for this small delegation, Mrs. Ziprin summons what had become the settlement movement's standard argument about the need for better and more affordable housing when she informs the committee that her ten-year-old son is "already estranged" from his tenement home because it is "not attractive to him." She passionately explains that "a home should be attractive and decent enough so that no barrier springs up between our children and ourselves. They must not become strangers!"[2] According to Mrs. Ziprin, the physical quality of the home determined the emotional quality of the feelings that bound families together. She attempts to persuade the Senate committee that the construction of attractive and structurally sound homes through government assistance would eliminate the affective barriers that had sprung up between children and parents who occupied the city's tenement flats. Public housing would, she assures the senators, restore emotional stability to her family and other families living in rundown buildings in cities across the nation.

The one hundred and fifty Lower East Siders who put on *A Dutchman's Farm* joined a much larger chorus of city dwellers who, during the 1920s and

1930s, pointed to inadequate and unaffordable housing as one of the most pressing issues facing U.S. cities. Although congested living quarters continued to be a problem about which city dwellers complained—especially in the neighborhoods where a rapidly growing number of black urbanites lived— many urbanists shifted their attention away from the number of people sharing a single tenement flat and focused instead on the quality and cost of a home in the city. As the labor and material expenses of urban housing rose dramatically over the first two decades of the twentieth century, lower- and middle-class urbanites found themselves in the position of having to pay a higher percentage of their income for an increasingly smaller percentage of the city's decent housing stock. Additionally, new modes of financing real estate developments in the city made it more profitable for developers to construct large-scale and upscale commercial and residential developments, thus diminishing the proportion of affordable and livable housing available to working-class urbanites. As the city settled into its early twentieth-century form of factory districts and residential neighborhoods tethered to downtown department stores, office skyscrapers, and luxury apartments by the railroad, subway, and streetcar, many urbanites struggled to secure attractive and affordable shelter. City dwellers such as Mrs. Ziprin tended to feel that the quality of their relationships, especially with their own family members, were threatened not by the number of people living under a single roof, but by the age and upkeep of the spaces in which they lived.[3]

While worrying that the interwar city had erected an emotional barrier between parents and children by physically destabilizing the urban home, many city dwellers simultaneously expressed concern about the ability of the city's informal organizations and formal institutions to continue to facilitate fellow-feelings among urbanites. Although many of the social structures that had supported patterns of affiliation and habits of interpersonal feeling among city dwellers persisted into the 1920s, the Great Depression crippled many of them. The churches, ethnic benefit societies, building and loan associations, and other neighborhood organizations on which working-class city dwellers had come to rely for material and emotional support were so weakened by the Depression that they had difficulty sustaining and facilitating the same degree of interpersonal connection that they had in previous years. The continued expansion of cities and metropolitan regions during the interwar period only added to the concerns of urban intellectuals that the social structures that had arisen to bring city dwellers into face-to-face contact and personal relations with one another were failing to do their jobs.[4]

Many urbanists responded to the crises of affect brought about by the transformation of the interwar city by pursuing and extending in their writing and city-making activities several strains of the urbanist discourse of sympathy that had been articulated by turn-of-the-century settlement intellectuals. Catherine Bauer, one of the period's leading advocates for public housing, blamed the lack of affordable and attractive urban housing on society's deeply felt desire to shelter and protect the "impregnable Family"—a desire that grew out of an almost irrational commitment to protect the "Rights of Man" and defend the "Freedom of the Individual" to "acquire, own, and dispose of property in any way which might benefit him." Both in her writing and public engagements, Bauer lobbied government officials, architects, and city planners to consider the "community as a whole" as the "real unit" of society, rather than the single family or individual citizen. She advocated treating the urban home not as a "barrack" from which to engage in battle with one's neighbors, but as a single "knot in a network" of other homes, shops, transportation lines, schools, and places of work. If "we want good cities," she insisted, society needed to develop an infrastructure capable of harnessing the "forces which keep people together and not of those which separate and individualize." Bauer argued for a philosophical and practical approach to urban housing that would facilitate the kind of public sympathy advocated by Progressive Era settlement residents rather than the emotional intimacies that held the "impregnable family" together.[5]

Other interwar urban intellectuals promoted alternative means by which city dwellers might engage in the type of face-to-face interactions in public spaces that would nurture fellow-feelings among them. Lewis Mumford, one of the most influential urban intellectuals of the interwar period, contended in his monumental *The Culture of Cities* (1938) that many of the efforts to address the city's problems through "housing and city planning" had been "handicapped because those who have undertaken the work have had no clear notion of the social functions of the city." Mumford shared with Bauer and Progressive settlement workers similar views about the ideal nature of social life in the city. He understood the city to be the "physical form of the highest and most complex types of associative life"—a life that consisted of interactions and associations forged among individuals beyond the boundaries of "tribe or family." Although Mumford shared Bauer's concerns about the role that housing played in facilitating or hindering fellow-feelings among strangers in public, he was more worried about the threat that "overgrown cities" posed to the vitality of the associative life. When cities became too big—as he felt many had become during the interwar period—Mumford argued that they became less effective in providing city dwellers with the institutions and social rituals that enabled them to establish emotional connections with one another. In addition to providing urbanites with the buildings, halls, and other physical spaces in which they might actualize their "social relatedness," city planners should, according to Mumford's particular urbanist discourse of sympathy, attempt to limit the size of the city. Rather than accept the megalopolis as the inevitable outcome of urban growth, he and his regionalist colleagues advocated the development of what he called the "polynucleated city": a cluster of cities "ranging in size from five thousand to fifty thousand" spread throughout a single region. These smaller cities would, he professed, provide residents the ideal setting in which to witness and participate in the "dramatization of communal life."[6]

Despite the efforts of Mumford, Bauer, and others to extend the particular urbanist discourse of sympathy that had been initiated by settlement intellectuals and that promoted the social and affective value of interactions among city dwellers in public and semi-public spaces, an increasingly large number of urbanists responded to the changing physical and social conditions of the interwar city by privileging the kind of intimate relationships most frequently experienced within the tribe and family. As the issue of affordable and adequate housing became the nation's primary urban concern during the 1930s, social scientists, city planners, politicians, and even some settlement residents, such as those at Henry Street Settlement, increasingly stressed the need to provide spaces in which city dwellers could maintain the intimate fellow-feelings among themselves that this particular phase of urban development appeared to threaten. Those who saw the city's dilapidated housing stock as its most pressing issue attempted to persuade the public to do something about it by depicting the city's unsafe and unsanitary homes as a threat to family relationships. According to this group of housing reformers, tenements and other residential buildings like them made it nearly impossible for the urban poor to get the affection they so desperately needed from their fathers, mothers, sons, daughters, and neighbors. Tenements, they reasoned, turned families and communities into strangers. Many of these urban housing reformers hoped to help elected officials and citizens see more adequate and affordable housing as essential to the nation's public health by dramatizing the urban housing crisis as a crisis of affect.

The public housing movement of the 1920s and 1930s marked a dramatic shift within an urbanist discourse of sympathy by stressing the singular importance of relationships founded on emotional intimacy—a shift that was, in many ways, a return to a mainstream nineteenth-century discourse of sympathy. Many public housing proponents contended not only that better, more affordable housing would improve the quality of fellow-feelings within families, but also that these new residential structures would create the physical environment in which similar but unrelated urbanites might acquire familial fellow-feelings for each other. The passage of the U.S. Housing Act of 1937—which created the political mechanisms through which cities received federal funds for slum clearance and low-income housing construction—signaled the codification in federal policy and, subsequently, in the city's built environment of the relatively narrow and conventional understanding of sympathy that was at the heart of the most prevalent discussions about urban housing. Although some settlement workers, social scientists, and public housing activists tried to use the language and logic of sympathy to account for the wide range of fellow-feelings and relationships that connected city dwellers to one another, New Deal political ideologies and cultural narratives calcified the conceptual possibilities of sympathy in such a way that an urbanist discourse that revolved around sympathy became nearly incapable of signifying and privileging anything other than emotionally intimate fellow-feelings and relationships. In its codified and calcified form, the interwar urbanist discourse of sympathy facilitated an approach to urban redevelopment that sacrificed local streets, small commercial establishments, community gathering places, and other public spaces for the construction of better and more affordable homes—an approach that was primarily invested in the development of private spaces and that would sustain the nation's urban renewal agenda for decades to come.

In interwar urbanist discourse, then, the concept of sympathy transitioned from being a term used to characterize and legitimize the value of interactions among city dwellers in public and semi-public spaces to one primarily used to indicate the kinds of emotional intimacies that could only emerge within domestic and other private spaces. The urbanist discourse of sympathy backslid, it could be said, to its pre-settlement house status—to the type of discourse pursued by Frederick Law Olmsted and many other nineteenth-century urban intellectuals. Sociologists at the University of Chicago such as Robert E. Park and Ernest W. Burgess laid the foundation for the conceptual regression of sympathy within twentieth-century urbanist discourse by dividing relationships into two categories: primary (intimate, face-to-face) and secondary (public, casual) associations. Although Chicago sociologists regularly pointed out the advantages of secondary relationships, they frequently pronounced these relationships—especially those forged in the city's tenement districts—to be emotionally inferior to the primary relationships rooted in the small town or rural village. Their evaluations of the city's social landscape influenced the way that a wide number of urban intellectuals thought and wrote about the city. In particular, Clarence Arthur Perry, one of the most influential urban planners of the 1920s and 1930s, translated the type of urbanism advanced by Chicago sociologists into the city's built environment. His concept of the "neighborhood unit" exaggerated the value of primary relationships and the emotional intimacies they facilitated while marginalizing the significance of secondary, public interactions among city dwellers. A sociological and planning discourse that increasingly revolved around a relatively narrow and conventional understanding of sympathy thus informed a public housing discourse powerful enough to reshape both the interwar urban imaginary and the city's built environment. This narrow understanding of sympathy and the implications of that understanding on the built environment was staged for the public in the Federal Theatre Project's popular production of Arthur Arent's *One-Third of a Nation* (1938).

The Chicago School's Sentimental Sociology

During the interwar period, sociologists at the University of Chicago acquired the type of explanatory power over urban life that settlement writers had possessed in the Progressive Era. Their extensive studies of Chicago's newcomers and neighborhoods shaped the way that a wide range of urban intellectuals thought and wrote about the city. Running through their sociological accounts of city life is a prominent storyline about the inability of urbanites to form meaningful relationships with one another. This potent plot of urban anomie exerted a particularly powerful influence on contemporary urbanists. In his foundational contribution to the Chicago school's canon, "The City: Suggestions for the Investigation of Human Behavior in the Urban Environment," Robert E. Park established the pattern of thinking and writing about the city's social landscape that his fellow sociologists would pursue in subsequent years. Writing in 1915, Park observed that the city's recent structural transformations, particularly the development of its transportation and communication networks, had led to the "substitution of indirect, 'secondary,' for direct, face-to-face, 'primary' relations in the associations of individuals in the community." According to Park, the city was no longer a place where neighborhoods and other social institutions brought individuals the same degree of emotional connection that they had experienced in "simpler and more primitive forms of society." Instead, the city forced "individuals and groups of individuals" who were "widely removed in sympathy and understanding" to "live together under conditions of interdependence, if not of intimacy."[7]

Chicago sociologists tried to be as open as possible to the social advantages of an urban life in which individuals reaped the rewards of the affiliations they experienced in the city and avoided the disadvantages of a moral order that had, in the past, been maintained through sometimes stifling intimacies. Writing over twenty years after Park's influential 1915 essay and from a vantage point that enabled him to perceive more clearly the benefits of an urban environment dominated by secondary relationships, Louis Wirth asserted in "Urbanism as a Way of Life" that city dwellers experience a "certain degree of emancipation or freedom from the personal and emotional controls of intimate groups" that enables them to "pursue their own diverging interests in their vocational, educational, religious, recreational, and political life." Wirth and other sociologists frequently acknowledged that, even though the city's demographic density and diversity made it difficult for urbanites to maintain the kind of "intimate and lasting acquaintanceship" that generated an emotionally satisfying sense of community, they were compensated with increased social and economic mobility.[8] In their most forward-thinking moments, early twentieth-century sociologists began to question the very standards with which they and others had been evaluating the social value of the urban community. Cecil C. North, a sociologist at Ohio State University, suggested that, although members of urban communities appear to have "little sympathy for, or understanding of, one another," it might not be useful to think exclusively of these communities as the product of "situations where simple, face-to-face relations prevail." Although important activities such as mail delivery and road building are typically "carried on in a highly impersonal manner devoid of conscious co-operation," North pointed out that these communal endeavors "would not be possible if there did not exist a very vital co-operative relationship between the citizens of the nation as well as between states and local groups."[9] One can perceive in the lines of sociological thought developed by Wirth,

North, and others the beginnings of a way of thinking about urban sociality that would be more fully developed in post-World War II urbanist discourse.

Despite the efforts of some urban sociologists to draw attention to the positive social aspects of an urban landscape dominated by secondary relationships, a sense of uneasiness about the health of urban communities and individual relationships pervaded interwar sociological discourse. The Chicago school's apprehensive assessments of an urban society no longer built on face-to-face interactions drew directly on the language and logic of eighteenth- and nineteenth-century Anglo-American social philosophy. Park's decision to signal his concern about the relationships formed in congested city neighborhoods by noting the lack of sympathy among individuals and groups of individuals rested on his and his colleagues' deliberate efforts to establish their discipline on the intellectual foundations of eighteenth-century moral philosophy. Aside from Albion Small's *Adam Smith and Modern Sociology* (1907),[10] nowhere is the intellectual bridge between moral philosophy and Chicago sociology more visible than in Park and Ernest W. Burgess's field-defining textbook *Introduction to the Science of Sociology* (1921). In the chapter on "Social Interaction," Park and Burgess included ten unedited paragraphs from Adam Smith's *The Theory of Moral Sentiments* (1759). The passages they excerpted contain Smith's classic description of sympathy as the imaginative power through which we "place ourselves" in another's "situation" and enter "as it were into his body and become in some measure the same person with him, and thence form some idea of his sensations."[11] Unless readers pay careful attention to the footnote, Smith's original account of sympathy's affective operations reads as though it were written by the authors of the textbook. Park and Burgess made no attempt through layout design or typography to indicate that the four pages following the section heading "Rational Sympathy" had been written by someone other than themselves. The *Introduction to the Science of Sociology*'s textual appropriation of Smith's prose conveys Chicago sociology's relatively unfiltered adoption of his social ideals in their evaluations of urban life. Unlike Jane Addams and other settlement workers at nearby Hull-House, Chicago sociologists did not feel compelled to modify the meanings with which Smith had endowed sympathy.[12] Their urbanist discourse did not seek to expose the alternate channels through which sympathy might flow among city dwellers, but instead called on their culture's conventional understandings of sympathy's affective processes and relational forms.

While Park, Burgess, and others continued to use the terminology and imagery of moral philosophy and the culture that had grown up around the concept of sympathy, they more frequently articulated their social ideals and corresponding misgivings about urban relationships through the more scientific sounding categories of "primary" and "secondary." As was made clear in Charles Horton Cooley's descriptions of these terms in 1909, these categories for evaluating social relationships were rooted in assumptions about the individual's need to give and receive sympathy. Cooley, who helped pioneer the field of sociology in the United States at the turn of the century and whom Park quoted extensively in his seminal 1915 essay, explained that the primary relationship is "characterized by intimate face-to-face association and cooperation" and "involves the sort of sympathy and mutual identification for which 'we' is the natural expression." Primary relationships allow individuals to fulfill the "sentiments and impulses"—namely "sympathy and the innumerable sentiments into which sympathy enters"—that constitute their "human nature."[13] Secondary contacts, by contrast, contain relatively little face-to-face interaction and therefore, according to sociologists, do not generate the type of intimate connections among individuals that lead to fellow-feelings. In interwar sociological discourse, secondary interactions were thought to be, according to political scientist and Chicago school collaborator Nicholas Spykman, "empty of content"; they are "merely the transitory meetings of strangers, in which the individual uniqueness of the participants remains hidden behind a shield of formal objectivity, aloofness, and indifference."[14] Without access to the hidden emotions and experiences of others, individuals would find it challenging to imagine themselves in another's position. Secondary contacts, according to many urban sociologists, fail to produce fellow-feelings.

Even Wirth's more seasoned and optimistic sociological discourse retained significant remnants of the discipline's habits of talking about secondary urban interactions as emotionally hollow. At the same time that he acknowledged the individual freedoms that the interwar city's social landscape made possible, Wirth repeatedly pointed out that its population size, density, and heterogeneity made it nearly impossible for city dwellers to achieve "bonds of kinship" and of "neighborliness," and instead led to the "segmentalization of human relationships." Even when contact among urbanites in the public realm was face to face, Wirth described these exchanges as "impersonal, superficial, transitory, and segmental." Echoing Georg Simmel's characterization of the city's influence on the individual city dweller's mental and social life,

Wirth suggested that the "reserve, the indifference, and the blasé outlook which urbanites manifest in their relationships" with one another was often the source of the city's well rehearsed social problems. Echoing the diagnoses of many of the urban sociologists that preceded him, Wirth reasoned that the "close living together and working together of individuals who have no sentimental and emotional ties" tend to "foster a spirit of competition, aggrandizement, and mutual exploitation"; "close physical contact" among city dwellers, "coupled with great social distance," too often gives rise to feelings of "loneliness" and "irritation."[15]

The Chicago school's assessments of interpersonal relationships inherited and perpetuated an earlier geographic bias. According to most late nineteenth- and early twentieth-century sociologists, primary relationships developed most naturally in the social and spatial environments of small, rural towns. In his formative description of the primary group, Cooley noted that the "village community" has always been the "chief sphere of sympathy and mutual aid" and "remains so in rural districts at the present day."[16] Although Chicago sociologists called attention to the social possibilities of city life, they did not overturn the assumptions through which Cooley and others mapped out the young discipline's approach to evaluating social behavior. In their *Introduction to the Science of Sociology,* Park and Burgess seemed to reinforce Cooley's assertions by noting that the village is the "natural area of primary contacts," for only in the village are individuals "in contact with each other at practically all points of their lives." The constant social contact stimulated by the village's limited physical boundaries bred the type of interpersonal intimacy that qualified a relationship as "primary": "lovers, bosom friends, and boon companions."[17] Chicago sociologists used the rural communities built on these primary relationships as a standard against which they often measured the urban communities they studied. They turned not just to Chicago's hinterland to find evidence of the village's social stability, but also to the European communities from which many of Chicago's immigrants had arrived.[18] C. Wright Mills pointed out the irony of urban sociological discourse when, in the early 1940s, he observed that the "operating criteria" of Chicago sociologists and other social pathologists of the city were "typically *rural* in orientation and extraction."[19]

For Chicago sociologists, the rapid physical and demographic growth of the interwar city created social circumstances that facilitated secondary contacts while stifling primary relationships. Given the increasing ease with which urbanites could move across the cityscape and communicate with those not in close physical proximity to them, the modern city undermined the spatial order and therefore the social logic of the village. The city, Park posited, is made up of a "mosaic of little worlds which touch but do not interpenetrate" and across which city dwellers move "quickly and easily."[20] This physical and social mobility allowed urbanites to participate in several different subgroups, freeing them to pursue their own interests and professions, but it also meant that they rarely spent enough time with a single community to develop primary relationships with others. Emory Bogardus and many Chicago sociologists described this paradox of physical proximity and emotional detachment as "social distance." They claimed that there was too much "social distance" among urbanites for them to achieve "fellow-feeling and understanding."[21] Chicago sociologists saw the social distance that pervaded the urban landscape as the fundamental cause for the social disorders that they spent two decades studying: gangs, delinquency, immorality, economic exploitation, transiency, and psychological instability. According to Park, the "breaking down of local attachments and the weakening of the restraints and inhibitions of the primary group, under the influence of the urban environment," must be seen as "largely responsible for the increase of vice and crime in great cities."[22]

According to the studies produced by Chicago sociologists in the twenties and thirties, nowhere were secondary contacts and the social ills that accompanied them more concentrated than in the city's tenement districts and slums. The suboptimal social conditions that Chicago sociologists diagnosed throughout the city in general were exacerbated for those who lived in tenements and lodging houses. In his study of Chicago's Near North Side, *The Gold Coast and the Slum* (1929), Harvey Zorbaugh asserted that there was "nothing of the nature of a community" in the section or the neighborhood dominated by lodging houses. He admitted that the lack of community in this particular Chicago slum may have had something to do with the "broken," "disorganized," and "ineffective" families who settled there, but suggested that the structures that sheltered these families were largely responsible for generating social distance among them. Zorbaugh argued that the "very physical conditions of lodging-house life" made "impossible that constellation of attitudes about a home, with its significant ritual, which affords the basis for that emotional interdependence which is the sociological significant fact of family life." Consequently, the "person who dwells in the lodging-house of the slum has to meet his problems alone."[23] Zorbaugh's evaluation of the Near North Side's slums rested on one of his culture's core assumptions: that a community's well-being ultimately depends on the ability of the individual home to cultivate familial fellow-feelings among its occupants. More specifically, Zorbaugh argued that the formation of emotional interdependence among individuals who shared a home depended not only on the quality of the individuals, but also on the condition of the physical structures within which they lived.

The Chicago school's narrative about the proliferation of secondary relationships and the corresponding decline of primary relationships in the city marked a distinct shift in twentieth-century urbanist discourse. Chicago sociologists intended to provide a mode of understanding the city's social landscape that was more suitable to the urban conditions of the interwar period than that provided by Progressive Era urbanists. The flaw in settlement thinking, Zorbaugh argued, was its refusal to account for the "inevitable trends in the growth of the city." In their efforts to "restore to local urban areas the neighborliness, sentiment, and face-to-face associations of the town," settlement workers ignored the city's growth trends, "which are clearly in the opposite direction—toward secondary contacts in local areas, toward anonymity in these areas, toward the organization of persons upon the basis of interest rather than of sentiment."[24] In many ways, Zorbaugh was right—the urban sociology to which he, Park, Burgess, Wirth, and others contributed was more attentive to and capable of making sense of the city's expanding physical form and the predominantly secondary relationships that it sheltered. But the particular language and logic of sympathy that permeated interwar sociological discourse simultaneously limited its ability to account for the social value of those secondary relationships. Because the interpersonal fellow-feelings that sociologists characterized as sympathetic tended to be the kind of emotionally intimate ones experienced among family members, close friends, and fellow tribesmen, their particular discourse of sympathy privileged a far narrower range of emotional connections and relational forms than those legitimized by a settlement discourse of sympathy.

Clarence A. Perry and the Neighborhood Unit

As many urbanists deployed the persuasive rhetoric of urban sociology to explain the shifting nature of city life in the interwar period, assess its social shortcomings, and propose solutions to urban problems, they picked up on and expanded its preferential treatment of primary relationships. The shift in an urbanist discourse of sympathy initiated by Chicago sociologists became especially pronounced in the emerging field of city planning. During the 1920s and 1930s, urban planners drew on urban sociological discourse as they fashioned the social objectives they hoped to achieve through the design and redevelopment of the urban environment. Ironically, in light of Zorbaugh's critique of Progressive urbanists and his confidence in city planning as a "new conception of action," interwar city planners often called on urban sociology in order to justify their efforts to create spaces in which urbanites could nurture intimate, neighborly, face-to-face relationships.[25] Taking their cues from urban sociology's characterization of primary relationships as more emotionally legitimate than secondary ones, planners were determined to create environments that would help individuals regain the intimate associations that the twentieth-century city seemed to have weakened. In translating the Chicago school's sociological discourse of sympathy to the vernacular of planning, interwar city planners amplified the value of intimate relationships. In the parlance of the growing discipline of city planning, sympathy signified an even narrower range of fellow-feelings than those to which sociologists used the term to refer. Shelby M. Harrison, the director of the social division for the Russell Sage Foundation's ambitious and important Regional Plan of New York and Its Environs (RPNYE), explained in the seventh volume of the *Regional Survey of New York and Its Environs* (1929) that it was time to "discover the physical basis for that kind of face-to-face association which characterized the old village community and which the large city finds it so difficult to re-create." City planners typically snubbed the settlement movement's progressive theorizations of sympathy and neglected sociology's more nuanced understanding of urban community. They tended instead to embrace the more conventional social and spatial ideals of the old village community in their efforts to reconstruct the city.[26]

Clarence Arthur Perry, one of the most influential urban planners of the 1920s and 1930s, became particularly invested in redeveloping an urban environment in which city dwellers might cultivate interpersonal intimacies. His concept of the "neighborhood unit"—a planning model that he developed and championed during the interwar period—was one of the most significant and influential ideas to come out of the young field of city planning. The neighborhood unit gained immediate traction with a wide range of urban intellectuals: city planners, architects, real estate developers, municipal and federal politicians, and social workers. Writing for the *American Journal of*

Sociology in 1934, Charles S. Ascher proclaimed that the neighborhood unit had already become "fundamental in planning thinking."[27] An ideological repository of the swelling cultural attitudes about the primacy of primary relationships, the neighborhood unit became a tool with which private developers and, eventually, municipal and federal governments could remake the urban landscape.

The neighborhood unit, as Perry defined it in his contribution to the *Regional Survey of New York and Its Environs*, refers to a "scheme of arrangement for a family-life community." Unlike Bauer and Mumford, Perry approached city planning with the assumption that the family unit contained the most valid relationships and that cities ought to facilitate domestic patterns of sociality. Not only did Perry design neighborhoods and urban communities that would meet "all the requirements which urban family life imposes upon its local environment," but he also used kinship as a model for understanding and advocating nondomestic social forms. He imagined public relationships as emotional extensions of private relationships, suggesting that city dwellers should feel connected to one another in the same way that they feel connected to their mothers, fathers, and siblings. Familial intimacy served as the social ideal toward which the neighborhood unit aspired. Perry hoped to help developers construct neighborhoods that would shelter family-life communities by following a few basic planning principles. Perhaps the best-known characteristic of the neighborhood unit is that it should contain just enough people to populate an elementary school. But Perry also claimed that neighborhoods should be clearly bounded by arterial streets that would discourage as much cross-neighborhood traffic as possible. He promoted ample park and recreation space and suggested that neighborhoods be centered socially and physically around family friendly institutions such as churches and schools. Believing that mixed-use environments generated blight, Perry encouraged planners to site shopping districts at the periphery of neighborhoods. If planners and developers followed these principles, Perry promised that neighborhoods would bring back to the city the "psychical conditions" that are the natural consequences of "face-to-face relationships."[28]

Perry invoked the authority of Chicago sociology as he tried to persuade others to buy into the idea of the neighborhood unit. In the closing section of his seminal study in the *Regional Survey of New York and Its Environs*, Perry rested his case for the neighborhood unit almost entirely on the "fundamental discoveries of modern research" made by sociologists. He cited the

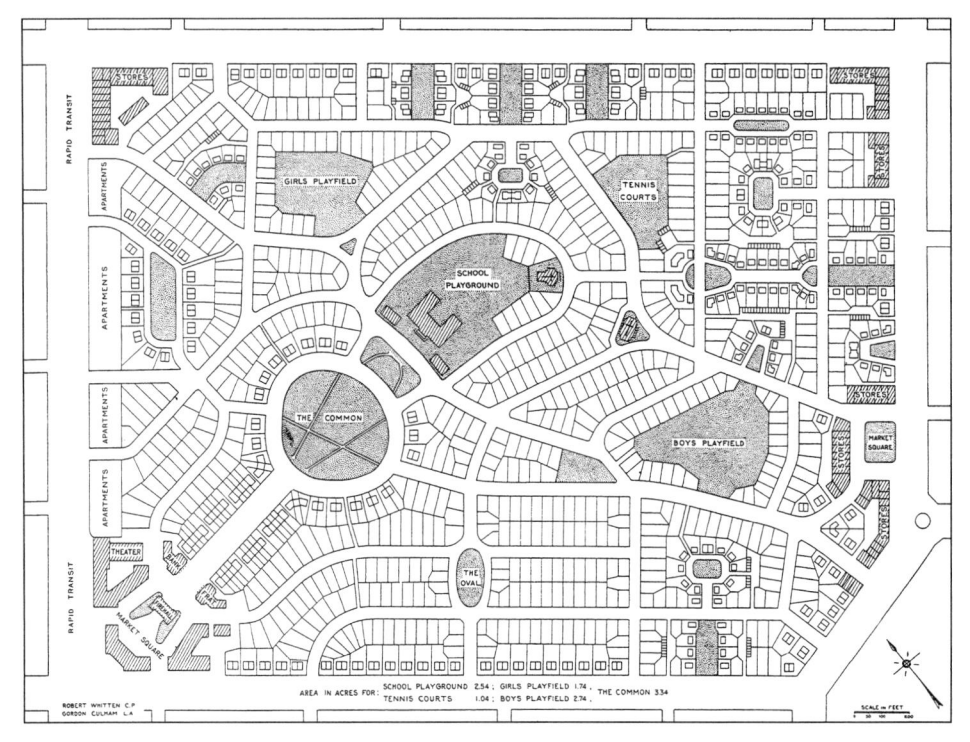

Figure 4. An example of a neighborhood unit plan that Perry used to illustrate his planning theories as he delivered lectures and lantern slide shows to audiences at New York University, Harvard University, and other groups during the 1920s. He included the plan in his contribution to the *Regional Survey of New York and Its Environs*, entitled *The Neighborhood Unit: A Scheme of Arrangement for the Family-Life Community*. Regional Plan Association.

writings of Cooley and Bogardus as evidence of the "psychical significance" and "tremendous influence" of the "primary group." He turned to Park and Herbert A. Miller to reiterate the "proper quality of community life in a populated district" that he had been describing throughout his study. And he called on Frederic M. Thrasher to illuminate the "vicious conditions" that arise where there is no "associate community environment."[29] In *Housing for the Machine Age* (1939), Perry's summative account of the neighborhood unit, he used the credentials of Burgess, Zorbaugh, William I. Thomas, and Roderick D. McKenzie to validate his credo that the "face-to-face condition is a normal feature of the environment of society and that man tends to degenerate when it is missing."[30] In his efforts to give credibility to the concept of the neighborhood unit, Perry overlooked the nuanced approach that Chicago sociologists had taken to the interwar city, omitting their discussions of the social value of secondary relationships and focusing instead on their frequent praise of primary relationships.

Perry inflated the social value assigned to primary relationships by Chicago sociologists by importing into his planning dialect a distinctly nineteenth-century urban imaginary. Perry repeatedly acknowledged the close connection between the neighborhood unit and the actual neighborhood where he had lived since 1912. Financed by the Russell Sage Foundation and designed by Olmsted, Jr., Forest Hills Gardens had been built as an experimental commuter suburb in Queens to model a new approach to suburban development. Perry praised Forest Hills Gardens's "fine quality of neighborly social life" and attributed its social character to a "real-estate plan which brought people of somewhat similar standards into proximity, and then promoted acquaintanceships and congenial groupings through the mere routine of caring for common values and facilities."[31] It is easy to hear in Perry's descriptions of Forest Hills Gardens distinct echoes of Olmsted, Sr.'s portrayals of his urban parks as spaces that made sympathy among city dwellers possible by removing them from the "restraining and confining conditions" of the city.[32] Perry's characterization of congeniality in Forest Hills Gardens as a social product made possible by groupings of people of similar standards also exhibits Olmsted Sr.'s skepticism about the ability of sympathy to help individuals overcome the social, cultural, and class differences present in an urban environment—only in a space such as Central Park could sympathy help city dwellers connect across their differences. Forest Hills Gardens materialized a nineteenth-century culture of sympathy that had never fully disappeared during the Progressive period. Perry's neighborhood unit provided a bridge across which the social and spatial forms belonging to this culture might migrate into a supposedly postsentimental urban society.

But Perry's commitment to return to the city the "primary group environment" about which Chicago sociologists had written and that Olmsted had tried to bring to life through his urban parks was distinct from the urban visions of his predecessors in the nature of its demand for homogeneity. Perry was convinced that sympathy could not be achieved among individuals living in socially diverse urban communities. The sympathetic process could not, as he and many of his contemporaries understood it, connect city dwellers to one another across the social, cultural, and economic distances that persisted in the interwar city. The neighborhood-unit scheme aimed to create a physical environment that nurtured intimate fellow-feelings among neighbors by replacing urban diversity with homogeneity. Perry repeatedly argued in his writings that the "great foe to community life is heterogeneity."[33] Standardizing the urban dwelling and its surroundings would standardize the type of residents attracted to a residential environment. Perry's unique real estate plan would, he promised potential residents, "automatically" draw "together a group of people of similar living standards and similar economic ability."[34] For urbanites accustomed to withdrawing from the city's public sphere because of the lack of socially compatible neighbors, the neighborhood unit's physical homogeneity would foster a demographic uniformity that would, in turn, provide residents with multiple opportunities to acquire the type of familial fellow-feelings that he valued above other types of affection. The neighborhood-unit scheme attempted to facilitate sympathetic exchanges among city dwellers by making it as easy as possible for them to identify with one another.

Given the neighborhood unit's mission to support a family lifestyle and return primary relationships to the city, Perry felt that the implementation of his real estate plan would do the most social good in those sections of the city most overrun by secondary contacts: the slums. He had been fully persuaded by the "recent sociological studies" that had "shown a high correlation between delinquency and the slum environment." He argued that the apartment house districts typically found in the slums created an objectionable and "unsatisfactory family environment" that was "hostile to primary grouping." The social conditions of these slum areas had become so degraded, in Perry's mind, that nothing could be done to their existing infrastructure to stabilize them as a healthy family environment. Regulatory measures would not eradicate the social and physical blight of the slums. In order to create an urban environment in apartment house districts that facilitated primary grouping, Perry insisted on the necessity of demolishing the slum's "present structures and internal streets" and preparing a "wholly new plan for that district" that would include a completely "new arrangement of dwellings, open-spaces, and institutions." He expressed optimism that the right kind of "city planning [would] hopefully act as a birth control upon slum conditions."[35] Perry's striking metaphor of city planning as family planning discloses not only his opposition to the spread of a particular type of built environment but also the nature of his dissatisfaction: he did not want the type of interpersonal relationships that slum conditions had bred to reproduce themselves through emotionally dysfunctional relationships. Perry reasoned that private and public partnerships that had not achieved the right style of emotional intimacy should not be allowed to enjoy the benefits of sexual intimacy.

Although the neighborhood unit—with its ample recreational spaces and meandering arterial streets—might be most fully and naturally implemented in the undeveloped properties on the city's periphery, Perry maintained that the scheme's essential planning principles should be adapted to the spatial conditions of the urban core. In the early days of promoting the neighborhood unit, he developed a five-block apartment house module that he claimed could be constructed in a deteriorating and dense urban neighborhood such as the Lower East Side. This downtown iteration of the neighborhood unit consisted of apartment buildings erected along the perimeter of a five-block property to enclose a common park and recreation space. Having been built over the preexisting city streets, thus shutting out the diverse human traffic that they carried, this common area would nurture the homogeneous primary grouping discouraged by the diverse neighborhood it had replaced. Although the neighborhood unit that Perry imagined developing on the Lower East Side would cater to businessmen and their families, he firmly believed that these five-block modules need not be limited to sheltering upper-class communities. When the "unit principles have become better understood, and architects and builders have had experience in applying them," he argued, then surely "other plans, within the means of quite a wide range of income classes, will be developed."[36]

While working up plans to restore intimate face-to-face relationships to cities through the implementation of the neighborhood-unit scheme, Perry realized that individual planners and private developers could not transform the city's physical and social orders on their own. He began to understand that expensive city real estate, high building costs, and the logistics of assembling multiple individually owned properties presented significant challenges to the production of neighborhood units during the interwar period. In the early stages of his survey of the Winfield neighborhood in Queens, Perry observed that the "cooperation of the municipality" would be crucial if "current costs [were to] be paid for the land, the demolition of the present structures, and the building of new apartments, and the whole development marketed at prices which would bring a modest commercial profit."[37] Even more problematic than financing these urban neighborhood units, though,

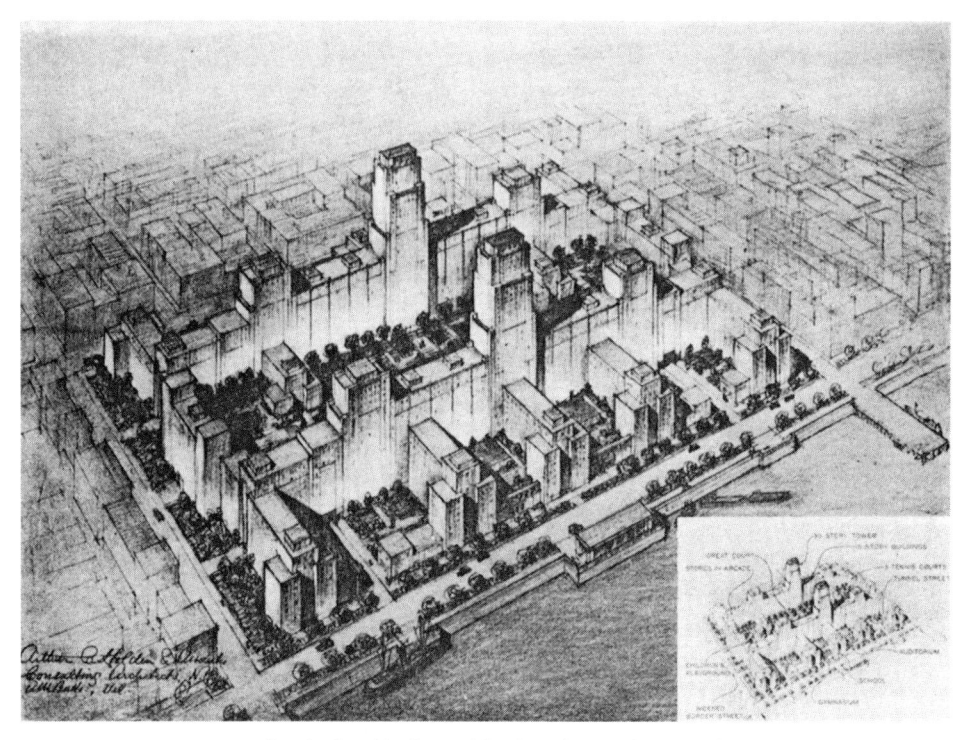

Figure 5. An example of a five-block neighborhood unit plan in a downtown setting that Perry used to illustrate his planning theories as he gave lectures during the 1920s on city planning. This particular five-block neighborhood unit was developed by Arthur C. Holden and Associates to be built at 131 East Twenty-Third Street, New York. The plan features sunlight, recreation spaces, local shops, school, gymnasium, and entertainment facilities for 1,000 families and limits exposure to traffic dangers. Perry included these sketches in his contribution to the *Regional Survey of New York and Its Environs*, entitled *The Neighborhood Unit: A Scheme of Arrangement for the Family-Life Community*. Regional Plan Association.

would be assembling the massive blocks of land on which they could be built. Perry and other city planners who aspired to construct neighborhood units needed the legal and rhetorical muscle to compel individual property owners to sell their land for the good of the comprehensive plan. The "plan of development," Perry reasoned, "leaves no room for abstentions"; the materialization of a neighborhood unit is "absolutely dependent upon a 100 per cent community action." Perry concluded that only the government possessed the ability to "coerce the unwilling minority into cooperation." In order to bring to the city the social conditions for which Perry and other urbanists yearned, the federal government would need to enter the private housing market. "The time has arrived," Perry announced in 1933, "when it is fitting to project 'a new deal' in the real estate world."[38]

Staging a New Deal for Public Housing

The federal government began to broker the new deal for which Perry and many others had been calling by establishing the Public Works Administration's (PWA) Housing Division in 1933 through the National Industrial Recovery Act. During the course of its four-year life, the PWA constructed fifty-one subsidized housing projects in thirty-six different cities. The government finalized the new deal it had initiated through the PWA when it passed the U.S. Housing Act of 1937. Often referred to as the Wagner-Steagall Act, this landmark piece of legislation gave city planners, private developers, housing activists, and municipal leaders both the legal authority and the financial resources to clear slums and construct the type of primary-group environments for which Perry and others had yearned. As historians of public housing have made clear, the Wagner-Steagall Act was the product of many competing approaches to the urban housing crisis; the legislative process marginalized some approaches while favoring others. Despite the varied opinions about what types of relational forms and interpersonal emotions public housing ought to cultivate, the view of urban social life solidified in the Housing Act of 1937 intensified the conceptual contraction of sympathy that had been advanced through the fields of sociology and city planning during the interwar period.[39] The Wagner-Steagall Act, which instigated the redevelopment of the city's physical and social landscape over the next several decades, consummated society's growing investment in a model of urban sociality that privileged private, intimate relationships. The Federal Theatre Project (FTP) production of Arent's *One-Third of a Nation*, which opened at New York's Adelphi Theatre on January 17, 1938, and was later performed in cities across the nation, dramatized the social ideals codified in the Wagner-Steagall Act. *One-Third* taught viewers how tenement housing interfered with the formation of intimate relationships among city dwellers and helped them understand and feel how public housing would enable urbanites to reestablish that lost intimacy. As urbanites watched *One-Third*, they felt for the actors on stage the kind of sympathy privileged within New

Deal urban policies and narratives—a fellow-feeling that consisted of intense intimacies rather than casual associations.[40]

One of several Living Newspapers produced by the FTP, *One-Third* staged the brand of sympathy that had become a prominent feature of New Deal urbanist discourse through blending agitprop and epic theater with traditional melodrama.[41] While *One-Third*'s enactment of the Living Newspaper's experimental features certainly appealed to audiences, its experimentalism did not mask the fact that the play was, as a critic for the *New York Times* observed, a "trenchant melodrama." Edward Carberry, writing for the *Cincinnati Post*, went so far as to suggest that the Cincinnati FTP unit's production of *One-Third* made "most melodramas seem tame."[42] In characterizing *One-Third* as a melodrama, these and other theatergoers were no doubt referring to the play's success in connecting viewers in emotionally intense ways to those who had become victims of the city's run-down tenements. Melodrama attempts to move viewers to experience the type of emotionally charged attachments toward the play's virtuous characters that they might feel for members of their family or close friends. By minimizing the complexity of its characters and the moral ambiguities of the circumstances in which they find themselves, melodramas strive to elicit from viewers the kind of deeply felt, interpersonal connections that simulate the more intense affections that tend to bind private relationships together. The genre does not usually traffic in the less forceful fellow-feelings that animate relationships formed in the public sphere.[43]

One-Third begins to educate its audience in melodramatic emotion as soon as the curtain lifts. In the opening scene, a fire breaks out in what theater critic Burns Mantle described as a "cross-sectioned four-story tenement"—a stage set that rivaled any "this town has ever shown" and that captured the physical inadequacy of urban housing that was the source of the period's primary urban concerns.[44] As the building burns, a "*crowd of* ONLOOKERS *and* PASSERS-BY *starts to gather*" and gaze up. Their attention fixes on a man stuck on a fire escape. As the crowd rushes to "*a spot directly underneath the fire escape*," they "*point to the* MAN *above who has been cowering on the fire escape*." Witnessing his immobility, the crowd gathered beneath the burning building instinctively imitates the man's physical and emotional position: they, too, "*freeze*."[45] Although a sudden blackout shuts down the dramatic action just as the actors and audience begin to connect emotionally with the endangered man, it would be inaccurate to interpret this modernist narrative break as the director's attempt to reject sympathetic identification as a dramatic tool in the mode of Bertolt Brecht. Rather, this moment puts the audience in a state of readiness to reenact repeatedly the affective process initiated, if not completely fulfilled, by this scene. *One-Third* incorporates the audience's impulse to identify with those on stage into its dramatic action when, one-third of the way through the show, a man makes his way from the auditorium seating to the stage. Driven to break the fourth wall by what he describes to the audience as his desperation to escape the terrible conditions of the tenements in which he had lived, this man never returns to his seat. Instead, Angus K. Buttonkooper remains on stage for the duration of the play and becomes its protagonist. As an everyman who was once a member of the audience, Buttonkooper's physical proximity to the scenes of tenement suffering facilitates the audience's emotional connection to the victims of the city's physically unsatisfactory and unaffordable housing stock. Through the figure of Buttonkooper, the audience more readily establishes intimate fellow-feelings with the virtuous tenement dwellers on stage. Buttonkooper, as one viewer of the Detroit Federal Theatre's production of *One-Third* reported, played a "very sympathetic part . . . in which every member of the audience can imagine himself."[46]

One-Third provides Buttonkooper and audience members multiple opportunities to sympathize with the tenement dwellers, not by staging more catastrophic events but by animating the social diagnoses of tenement life that had been delivered by sociologists, city planners, and other urban intellectuals—namely, that tenements deprived their inhabitants of primary, intimate relationships. The relational depravity to which tenement dwellers had been pushed by their living conditions can be seen most clearly when Buttonkooper's "Guide" takes him uptown to Harlem's "Hot Bed" district, where, in the tenements off Lenox Avenue between 135th and 145th Streets, urbanites sometimes arranged to split up the cost of renting a single bed over the course of a day. The Hot Bed episode opens as a light slowly illuminates the upper right cubicle of the tenement stage set and a man (First Negro) stands in the center of the cubicle as he prepares for bed. When he finds another man (Second Negro) still sleeping in his bed, the play momentarily invokes the tender intimacies that, in other plays and novels, typically accompany these bedside moments. In sentimental narratives such as Harriet Beecher Stowe's *Uncle Tom's Cabin* (1852), the bed is often where interpersonal intimacy is most intensely felt and expressed. Too consumed by his own need to sleep, however, the First Negro cannot afford to imagine himself in the position of the slumbering man and act out the compassionate

Figure 6. The opening scene of Arent's *One-Third of a Nation* during a performance at the Adelphi Theatre in 1938. The scene showcases Howard Bay's masterful stage set, which he designed as a cross section of a four-story tenement building. Federal Theater Project Collection, Music Division, Library of Congress, ftp0068.

feelings that might arise from this sympathetic process. Instead, he barks, "Hey, wake up!" (89). The spatial and economic logic of the tenement denies the First Negro the physical and emotional distance he needs to participate in a sympathetic exchange. The scene literalizes Park's fears about the consequences of forcing "individuals and groups of individuals" who are "widely removed in sympathy and understanding" to "live together under conditions of interdependence, if not of intimacy." It also acknowledges the ways in which the intensification of the migration of Southern blacks to Northeastern, Midwestern, and Western cities during the 1920s and 1930s had exacerbated the problem of urban housing. According to the rationale of the Hot Bed scene, tenements stripped their inhabitants of the emotionally satisfying relationships that should be grounded in the family unit and replaced them with a series of hostile exchanges among strangers.

By dramatizing the lack of intimate fellow-feelings among tenement dwellers, *One-Third* invited audience members to supply those on stage with the sympathy of which they had been deprived. While the First Negro does not initially have the physical and emotional space that he needs to engage in the sympathetic process, the audience does. This sympathetic process intensifies when, after being shoved out of bed by the First Negro, the Second Negro delivers the play's lengthiest and most impassioned speech. While crawling on the floor of the cubicle to the top step of the ship ladder leading down to the stage, the Second Negro complains of his "sick belly" and demands to know what "kind of thing I gotta put up with anyhow" (90). While struggling to sort out the injustices of his living conditions, he recalls what his "grandpop used to tell me—'bout the old country where he come from": "When a man's got more misery'n he kin stand, and his bones ache and his eyeballs burnin' with fire and there's hot pain runnin' up and down his arms and legs—you know what he do? You know what? He grab his machete, and run out into the clearing where all the planters are stan'in' with their whips in their hands and he yell as loud as he can, *Amok, Amok!* . . . You know what that mean? It mean I can't work no more! I'm crazy from work and I don't wanta live!" (91). By eliding the misery of his living and sleeping arrangements—the aching bones, burning eyes, and sore muscles—with those his grandfather experienced as a slave, the Second Negro not only communicates the severity of his suffering but also triggers within the audience the type of sympathetic response that had been cultivated by abolitionists and Reconstruction Era Republicans over several decades. When he asks, after delivering his speech, "Did you hear, did you hear me?" (91), the audience knows exactly how it should respond because it had been taught how to hear and feel by the abolitionist archive of interracial storytelling. By imagining black tenement dwellers as the inheritors of the physical conditions of slavery, viewers could slip into the structures of familial fellow-feelings *Uncle Tom's Cabin* and so many other abolitionist narratives had built up within the culture.[47]

While *One-Third* elicits relatively conventional domestic forms of sympathy for tenement dwellers through fairly straightforward melodramatic strategies, it is much more innovative in its efforts to prod viewers into acting correctly on these intimate attachments. What type of action audience members should take is the central problem that *One-Third* seeks to solve. In a typical melodrama, the villain not only solidifies the audience's affections for the virtuous victims but also provides it with a clear sense of how to act on its fellow-feelings for those victims. Because the villain embodies the forces that unjustly oppress the distressed, the crowd feels compelled to channel its emotional attachments to these sufferers into actions that undermine the villain's ability to continue inflicting harm on them.[48] *One-Third* initially seems less interested in identifying a villain than in dismissing the usual suspects. There is no evil arsonist lurking in a dark corner of the stage watching the opening scene's conflagration. And although the burning building's landlord, Mr. Schultz, appears to be a likely candidate to play the role of villain, he convincingly insists that he cannot be blamed for violating the housing codes established by the New York City Tenement House Commission—violations that most likely sparked the fire. After seeing the play, Richard Watts, Jr., observed that *One-Third* is "passably courteous" to Mr. Schultz and the other "tenement landlords, showing them as natural products of an existing condition, rather than melodramatic ogres."[49] Even the tenement structure, which had become a popular whipping boy among housing reformers, is partially exonerated. Rather than loom threateningly over its inhabitants, the tenement within which much of the play's action takes place becomes a character that voices its grievances to the audience. Tired of being blamed for physically and socially wounding its residents, the tenement house calls attention to its own suffering: "Do you see that broken balustrade? That crumbling plaster? And that sink down there under the steps? Do you see that rubbish piled up? That's me" (67). The voice of the tenement aligns its physical indignities with the anguish experienced by those it shelters. Both parties, the voice of the tenement implies, suffer at the hands of a common enemy.

The real enemy of the victimized tenement dwellers is, the play slowly reveals, an economy that failed to give landlords and landowners the incentive to maintain their property and therefore to provide the urban poor with adequate shelter. *One-Third*'s villain turns out to be the economics of urban land—what I will refer to as the tenement economy—that had, especially during the interwar years, "made New York real estate the soundest and most profitable speculation on the face of the earth" (23). The play devotes significant dramatic energy to explicating the bizarre logic and history of land speculation that placed landlords such as Mr. Schultz in an affective bind and sunk tenement buildings into a state of physical and existential despair. Mr. Schultz, who had been blamed for the fire with which the play opens, attempts to establish his innocence by explaining that, in an urban economy where the value of land "goes up, all the time," landlords like himself "cannot fix up the apartments" or "lower the rents" because the "land cost too much!" He persuasively pleads that he'd do anything he could for Mr. Rosen, the tenant who had lost his wife and two children in the fire that broke out in the building, but reasons that, if Mr. Rosen "can only afford to pay $24 a month," he'd be forced to "live in my house or one just like it—and you cannot blame me" (23). *One-Third* invites the audience to see Mr. Schultz not as an unscrupulous character evading responsibility for his actions but as someone whose goodwill and neighborliness had been arrested by the fiscal system in which he had been trapped. The audience comes to understand the irrationality of an economic system that rewards a small number of property owners for the increased value of land created through the "industry" of thousands of urbanites (35). In such an inherently unjust system, the landlord takes his place alongside his tenants and his building as a victim of the fire that consumed his property.

According to *One-Third*, the power, scope, and elusiveness of the tenement economy's villainy overwhelmed anyone who had attempted, over the course of the two-plus centuries of urban history reenacted by the play, to turn their sympathy for the urban poor into improved housing conditions. As the dramatic action unfolds, *One-Third* blockades nearly every possible course of action available to an audience yearning to connect emotionally with those urbanites on stage. Even when *One-Third* arrives at the solution to the urban housing problem that it clearly endorses—razing the tenements and building affordable housing in their place—the tenement economy's complexity and deep entrenchment in the city make it difficult for the audience to know what, exactly, it might do to help bring about this radical transformation. The play paralyzes spectators by demonstrating for them the seemingly unavoidable ways in which the high costs of land, labor, and material, in addition to the excessive commissions exacted by businessmen involved at every stage of the building process, will inevitably produce a housing product that Buttonkooper and others like him cannot afford. These victims of the tenement economy will remain stuck in their dangerous living conditions because the private housing market has failed, and always will fail, to produce adequate shelter for them. *One-Third* compellingly argues that the reason "there's no incentive to the commercial builder to build for the low income group is this: there's no money in it" (97). In delivering this assessment of the economic stalemate facing city dwellers and urban professionals, Arent espoused the argument that housing reformers such as Bauer and Edith Elmer Wood had been making for several years about the failure of the private market to provide adequate shelter for the majority of the population. When left to its own devices, they insisted, capitalism would never produce decent housing for all. Little, it must have seemed to the audience, could be done to short-circuit the tenement economy.[50]

That *One-Third* offered up the government as the only actor capable of thwarting the tenement economy's villainous domination of the urban poor would not have surprised many, but Arent's efforts to frame the government's intervention into the private housing market as a natural extension of the audience's intense fellow-feelings for tenement dwellers would have been somewhat startling. Arent reasoned that, because the engine of the tenement economy was the "profit motive," the remedy for the "human misery" manufactured by that fiscal system had to be a financially disinterested participant in that economy (104).[51] According to *One-Third*, the U.S. government possessed the type of unselfish behavior that would liberate not only Buttonkooper and his neighbors but also the landlords and landowners who had been dehumanized by the tenement economy. Having been incapable of consummating the emotional intimacies instigated by the play's dramatic action because of the need to survive the inequities of the tenement economy, tenants and landlords would be freed by the government to let go of their self-interests and to more fully connect with one another. After seeing a performance of *One-Third* at the Adelphi Theatre, Howard H. Spellman grasped the affective implications that a federal intervention in the private housing market would have on the relationships among these city dwellers: "Unless the government steps in to assist both the landowner and the person who lives on his property, we cannot expect a miracle of self-effacement on either side." The government would, the play hoped to persuade viewers, enable city dwellers to efface the boundaries that limited them to their own hearts and minds so they might more fully attach themselves to each other and deepen their emotional ties to one another.[52]

One-Third helped its audiences grasp and become comfortable with the federal government's function in the New Deal city by helping them experience what it felt like to depend on an outside party to complete the circuits of sympathy in which they had been engaged throughout the play. The government's role in facilitating emotional intimacies among city dwellers is dramatized most clearly in a scene near the end of the play that reenacts the debate about the Wagner-Steagall Housing Bill in the Senate. In the process of haggling over the bill's details, Senator Wagner instructs his fellow senators and, indirectly, theatergoers that their concern for the well-being of "individuals who live in the slums" will be most effective when bound up in "sympathy with [the government's] efforts to do something for the one-third of the people of the United States who are ill-housed—something to give these unfortunate people who have not sufficient income to enable them to live in decent quarters a chance for life" (109). In this moment, Arent calls the audience's attention to the New Deal's appropriation of and improvisation on the culture's discourse of sympathy. *One-Third* attempts to convince urbanites that the only way to restore primary relationships to their communities is to refract their emotional connections to one another through the welfare state. To embrace the federal government's efforts to do something for the urban poor is actually to sympathize with them. Given these new affective coordinates, the clerk of the Senate's reading of a section of the Wagner-Steagall Housing Bill feels very much like the melodrama's emotional highpoint.[53] The bill's intent to "create a United States Housing Authority, to provide financial assistance to the States and the political subdivisions thereof for the elimination of unsafe and unsanitary housing conditions," resonates with the melodramatic register of emotions within which it is couched (107). The federal government accomplishes what the audience yearns to do but ultimately cannot: save the tenement dwellers from the villainy of the tenement economy. The clerk of the Senate acts as a proxy for the sympathetic spectators in the same way that Buttonkooper acts as their proxy.

Although *One-Third* offers a creative solution to the affective problem posed by the welfare state's mediation in urban relations, its enactment of the social ideals at the heart of the Wagner-Steagall Act and other New Deal urban policies through the genre of melodrama exhibits the exhaustion of an urbanist discourse of sympathy. The play's adherence to melodramatic conventions prevents viewers from experiencing any form of fellow-feeling other than intense intimacy. Melodrama excels at the task of mobilizing political will, and *One-Third* did just that—politicians, activists, and other urban intellectuals used *One-Third* to help them accelerate the process of razing and rebuilding tenement districts in cities across the country.[54] But melodrama is not a cultural form adept at helping participants experience and acknowledge the validity of a broad range of interpersonal emotions and relational forms. Rather, melodrama initiates a limited range of interpersonal emotions: vehement hatred for the villain and intense identification with the victim. By using the melodramatic form to instruct viewers how urbanites should feel toward one another, and would have the opportunity to feel in the newly built public housing projects, *One-Third* reveals that an urbanist discourse that relies on the language and logic of sympathy to explain the affective nature of relationships among city dwellers will inevitably fall short of conveying and legitimizing the wide range of interpersonal emotions and relational forms that connect urbanites to one another in public and semi-public spaces.

Building Sympathy in the Williamsburg Houses

At one point during the performance of *One-Third*, Buttonkooper's wife insists that he "come with [her] this instant!" After getting his attention, she informs him in a loud whisper that there is a "new Housing Development. Williamsburg. They're taking applications!" (87). She had hoped to be among the first to apply for one of the project's 1,622 apartment units, unaware that 25,000 other applicants were also hoping to secure a spot in the new development. The housing project in which Buttonkooper's wife hoped to live was the recently completed Williamsburg Houses. Built with funds made available by the PWA Housing Division, Williamsburg Houses welcomed its first tenants in 1937. Consisting of twenty four-story buildings sited on twenty-five acres of cleared urban land and costing nearly fourteen million dollars, the housing development was by far the largest and most expensive of the federal government's public housing endeavors at the time. Langdon W. Post, chairman of the New York City Housing Authority, pronounced Williamsburg Houses to be "the most valuable contribution to social progress that the New Deal has made" and insisted that the overwhelming demand for apartments in the project revealed "the absolute necessity for a large scale public housing program." Williamsburg Houses achieved the social progress that Post, Perry, and many other urban intellectuals desired by materializing a built environment in which the kinds of fellow-feelings privileged within interwar urbanist discourse could be achieved by city dwellers.[55]

Williamsburg Houses offered urbanites an alternative not only to the inadequate domestic environment provided by the city's rundown housing stock but also to the public spaces that harbored the city's increasingly diverse population. William Lescaze and others at the NYCHA who designed Williamsburg Houses clearly intended to set the project apart from the interwar city's urban fabric. According to *Williamsburg Houses: A Case History of Housing*, a 1937 publication by the Federal Administration of Public Works, the new housing project "nestles in the heart of the historic Williamsburg section of Brooklyn." Williamsburg Houses aspired to achieve a spatial relationship to its surroundings similar to that between a small hamlet and the rural valley in which it nestles. The two images greeting the reader on the booklet's opening pages echo the pastoral imagery invoked by the text. An aerial photograph of Williamsburg Houses depicts the project as a clean and illuminated tract of land distinctly set apart from the dark and indistinguishable urban area surrounding it. The forty-five-degree angle at which the lines of the project's buildings are set off from the preexisting neighborhood grid reinforces the image of a settlement both nestled securely in and set apart from its surroundings. On the facing page, a pencil sketch of the Remsen Farm that once stood on the site of Williamsburg Houses in 1700 reinforces the idyllic social values elicited by the text and photograph. The drawing explicitly underscores the publication's reminder that Williamsburg was once a "thriving farming community" that gradually evolved into a "village." The PWA hoped to convince the public that Williamsburg Houses would return the neighborhood to its village roots—to a past when Williamsburg "offered a quiet haven to persons desiring snugness and privacy." The privacy made possible through the built environment of Williamsburg Houses would, the booklet implied, enable residents of the new development to form snug relationships with one another.[56]

The first tenants of Williamsburg Houses saw themselves as active participants in realizing the social vision that had been projected on their new home by municipal and federal officials. Charles S. Bilker, one of the first residents of Williamsburg Houses, spelled out the type of "neighborliness" that he had begun to experience in his new home and that he hoped his new community would continue to pursue. In a poem titled "Friendly Neighbors One and All," Bilker depicted the housing development as a place where residents "just sit around and chat / And forget our daily troubles." Although he did not specify where, exactly, he and his neighbors sat around chatting, the project's architect, William Lescaze, had designed spacious basements with laundry facilities, social units, and craft rooms in each building where residents could interact with one another. Unlike the busy sidewalks and streets Williamsburg Houses had replaced, each apartment building's communal spaces enabled residents like Bilker to cross paths repeatedly with the same set of neighbors. The development's physical layout invited them to

Figure 7. The Federal Administration of Public Works included this aerial photograph of Williamsburg Houses in its *Williamsburg Houses: A Case History of Housing* to draw attention to the difference between the new housing project and its larger urban context. Library of Congress Prints and Photographs Division, LC-USZ62-134605.

imagine their new living environment as a return to the communal life of a small rural town—a place where neighbors were able to "talk and laugh and joke / To sympathize and smile / To pat a neighbor on the back." As if he were fulfilling the prophecies of those who had funded and designed the country's largest public housing development, Bilker deployed an interwar discourse of sympathy to characterize the intimate interpersonal relationships that he had formed at Williamsburg Houses. The project's built environment had created for Bilker a sense of time and place distinct from the city's spatiotemporality. Bilker's ability to sympathize with his neighbors was closely linked to the social patterns made possible by the physical design of Williamsburg Houses. Even if the workday had "been a hard one / And evening finds us blue," Bilker promised his fellow residents that Williamsburg Houses would enable them to "mingle with the neighbors" and thereby give "life a rosier hue."[57]

The residents of Williamsburg Houses and other public housing projects built in the 1930s assured themselves and others that these new urban environments had cultivated the type of familial feelings for one another that interwar urbanists had claimed were so difficult to develop in the city's tenement districts. Soon after Williamsburg Houses had opened its doors, Lillian Cicio expressed her hope that she and her new neighbors would soon "feel like one big family sharing our woes and joys together."[58] Cicio's social aspirations appear to have been fulfilled when, after the residents had been living together in Williamsburg Houses for a year, the editors of the development's community newspaper confidently asserted that, although they were "at first strangers," they had become, "through our various unit clubs, social clubs and the Inter-Unit Council, . . . a closer, more harmoniously-knit group." The editors concluded their celebratory column by congratulating "Mr. and Mrs. Tenants" on their "first anniversary."[59] In pronouncing the tenants husbands and wives, the editors made their case that Williamsburg Houses had achieved the social purposes for which it had been built. If concerns about tenement life had been articulated through fears and reports of the dissolution of the family unit, the image of public-housing residents working together in marital harmony signaled the return of a vibrant social order to the city. Tenants claimed that they had forged the kind of intimate relationships signified by their culture's ultimate form of sympathetic exchange: marriage.

Public housing and the cityscapes that they brought into being gave physical form to the social ideals that had clustered around the concept of sympathy at the heart of interwar urbanist discourse. The desires and efforts of urban intellectuals to create space in the city in which inhabitants might reap the social benefits of primary, face-to-face relationships help explain where, how, and for whom public housing projects were built. As Bauer and her fellow modern housing planners vehemently argued, it would have made much more economic, social, and practical sense to follow the example of many European countries and construct public housing on vacant land rather than on demolished slum sites and to allow a broader cross-section of the population than just low-income urbanites to inhabit the subsidized dwellings.[60] While Bauer's vision of what public housing should look like, whom it should serve, and how it should be funded shaped some of the New Deal's housing legislation, many of her core convictions were sidelined, at least in part, because they did not resonate with the language and logic of sympathy that had been rapidly accumulating cultural capital among urban professionals since the end of the Progressive Era. The conceptual exhaustion of sympathy that urban sociologists, city planners, culture makers, and public officials had carried out during the interwar period demanded slum clearance and affordable housing in the industrial city's dense tenement neighborhoods. The relatively simplified and unimaginative discourse of sympathy codified in the 1937 Housing Act would persist through the next several decades and continue to shape an approach to urban redevelopment that sacrificed local streets, small commercial establishments, and public gathering places for the construction of housing projects and other private spaces.

CHAPTER 3

Literary Urbanists and the Interwar Development of Urban Sociability

Just six years after Williamsburg Houses opened its doors to many enthusiastic residents, Betty Smith published her wildly popular novel *A Tree Grows in Brooklyn* (1943). Near the end of Smith's novel, the narrator laments that Francie Nolan, whose childhood she had carefully documented for readers, would never be able to return to the Brooklyn neighborhood in which she had grown up because "there would be no old neighborhood to come back to." The "city was going to tear down the tenements" where Francie had lived and "build a model housing project on the site; a place of living where sunlight and air were to be trapped, measured and weighed, and doled out so much per resident."[1] The narrator's cynical opinion of the housing project—which was unnamed in the novel, but which clearly referred to Williamsburg Houses—is not difficult to hear in the narrator's language. The airy and sunny apartments of the new housing project had failed, in the narrator's estimation, to reproduce the thriving social landscape that Francie had experienced as a child and teenager in Brooklyn. Rather than liberate tenement dwellers, the narrator asserts that Williamsburg Houses had "trapped" them in a socially sterile environment. By juxtaposing the natural elements of sunlight and air with the mechanical processes of measuring and weighing, the narrator suggests that the public housing enterprise is an artificial one. This unnatural approach to urban redevelopment created a "place of living" that isolated residents from one another.

A Tree Grows in Brooklyn told a very different story about the interwar city's physical and social landscape than the one that had been broadcast by many sociologists, city planners, private developers, and housing reformers, and that had been codified in the establishment of the Public Works Administration's Housing Division and the passage of U.S. Housing Act of

1937—shifts in the federal government's organization and policy that made the construction of Williamsburg Houses and other similar public housing projects possible. Unlike Robert E. Park, Clarence A. Perry, Arthur A. Arent, and Langdon W. Post—who tended to see urban relationships as emotionally inferior to those grown in the small town or village—Smith validated the affiliations among urbanites in the city's public and semi-public spaces. She described the fellow-feelings that Francie forged with neighbors, shop owners, co-workers, and strangers while making her way through Williamsburg's sidewalks, commercial establishments, and public institutions as "companionable" feelings.[2] Smith did not ignore the significance of the familial and intimate emotions that bound Francie to her father, brother, aunt, and lover, but she also captured and legitimized the less intense interpersonal affections that connected Francie to other urbanites in the city's public sphere. According to Smith, the tenements, businesses, schools, and streets that were torn down to make way for Williamsburg Houses had once sheltered a healthy social order that consisted of a wide variety of relationships held together by a range of fellow-feelings.

Although the urbanist discourse of sympathy that helped underwrite the destruction of Francie's old neighborhood and the construction of Williamsburg Houses would persist throughout the postwar years, *A Tree Grows in Brooklyn* contributed to the emergence of a very different way of understanding and assessing relationships among city dwellers. Smith's widely read novel rejected the urbanist discourse of sympathy and instead gave voice to an urbanist discourse of sociability that privileged the interactions that urbanites experienced in the city's public spaces. This discourse of sociability was cultivated, in large part, by literary urbanists during the interwar years. Proletarian urban novelists such as Smith, James T. Farrell, Mike Gold, Henry Roth, and Pietro Di Donato joined the efforts of city journalists such as those writing for the *New Yorker* in attending to the broad spectrum of social processes and emotions that activated and signified fellow-feelings among city dwellers. These literary urbanists captured what Georg Simmel had described in 1911 as the "worth of association" and the "structure of sociability" built on associative relationships that were held together by "amiability" and "cordiality." Sociability, Simmel explained, generated relational forms in which participants remained "above all individual intimacy, beyond everything purely personal."[3] Rather than privilege the primary, intimate relationships espoused by so many other interwar urban intellectuals, these literary urbanists called attention to the ways city dwellers experienced an awareness of and appreciation for the more informal relationships in which they were inevitably and often involuntarily involved. This awareness, these writers suggested, produced fellow-feelings that linked urbanites to one another in emotionally meaningful and socially satisfying ways, even though these fellow-feelings may not have been as intense as those experienced within intimate relationships. These literary urbanists spent their time exploring the webs of secondary rather than primary interdependencies in which city dwellers were enmeshed.

Many literary urbanists located their accounts of sociable urban relationships in spaces within the city's built environment that had been marginalized by the interwar urbanist discourse of sympathy. These writers did not entirely ignore domestic and other private spaces, but they tended to investigate the interactions among city dwellers in the urban spaces carved out by the city's commercial establishments, public institutions, and social enterprises. During the 1930s and 1940s, city journalists, tenement novelists, and other literary urbanists validated the encounters among city dwellers in restaurants, theaters, movie houses, cabarets, nightclubs, laundries, grocery stores, butcher shops, cigar stores, pawnshops, small office buildings, subway stations, boxing gyms, libraries, post offices, schools, and social clubs. The intensified decentralization of the city during the interwar years not only dispersed residents beyond the urban center to its peripheries, but also spread the city's commercial establishments and public institutions throughout the city—making the kinds of spaces that supported sociable affiliations among urbanites more accessible to them. Although the Great Depression and the early stages of the transition from an industrial to a postindustrial economy were hard on these commercial and public enterprises—especially downtown, where construction came to a near standstill and property owners frequently tore down unoccupied buildings—literary urbanists used these spaces to formulate an urbanist discourse of sociability.[4]

During the interwar years, then, when the urbanist discourse of sympathy became nearly incapable of signifying anything other than emotionally intimate fellow-feelings, literary urbanists offered an alternative mode of representing and legitimizing the multiplicity of relational forms and fellow-feelings that connected city dwellers to one another. The city journalists and novelists featured in this chapter pushed the public's understanding of the affective possibilities of urban affiliations in new directions. Whereas early settlement writers thought of urban sympathy as the fellow-feelings among city dwellers that grew out of daily contact and that ultimately resulted in friendship, *New Yorker* journalists and tenement novelists conceived of sociability as a relational process that depended less on frequent interactions and familiarity among urbanites than on their co-occupation of the city's spaces. These writers were interested in exploring and validating the affective connections among acquaintances and even strangers who shared a particular city street, building, or neighborhood. As city dwellers participated in the social and economic processes embedded in the city's public and commercial spaces, they became aware of the many ways in which they depended on those with whom they were not very familiar or whom they did not know. This awareness of and appreciation for the relatively impersonal interdependencies that made it possible for urbanites to carry out their lives in the city generated fellow-feelings that operated well beyond the affective boundaries of intimacy. These literary urbanists were interested in calling attention to a type of sociability produced through the involuntary accumulation of public contacts rather than the purposeful cultivation of friendships and domestic relationships.

Profiling Urban Sociability in the *New Yorker*

In the two decades after Harold Ross established the *New Yorker*, the magazine's writers cultivated a new vocabulary for writing and talking about urban encounters and relationships. In its attempt to fashion a "reflection in word and picture of metropolitan life," as Ross put it in a prospectus for his yet-to-be-published magazine, the *New Yorker* explicitly sought to distance itself from sentimental and sensational characterizations of city life and to establish its own representational habits. Changes in the city's physical, economic, cultural, and social orders since the late nineteenth century, Ross suggested, demanded a new approach to representing urban life. He envisioned a magazine whose literary and artistic content would give an account of and attend to what he described as the proliferation of "public and semipublic smart gathering places" throughout the city—its "clubs, hotels, cafes, supper clubs, cabarets and other resorts." Ross hoped that his magazine would replace the inadequate vocabularies of newspapers and other magazines with a discourse that was more "sophisticated"—a term that the *New Yorker*'s editors, writers, and readers would use to brand the magazine. Articulating the magazine's particular model of sophistication required *New Yorker* writers to finesse literary forms and styles that would, as Ross professed in his prospectus, simultaneously "hate bunk" and "be human." These seemingly conflicting demands called for a discourse that could be both hardboiled and sensitive—a rhetoric that communicated, as one midcentury reader attested, a "cozily human but never sentimental understanding of the doings of our time." The representational styles and strategies that grew out of Ross's founding vision challenged the authority of sociologists, city planners, and housing activists to determine the value of urban relationships.[5]

More fully than the pieces produced within the magazine's fiction and humor departments, *New Yorker* fact writing assumed the task of representing the sociable encounters among urbanites within the city's public and semi-public gathering places.[6] "A Reporter at Large" served as the primary rubric within which journalists such as E. B. White, Meyer Berger, Joseph Mitchell, A. J. Liebling, Alva Johnston, Niven Busch, Jr., and St. Clair McKelway initially experimented in their efforts to describe urban sociability. In the October 28, 1933, issue of the *New Yorker*, White wrote under the pseudonym E. Bagworm Wren about the Yosian Brotherhood, a walking club dedicated to exploring the city's pockets of nature. On the day White joined one of the brotherhood's outings, the group of amateur naturalists consisted of a "buoyant Russian girl in a yellow sweater, a tiny fat man who smiled relentlessly, a woman who was hoarse but wouldn't gargle, an amateur philosopher in a green hat, a quiet young man who carried a magnifying glass and looked for newts under rocks, a tittery blonde girl with big bones, [and] a seventy-seven-year-old husband from Sheepshead Bay." Rather than perceive social chaos in such a random assortment of individuals, White perceived the subtle emotional connections that gave the relationships within this group meaning. The city dwellers on this particular excursion became Yosians, White claimed, because the organization gave them a "chance to make friends, a lonely-hearts club of the outdoors."[7] Although some of the Yosians may have been looking for deep friendships, most were simply hoping to take the edge off of a loneliness that could only be eased by casually associating with other urbanites in a public setting. The Russian girl, tiny fat man, hoarse woman, amateur philosopher, quiet young man, tittery blonde girl, and seventy-seven-year-old husband were not seeking the kind of emotionally intense relationships that would erase their significant social differences but looking for affiliations that might ease the pain of their solitariness. The husband from Sheepshead Bay may have had deeply satisfying domestic relationships, but White suggested that his outings with the Yosian Brotherhood fulfilled an emotional need that could not be met through domestic patterns of intimacy. The structure of sociability he found in the Yosian Brotherhood satisfied his need to see how he fit into a larger social order.

In their efforts to help readers recognize the presence and validity of sociable affiliations among urbanites, White and other *New Yorker* journalists sought to illuminate various social orders in areas of the city where the public had been taught to see disorder. They knew that only when readers perceived these larger social worlds within which city dwellers encountered one another would they acknowledge the possibility of meaningful interactions among them. *New Yorker* reporters became especially interested in writing about urban districts and neighborhoods that had been dismissed by sociologists, city planners, politicians, and residents as slums. Johnston's "A Tour of Minskyville," which appeared in the August 6, 1932, issue, was just one of many pieces published under "A Reporter at Large" in the 1930s that undermined the urban narratives that defined certain areas of the city as rundown or indecent and, therefore, as incapable of staging socially substantial encounters among individuals. Johnston offered readers a detailed tour of Minskyville that produced a very different picture of the district than the one that had been used by private developers and city officials to generate support for their plans, as he put it, to "clean up" the area. Beginning at the racy Salon des Arts at Fifty-Second and Broadway, the northern tip of Minskyville, Johnston walked his readers south past the recording-phonograph laboratory and the Psychograph studio to the Central Theatre at Forty-Seventh and Broadway. According to Johnston, the Central Theatre, which programmed continuous burlesque shows to give patrons "something else to think about" during the Great Depression, was the "heart of Minskyville."[8] Johnston's virtual tour of the district neutralized its critics by giving the area a distinct physical form and social purpose. Assigning the district a "heart" not only gave readers a sense of the district's spatial dimensions but also suggested that it sustained the social lives of those who lived and recreated there. According to Johnston, Minskyville possessed a coherence and vitality capable of providing those who encountered one another in its salons, studios, and theaters with a sense that their interactions had meaning because these institutions connected them not just to one another but to the larger social world of Minskyville.

New Yorker reporters deepened their readers' awareness of the sociable relations in which city dwellers participated by investigating the ways in which individual institutions sustained these broader social orders. These writers were especially interested in exploring the role that commercial enterprises played in generating opportunities for city dwellers to affiliate with one another. Sherwood Anderson, author of the important short story cycle *Winesburg, Ohio* (1919), demonstrated a clear understanding of the cultural work that "A Reporter at Large" was capable of performing in his lone contribution to the rubric. In the *New Yorker*'s June 9, 1934, issue, Anderson used Stewart's Cafeteria in Sheridan Square as a lens through which he could "check on city life." The restaurant was invaded by several different social circles throughout the day, but Anderson was most interested in the crowd that took over Stewart's during the evening and early morning hours—the young urbanites who wanted "to be great actors, singers, sculptors, painters." As one of these aspiring artists explained to Anderson, the "children of the arts" gathered at Stewart's en masse because the "outer world is too harsh, too brutal" and they needed a place to establish their "own little world."[9] Rather than think of Stewart's primarily as a place for purchasing and consuming food, Anderson and his subjects characterized the cafeteria as a space capable of giving shape to social worlds. Stewart's functioned as a home to the "children of the arts" and other groups of urbanites in the sense that it created a contained environment within which city dwellers could perceive the nature of their connections to one another in ways that they could not in the world outside the restaurant. Even though each group that patronized Stewart's throughout the day followed a set of social codes that may have conflicted with the financial interests of the cafeteria, the institution proved capable of modifying or relaxing its protocols to accommodate the various social orders that gathered there.

While "A Reporter at Large" took the lead in documenting the city's various social worlds and the built environments that gave them coherence, its conventions did not allow reporters to explore deeply the affective dynamics of the associations that constituted these social orders. In an attempt to examine and articulate more precisely the nature of the ties that connected individual city dwellers to one another, journalists turned to the magazine's "Profiles" rubric. This rubric gave journalists room to reconsider the very nature of urban identity. By reimagining the identity of the individual urbanite, *New Yorker* journalists helped readers consider a wider variety of social possibilities for that individual. Margaret Case Harriman, who began writing profiles for the *New Yorker* in 1933, distinguished the rubric from other similar forms by insisting that profilers "are not fan-magazine authors, they have not reached the full dignity of biographers, and they are definitely not interviewers."[10] Harriman's comparisons call attention not only to the even-tempered tonal quality toward which profiles aspired but also to the rubric's efforts to reconsider the process by which individuals constructed their identities. Profilers did not rely too heavily on an individual's genealogical past as the principal source of identity; nor did they put too much weight on an individual's self-constructed image. Profilers instead saw identity as the product of an individual's relationship to a specific physical environment and the social orders that this environment supported.

Particular places in the city marked upon urbanites an indelible identity, an ontological process to which *New Yorker* journalists called explicit attention in their reportage. Johnston's 1933 profile of Lou Stillman, owner of a boxing gym on the Upper West Side, exaggerated the connection between identity and the city's built environment that *New Yorker* writers had begun to work out in their early profiles. Johnston informed readers of his surprise on learning that the gymnasium Stillman owned was not named after him, but rather that Stillman was "named after the gymnasium." Born as Lou Ingber, Stillman had grown so tired of the gym members mispronouncing his name that "he finally took the name of the gymnasium as his own."[11] It would be crude to understand the process by which Stillman changed his Jewish surname to a more ethnically neutral one strictly as a response to xenophobic pressures. Johnston suggested to readers that Ingber's adoption of the surname Stillman reflected not his desire to disavow his ethnicity, but his acknowledgment of the deep connection between his identity and the public world of buildings, businesses, and consumers in which he operated. He recognized that his encounters with those who patronized his gymnasium were produced by and mediated through its spatial dimensions and location. His willingness to change his name manifested his understanding of the sociable, rather than intimate, nature of the relationships between himself and the city dwellers with whom he affiliated in his gymnasium. Stillman's seemingly casual decision to take a new name simultaneously registered the almost impersonal quality of his associations with the aspiring boxers and the significance of the obligations he felt toward them.

In helping readers understand the degree to which the public world of people and buildings shaped urban identity, *New Yorker* journalists pushed readers to reconsider the nature of the connections between profiled individuals and those with whom they affiliated in the city's gathering places. In his profile of Mazie P. Gordon—a woman who had "presided for twenty-one years over the ticket cage" of a Bowery movie house called the Venice—Mitchell located his subject at the heart of a network of urban relationships.

Unlike the "glass-topped Bowery and Chinatown rubberneck wagons [that] often park in front of the Venice" and unload a "band of sightseers [who] stand on the sidewalk and stare at Mazie," Mitchell saw her not as an isolated spectacle at which to gawk or a curiosity to pity but as a member of a particular urban community and locale. He reported that the

> people who stopped by to talk with [Mazie] between noon and 6 P.M. one Saturday this Fall included Monsignor Cashin, Fannie Hurst, two detectives from the Oak Street station, a flashily dressed Chinese gambler whom Mazie calls Fu Manchu . . . two nuns from Madonna House . . . a talkative girl from Atlanta, Georgia called Bingo . . . the bartender of a Chatham Square saloon . . . and the clerk of a flophouse.[12]

In addition to fixing Mazie to a particular plot of the cityscape—a tactic utilized, after all, by many sensational slumming narratives—Mitchell revealed the ways her location and trade enabled her to associate with a wide variety of city dwellers. The public nature of her interactions with her fellow urbanites allowed her to engage with individuals from across the ethnic, religious, and class spectrum and with whom she most likely would not have been able to maintain a close friendship. Mazie's fellow-feelings for Fu Manchu, Bingo, and others grew out of what Mitchell described as a "wry but genuine fondness" for them, rather than an emotionally deep commitment to them. While the equivocal quality of her affections for other city dwellers may not have landed her an invitation to dine in Fannie Hurst's home, her wry fondness for them nevertheless enabled her to form genuine connections that obligated her to treat those whose lives intersected with her ticket cage "as an equal."[13] City dwellers were, Mitchel and other *New Yorker* journalists suggested, more commonly bound to one another through involuntary accumulation of sociable associations than through purposeful cultivation of private intimacies.

Just a few months after the *New Yorker* published Mitchell's profile of Mazie, the magazine offered readers what might be considered its manifesto of urban sociability. Published in the spring of 1941, A. J. Liebling's three-part profile of the Jollity Building—one of New York's "dozen or so buildings in the upper stories of which the small-scale amusement industry nests like a tramp pigeon"—crystalized for readers the *New Yorker*'s distinct vision of the interwar city's social landscape and the nature of the sociable affiliations that proliferated within it. Likely a composite of several buildings located on or near Broadway, such as the Brill Building at 1619 Broadway, Liebling's six-story Jollity Building contained street-level shops and a dance hall on its lower floors, while its upper floors consisted of cubicles and unfurnished offices. Liebling's decision to represent metropolitan life by focusing on a building, rather than an individual, might have initially struck readers as a bizarre twist on one of the *New Yorker*'s longest-standing rubrics, but his profile in fact synthesized and recombined many of the form's discursive commitments. Where previous profilers had been somewhat limited in their efforts to portray the social dynamics of urban sociability by the genre's inclination to single out individuals from the crowd, Liebling's unusual approach enabled him to investigate fully what he referred to as the city's "social structure."[14]

Like many previous pieces of *New Yorker* fact writing, Liebling's profile of the Jollity Building exposed the intricate interconnections that constituted the social worlds to which it and other physical spaces had given definition. Formally, the three-part profile consisted almost entirely of traditional, but miniature, interlocking profiles. In the first installment, a brief profile of Hy Sky—the "senior tenant in the building" and the "proprietor of the Quick Art Theatrical Sign Painting Company, on the sixth floor"—naturally lead to mini-profiles of various other occupants in the building. Among the other individuals connected to Sky are the Jollity's bandleaders, who regularly hire him to paint their door signs and music racks. When one of the building's bandleaders gets a gig and purchases Sky's goods, he "hurries out to the curb on Seventh avenue in front of Charlie's Bar & Grill, where there are always plenty of musicians, and picks up the number of fellows he requires, generally four." After being chosen by the bandleader, these musicians, in turn, rush to reclaim their instruments from the pawnshop. If, however, one of them "lacks the money to redeem an instrument, he borrows the money from a Jollity Building six-for-fiver, a fellow who will lend you five dollars if you promise to pay him six dollars within twenty-four hours." Liebling's profile convincingly demonstrated for readers how the "life cycle" of an individual urbanite inevitably intersected with the life cycles of several other city dwellers. Consisting of these inextricably intertwined relationships, the Jollity Building looked less like a standard corporate office building than an intricate ecosystem.[15]

In the process of tracing the many social and economic interconnections that sustained the Jollity Building's occupants, Liebling's profile dramatized the nature of the emotional attachments that grew out of the interdependencies among them. Given the inability of most tenants to hold on to what little cash they generated, the building's renting agent claimed that he had to make "an average of fifteen calls to collect a month's rent on an office"; as a result, he "acquires a much greater intimacy with the tenants than the agents of a place like Rockefeller Center or River House."[16] Liebling's syntax drains "intimacy" of its traditional domestic connotations, but his use of the term was not entirely sarcastic. Instead, he staked out a new set of emotional possibilities signified by intimacy by embedding the term in the social spaces created by the Jollity Building. The Jollity's residents, in turn, helped Liebling sustain the tricky tone he grafted onto emotional concepts like intimacy. Jerry Rex, an agent who supplied acts for local cabarets and theaters, refused to collect extra cash by emceeing the shows he booked because, as he put it, "When I get out on the stage and think of what a small buck the performers are going to get, I feel like crying." Sounding as if he had just stepped out of a hard-boiled novel, Rex empties his diction of tenderness while maintaining the affective implications of such language; he may not really want to cry, but readers would have understood that he did feel for the performer's economic and emotional plight. Like Mazie P. Gordon, Rex might be said to have a "wry but genuine fondness" for the performers. In describing the kind of relationships that existed among those who "wander through the grimy halls of the Jollity Building looking for work," Liebling hoped to supply readers with an "appreciation of meretricious types."[17] The concept of appreciation much better captures the nature of the emotion connecting urbanites to one another than do intimacy, love, friendship, or any of the many other terms privileged within an urbanist discourse of sympathy.

Locating Sociability in *A Tree Grows in Brooklyn*

After publishing city journalism in the *New Yorker* for much of the 1930s, Meyer Berger reviewed *A Tree Grows in Brooklyn* for the *New York Times* in 1943. His review made visible the connection between the discourse of urban sociability that he had helped develop at the *New Yorker* and that which Smith and other urban novelists articulated during the interwar period. After admitting that he had always hoped to one day write a novel about his "old block in Williamsburg in Brooklyn," Berger conceded that there was no longer a need to fulfill that dream because Smith had just published the type of novel that he had hoped to write. He praised Smith for reproducing the "cries, the odors and the squalor of old Graham Avenue and its tenements: the hot-eyed old pickle peddlers, overstuffed mothers, breast-feeding their babies with Oriental disregard for the stares of passing little boys and girls." According to Berger, the novel "swarms with living people" who move through the "dream world that was bounded, more or less, by the awesome atmosphere of the local public library, by the streets that lead to the neighborhood stores and by the view from the fire escape."[18] Unlike many reviewers who read *A Tree Grows in Brooklyn* primarily as a character study of the novel's young protagonist, Francie Nolan, Berger recognized it as a story about an urban community and the built environment in which that community operated. Smith's novel was, as another reviewer observed, "the story of Williamsburg."[19] As an attempt to represent the sociable affiliations and encounters that made urban communities like Williamsburg viable, *A Tree Grows in Brooklyn* extended the work that Berger, Liebling, Mitchell, and others had been doing in the *New Yorker* and city newspapers for over a decade. Like the early *New Yorker* journalists, Smith located urban sociability in the libraries, stores, streets, and tenements of the interwar city.

But because Smith chose to write her story of Williamsburg in the form of a novel—a genre with a different set of expressive capabilities than journalism—she offered readers a deeper understanding of the affective possibilities of urban relationships than city journalists were capable of providing. *A Tree Grows in Brooklyn* did not, as Orville Prescott noted in his review of the novel, sound like the "sour, sordid sociological report" of Williamsburg and other tenement districts to which the public had grown accustomed during the 1920s and 1930s.[20] Instead, Smith illuminated for readers the social significance of the interpersonal connections that Francie and her neighbors forged within Williamsburg's public and commercial spaces. She abandoned the standard by which urban relationships had been evaluated during the New Deal Era—a standard that privileged the type of intimate face-to-face interactions that many felt were necessary for initiating and sustaining fellow-feelings—in favor of a social model that generated fellow-feelings through the far less intimate contacts and exchanges that took place in the city's gathering spaces. Unlike many sociologists, city planners, and housing reformers who viewed the city's tenement districts as the most socially depraved locations in the city, Smith saw Williamsburg's built environment as one that facilitated the formation of a healthy urban community. Given its immense popularity, *A Tree Grows in Brooklyn* made a significant contribution to the urbanist discourse of sociability.[21]

Smith signaled her commitment to developing a discourse of sociability by clearly rejecting the type of urbanism embraced by sociologists, city planners, elected officials, and some of those with whom she had worked on the Federal Theatre Project. When *A Tree Grows in Brooklyn* ridicules the transformative aspirations of those who created the "modern housing project" that had, by the time of the novel's publication, razed one of Smith's childhood homes and much of Francie's neighborhood, it rejects the social ideals upon which Williamsburg Houses and other public housing projects were built and operated. While Smith's novel does not directly criticize Williamsburg Houses at any other point of the narrative, its repudiation of the brand of urbanism that public housing sought to actualize retroactively suffuses her story. The novel's titular symbol—the ailanthus tree that "grew lushly, but only in the tenement districts"—should be understood as a direct challenge to the arguments forwarded by public housing advocates about the tenement district's lack of sunshine, air, and greenery. By characterizing Williamsburg as uniquely capable of nurturing the ailanthus tree, Smith reasons that the urban poor who live in tenements already possessed the moral and social benefits that her culture associated with the natural world. Rather than view the tenement phase of a neighborhood's life cycle as its low point, *A Tree Grows in Brooklyn* characterizes this phase as the high point of an urban community's evolution. The novel upends the decline narrative that had been used by many urban intellectuals to narrate her neighborhood's history by reminding readers that "people called" the ailanthus tree the "Tree of Heaven." By mapping the teleology of Christian mythology onto Williamsburg's hardscape, Smith's novel undermines the claims of those who saw public housing as the most desirable afterlife for Williamsburg's tenements.[22]

More specifically, *A Tree Grows in Brooklyn* calls into question the claims made by public housing advocates about the social benefits of the close-knit, residential communities that Williamsburg Houses would bring back to tenement districts. The undesirable side effects of these village-like relationships on the city's public social orders are made particularly visible in one of the novel's most disturbing scenes. After returning from running their afternoon errands, a group of the neighborhood's "good housewives" gathers "into little knots" (232). These women collectively taunt Joanna, a neighborhood teenager who liked to walk her illegitimate child up and down the street.

They repeatedly goad her to "get off the street," and, when Joanna refuses to heed their threats, the women begin to throw stones at her (233). At one point, an errant rock strikes the baby and draws a "trickle of blood." Joanna immediately picks up her infant from the carriage to inspect its wound and withdraws into her home. The neighborhood women had "won," the narrator notes; they had managed to "drive Joanna off the street" (234).

The stoning scene dramatizes on a very small scale the social costs of privileging intimacy above sociability. The novel, of course, does not entirely dismiss the value of intimate kinship and friendship. *A Tree Grows in Brooklyn* spends significant time detailing Francie's meaningful and warm relationships with her father, mother, brother, and aunts. And the novel suggests that the neighborhood's housewives enjoy the emotional advantages of close friendship—they spend significant time together and support each other through their common trials. Despite living in a tenement district, the relationships among these women would have been described by Chicago sociologists as primary contacts. Contrary to sociological wisdom, though, the narrator claims that these primary relationships are not the only type of valuable relationship and should, therefore, not be pursued at the expense of other, less intimate relationships. When the private relationship is perceived by city dwellers as the only viable form of sociality, as it is for the women who stone Joanna, the novel contends that this "bond" will shrink the "hearts and . . . souls" of city dwellers (237). Incapable of making room in their lives for those not included in their small social circle, the neighborhood women attempt to realign the urban landscape to mirror the narrow boundaries of their affective geography. Their private relationships produce a desire to shrink and control public space, to expel those who do not share their social values off the street. Much like the planners, architects, and municipal leaders who designed Williamsburg Houses, these women attempt to domesticate Williamsburg's streets and sidewalks. They are unwilling to share public space with those with whom they do not wish to have a private bond. In *A Tree Grows in Brooklyn*, the primary group appears to be, at times, public enemy number one.

Smith addresses the social injustices that Joanna and her baby suffer at the hands of the neighborhood women's private bonds by promoting an alternative to urban relationships held together by intimacy. While most nineteenth-century sentimental literature uses the undeservedly mistreated child or mother figure to generate an intense identification with the individual and the moral cause that she represents, the stoning scene in *A Tree Grows in Brooklyn* fails to engender this same type of attachment to Joanna and her baby. Francie, who witnesses the hostile exchange between Joanna and the neighborhood women, had, in fact, been warned by her mother not to associate with the unwed mother. Francie's mother informs her that there's "no use getting sentimental" about what happened to Joanna; "I wouldn't feel too sorry for her," Francie's mother cautions, before adding, "Let Joanna be a lesson to *you*" (232). Francie may not necessarily feel sorry for Joanna and her child, but she does feel sharp pains of remorse for failing to have returned Joanna's casual smile when crossing paths with her on the sidewalk prior to the stoning incident. Francie does not respond to Joanna's mistreatment by pursuing an intimate relationship with the victimized mother but instead feels bad for having violated the unspoken rules governing social exchanges among urbanites in Williamsburg's public spaces. Because she had not conveyed the appropriate public expression of fellow-feeling for Joanna, she responds to the stoning episode by extending sociability to Joanna. Hoping to "sacrifice something to pay for not having smiled at Joanna," Francie places her only copy of the school magazine, which contained her first published story, in Joanna's empty baby carriage. Francie's sacrifice entails giving up the "nice warm feeling" she would have received from showing the magazine to her family in order to re-enter Williamsburg's public sphere (234). Because Francie makes her offering anonymously, her act restores to both herself and Joanna an emotional connection to the broader urban public that had been severed immediately before and during the stoning episode. Francie may forfeit the "warm feeling" made available through intimate kinship, but her sacrificial gesture demonstrates that sociable relationships, in which individuals may not respond to one another in personal and familiar ways, possess their own type of emotional satisfaction.

Francie's commitment to sociability in this particular moment must be seen not as the result of the moral lesson that her mother hoped she would learn from Joanna but as the outcome of the many lessons that Francie had absorbed about the maintenance and value of urban affiliations while making her way through Williamsburg's gathering places. Francie had received much of her social education in Williamsburg's commercial establishments; "neighborhood stores," the narrator explains, "are an important part of a city child's life" (135). Smith had, in fact, been interested in writing about these overlooked urban institutions from the very beginning of her writing career. While auditing a journalism course at the University of Michigan in the late 1920s, Smith wrote a piece about the "five-and-ten cent stores" that flourished

Figure 8. A photographer for the New York City Housing Authority and Works Progress Administration photographed children playing at the corner of Ten Eyck Street and Manhattan Avenue in Williamsburg during the summer of 1934. Four years later, the streets and buildings in this photo would no longer exist, having been razed to build Williamsburg Houses. New York City Housing Authority Records, La Guardia and Wagner Archives.

in "large cities." She liked to "prowl around" these types of stores "on a Saturday afternoon," she explained to her friend, Murry Godwin: "It's all so gay and carnivally. People so obviously enjoy living."[23] In addition to putting the city child in contact with what the narrator of *A Tree Grows in Brooklyn* describes as the "supplies that keep life going" and the "beauty that his soul longs for," the neighborhood stores are also where children like Francie learn how urbanites go about the business of living with all kinds of people in the city (135). Williamsburg's five-and-ten cent stores, pawnshops, bakeries, butcher shops, groceries, penny candy stores, paint shops, cigar stores, and laundries teach Francie how urban sociability works.

As Francie patronizes Williamsburg's neighborhood stores while carrying out her family responsibilities, she enters into and becomes aware of her position in the neighborhood's intricate social network. While waiting for her turn to buy bread at Losher's bread factory—a Williamsburg institution that supplied the neighborhood stores with fresh bread and then "redeemed the stale bread from the dealers and sold it at half price to the poor"—Francie often "sat on a bench and watched" the customers. In addition to observing the other children who had been sent by their families to buy bread, she always noticed a collection of "old men." These men, the narrator notes, were "pensioners on their families" and were often "made to run errands and mind babies, the only work left for old worn-out-men in Williamsburg." Waiting on the benches at Losher's for the bakery wagons to deliver the bread gave these men a "purpose in life for a little while and, almost, they felt necessary again" (15). Without establishments such as Losher's, these old men would have become purposeless and socially dispensable. Francie realizes that the commercial infrastructure of the neighborhood had evolved in ways that made room for different types of individuals. Losher's was just one of many neighborhood stores that not only enabled working-class city dwellers to get by but also pushed them to recognize the value of each other's lives. While buying bread at Losher's, Francie comes to acknowledge that the purpose of the old men's lives overlaps, to some degree, with the purpose of her own—a realization that gives her a sense of fellow-feeling for the old men, despite the fact that she never verbally interacts with them.

Although Francie does not form close friendships with other customers and proprietors in Williamsburg's commercial establishments—her encounters with shop owners are, in fact, often abrasive—*A Tree Grows in Brooklyn* goes out of its way to depict these relationships as socially and emotionally significant ones. Francie's relationship with the "Chinaman" that laundered her father's soiled shirts typifies the affective complexities of the social interactions that occur in Williamsburg's stores. Francie's approach to the laundry's immigrant proprietor is tinged with orientalism, but Francie's desire "to be a Chinaman . . . and have such a pretty toy to count on" and to "eat all the lichee nuts she wanted" grows out of and sustains a meaningful interpersonal connection that is hard to overlook (138).[24] Francie's inability to fulfill her desires to *be* the Chinaman preclude her from identifying with him, but it does not prevent her from establishing an emotionally valuable association with him. The economic exchange that she makes with the Chinaman—she receives two lichee nuts and her father's clean garments for the dime she slides across the counter—produces her "first experience with infinity." Francie's encounter with "infinity" may have something to do with the neighborhood's belief that the stone of a lichee nut "contained a smaller stone and that the smaller stone contained a smaller stone which contained a yet smaller stone and so on," but the metaphysical nature of this experience might also be understood to refer to Francie's encounter with the infinite variety of human experience signified by the Chinaman. Here, the "mystery of the Orient" seems to function less as a cultural force oppressing the Chinaman—though he certainly may feel marginalized by mainstream Williamsburg society—than as the source of Francie's recognition of the value of engaging with those with whom she cannot identify (138). The "wonderful barter" Francie makes with the proprietor of the laundry serves as a compelling metaphor for the social model privileged by the novel (137). While we do not know what the Chinaman receives from Francie, other than money, he unwittingly offers her an understanding of the irreducibility of those with whom she shares the city and the experience of encountering those who are radically different from her. Francie's recognition of the infinite differences between her and the Chinaman stimulates rather than stifles her fellow-feelings for him.

The affective dynamics of Francie's fellow-feelings for the Chinaman and other merchants with whom she interacts may not resemble the emotions generated within a friendship, but these interpersonal feelings do connect her to these merchants in emotionally rewarding ways. Francie's interactions with one of Williamsburg's Jewish pickle vendors provide valuable insights into the emotional complexity of these public relationships. When Francie walks down to Moore Street to buy "fat Jew pickles" from a "patriarch with a long white beard, black skull cap and toothless gums," she asks the man for a "penny sheeny pickle." The vendor takes offense at Francie's use of the derogatory term "sheeny" and stares her down with his "fierce red-rimmed eyes." Francie insists that she "did not know what the word meant really"; she used "sheeny," the narrator explains, to describe "something alien, yet beloved" (45). Francie's complicated affection for the pickle vendor—he is simultaneously both "alien" and "beloved" to her—is powerful enough to enable Francie to reject the rumors circulated by the neighborhood children that he "spat or did worse" in the vat from which he sold pickles to his gentile customers (45). Even though the Hebrew patriarch mutters "curses into his stained white beard" while fishing out a pickle for Francie, her fellow-feelings for him allow her to weather his antagonism toward her and to counteract her peers' misgivings about him. Francie had, no doubt, cultivated these fellow-feelings through repeated encounters with him in the shared public space of Moore Street. These transactions with the pickle vendor in Williamsburg's public realm enable Francie to develop a connective affection that hovers between alienation and fondness. She might be said to feel for the Jewish pickle vendor the same feelings she has for her co-workers who endlessly tease her: "companionable" (367–68).

Although Francie senses that her public interactions with those who circulate through Williamsburg's stores, libraries, playgrounds, and streets enable her to feel, much as she did at school, a "definite part of something, part of a community" (163), she has difficulty articulating to others the emotional complexion of this sociability. While standing on the Brooklyn Bridge with Lee Rynor, a soldier from Pennsylvania on his last leave before his deployment to France, sixteen-year-old Francie attempts to express to her first love the affective infrastructure of her community. When Lee shares his excitement about seeing the Manhattan skyline for the first time, Francie directs his attention to the other side of the East River. She enthuses to him that "there's a *feeling*" about Brooklyn but has trouble explaining to Lee exactly what that feeling is. She rationalizes her inarticulateness by adding, "You've got to live in Brooklyn to know" (452). Francie may be right to conclude that an outsider like Lee cannot fully understand the feeling that Brooklyn's public spaces produced among residents for one another, but at least part of her inability to communicate the emotional nature of these interpersonal bonds to others grew out of her culture's inability to make sense of the city's structure of sociability. Many urban intellectuals, including those responsible for demolishing a large swath of Francie's neighborhood to build Williamsburg Houses, had insisted that the feeling that made Brooklyn so appealing to Francie did not actually exist—especially in tenement districts such as Williamsburg. *A Tree Grows in Brooklyn* embodies Smith's attempt to supply the public with that which Francie could not quite verbalize: a conceptual framework for understanding and elucidating the "companionable" feelings that connect neighbors and strangers to one another in neighborhoods like Williamsburg.

Smith's novel uncovered the value of the sociable affiliations that connected tenement dwellers in Brooklyn's Williamsburg neighborhood to one another despite—or, more accurately, because of—the area's built environment. The neighborhood's run-down residential buildings, small commercial spaces, and public institutions played a critical role in facilitating the fellow-feelings that residents had for each other. As Francie and her neighbors participate in the social and economic activities supported by Williamsburg's streets and stores, they acquire a fellow-feeling for one another that does not necessarily diminish ethnic and economic differences. The companionable affections that Francie feels for those alongside whom she works, walks, and shops in Williamsburg should not be mistaken as a product of, or as a path toward, close friendship and other intimate relationships. Rather, the sense of companionship that Francie feels for her fellow city dwellers is born out of the recognition that her physical and emotional well-being depends on the wide variety of urbanites—companions in the most spatial sense of the word—that made her life in the city possible.

The Complexion of Urban Sociability

The discourse of urban sociability that Smith and other literary urbanists developed during the interwar period proved capable of legitimizing a range of relational forms and fellow-feelings that connected urbanites to one another, but these writers did not offer alternative city-building strategies to those that had been codified in New Deal legislation. Their inability to recognize the need to intervene in the redevelopment of the city's built environment might be attributed, in part, to the nostalgia that motivated and infused their work. These literary urbanists set out to document urban social orders and built environments that had already or would soon disappear as the city transitioned from an industrial to postindustrial economy and as new patterns of urban migration changed the demographic composition of urban neighborhoods. Liebling's profile of the Jollity Building was clearly inspired by his understanding that it and buildings like it would be "pulled down" and "replaced by a one- or two-story taxpayer"; he wrote to record the workings of the social orders that these buildings had sheltered in the past, not necessarily those it would need to harbor in the future.[25] And *A Tree Grows in Brooklyn*, though narrated from the vantage point of 1943, spends nearly all its time documenting Francie's life during the 1910s. In her efforts to capture a social world that had been partially wiped out by the construction of Williamsburg Houses, Smith transported readers back to a time just before the social, economic, and demographic transformations that culminated in the Housing Acts of 1937 and 1949 began to manifest themselves in hard-to-ignore ways on the urban landscape. This nostalgic dimension of the interwar discourse of urban sociability developed by literary urbanists prevented these writers from seriously considering the tactics necessary to both protect and create the kinds of urban spaces that would facilitate sociable interactions among city dwellers.

The nostalgic element of the interwar discourse of urban sociability also limited its ability to make sense of interracial urban relations and to recognize the ways the built environment increasingly obstructed interracial interaction. The relative absence of black urbanites in Smith's novel and in the *New Yorker*'s urban journalism is striking given their growing presence in the interwar city. The Great Migration was in full swing when Smith, Liebling, Mitchell, Johnston, and White were helping readers make sense of urban life, but their work hardly registers the demographic and material transformation of the city brought about by this massive folk migration. Interracial sociability ultimately depended on the access of black and white urbanites to shared urban spaces. But when black migrants arrived in Chicago, New York, Philadelphia, and other urban destinations, they had limited access to residential, educational, recreational, commercial, and public spaces in which they might sociably affiliate with white urbanites. As urban historians have shown, spatial segregation persisted and, in many ways, intensified throughout the first half of the twentieth century.[26]

Richard Wright, Jean Toomer, Dorothy West, Chester Himes, Nella Larsen, and other black literary urbanists writing during the interwar period called attention to the spatial segregation that limited opportunities for interracial interaction. The protagonist of Wright's *Native Son* (1940), Bigger Thomas, compares his experience living in Chicago's Black Belt to "living in jail": "We live here and they live there. We black and they white. They got things and we ain't. They do things and we can't. . . . Half the time I feel like I'm on the outside of the world peeping in through a knothole in the fence." While not all black city dwellers experienced the city as the kind of radically segregated place that Bigger describes—many associated with white individuals at places of work, entertainment, and consumption—Wright argued that the racial logic of the interwar city's spatial order significantly undermined the possibility of interracial sociability. When Jan and Mary, who think of themselves as racially progressive members of the white community, ask Bigger to take them to a "*real* place" to eat on Chicago's South Side in hopes of the chance to interact casually with him and other black urbanites, Bigger struggles to connect with them in any meaningful way. Sitting at a table with Mary and Jan in Ernie's Kitchen Shack makes Bigger so uncomfortable that it "altered" the "very organic functions of his body." In his "relations" with Mary, in particular, Bigger "felt that he was riding a seesaw; never were they on a common level."[27] Wright claimed that attaining the socially common ground on which Bigger, Mary, and Jan might build fellow-feelings for one another was ultimately predicated on their ability regularly to co-occupy the same physical spaces within the city. Living in a city in which black residents were fenced into spaces that operated outside the places in which the white world existed obstructed the experience of interracial sociability.

If black literary urbanists reminded the public of the inability of the growing urbanist discourse of sociability to account adequately for the unjust interracial social dynamics in the interwar city, they nevertheless called attention to the social value and emotional legitimacy of the sociable affiliations that black city dwellers experienced among themselves within what St. Clair Drake and Horace Cayton called the "black metropolis."[28] While the interwar city limited the occasions for interracial encounters, it provided black residents with unprecedented opportunities to associate with one another in the restaurants, nightclubs, theaters, movie houses, cabarets, pool halls, stores, butcher shops, churches, and social clubs that sprang up in urban neighborhoods such as Harlem, Chicago's South Side, and Philadelphia's Seventh Ward.[29] When the protagonist of Nella Larsen's *Quicksand* (1928), Helga Crane, arrives in Harlem, she immerses herself in the nightlife of the black metropolis. As she affiliates with other black urbanites in its "shops, its theaters, its art galleries, and its restaurants," she "lost that tantalizing oppression of loneliness and isolation which always, it seemed, had been a part of her existence." In giving herself up to the "miraculous joyousness of Harlem," Helga's sociable affiliations with other black city dwellers acquired meaning by giving her the sense that she belonged to a larger social world than had been available to her through the "feeling of smallness which had hedged her in, first during her sorry, unchildlike childhood among hostile white folk in Chicago, and later during her uncomfortable sojourn among snobbish black folk in Naxos." While her encounters with other urbanites in Harlem's gathering places do not result in a wide circle of friends, they do take the edge off her loneliness and isolation. But, despite the emotional advantages that Helga discovers within Harlem's structures of sociability and the absolute lack of desire for those "pale and powerful people" beyond Harlem to signal an "awareness" of her existence, the socially circumscribed nature of these structures of sociability cause her to "lose confidence in the fullness of her life. She eventually begins to feel "shut in, trapped," and, as a result, begins to "draw away from those contacts which had so delighted her." According to Larsen, a physical and social landscape that obstructed the probability of interracial affiliation would inevitably undermine the social power of an intraracial structure of sociability.[30]

As the city continued to transform both physically and socially in the postwar era, urban intellectuals modified and deepened the discourse of sociability developed by literary urbanists during the interwar period in an attempt to account for an even broader range of affiliations among urbanites and to develop city-building strategies that would facilitate these affiliations. The tyranny of intimacy at the heart of the New Deal Era's urbanist discourse of sympathy persisted in the postwar years and continued to shape the efforts of those responsible for redeveloping the city. But many urban intellectuals worked to tweak and expand the interwar urbanist discourse of sociability to provide the public with new ways to think about and legitimize the connections and relationships forged among city dwellers. This postwar discourse of sociability enabled urbanists to perceive and validate forms of interracial and cross-class relationships that remained obscure in an interwar discourse of sociability. Postwar urbanists would become more aware of and outspoken about the need to create urban spaces that would allow city dwellers opportunities to affiliate with and feel connected to those who did not inhabit their racial, ethnic, class, or geographic boundaries.

CHAPTER 4

The Ecology of Sociability in the Postwar City

In the June 2, 1951, issue of the *New Yorker*, readers of the magazine encountered the first installment of a rather unusual three-part profile: Rachel Carson's profile of the sea.[1] While recognizing the significance of this and subsequent publications in the *New Yorker* for Carson's career, many have found it difficult to make sense of her appearance in a magazine targeted, according to founder Harold Ross, at "persons who have a metropolitan interest."[2] It seemed strange, Harrison Smith noted in his review of the book from which the Profile of the Sea had been taken, that the "*New Yorker* would print a great part of a book that is so alien to its normal purposes." Dr. T. McKean Down voiced a similar response when he informed the magazine's editors that, while he greatly enjoyed Carson's essays, he "would not have supposed . . . that they would appeal to the majority of your clientele." Echoing Down's surprise, Miriam Teichner wrote Ross to explain that Carson's work was the "sort of thing that might well be taken for granted in the *National Geographic* or *Natural History* magazines, but in the *New Yorker*, it brings a tingling drench of astonishment and delight."[3] Smith, Down, Teichner, and others could not fathom why Carson's ecological lens had been placed within the metropolitan monocle of Eustace Tilley, the *New Yorker*'s sophisticated cover boy. But Carson's ecological ideas were not at all alien to the magazine's purposes. In fact, the "Talk of the Town" section of the June 9, 1951, issue, in which the second installment of Carson's Profile of the Sea appeared, celebrated the opening of the American Museum of Natural History's (AMNH) Felix M. Warburg Memorial Hall, which consisted of "some twenty exhibits illustrating the ecology, or environmental interrelationship, of plant and animal life."[4] Ecology, it might have been suggested to those reading the *New Yorker* in the summer of 1951, clarified rather than obfuscated the metropolitan magazine's vision of urban life.

What readers witnessed in the surprising appearance of ecology in the *New Yorker* was the evolution of a discourse of sociability that interwar literary urbanists, especially those who had written for the magazine in the 1930s and 1940s, had cultivated in their efforts to legitimize a wider range of relationships among urbanites than those acknowledged within the urbanist discourse of sympathy. New ecological research provided midcentury urbanists with the scientific evidence and conceptual framework through which they could more persuasively call attention to the various types of affiliations that city dwellers forged with one another. The ecological paradigms that emerged during the interwar and postwar periods—paradigms that differed in significant ways from those embraced by early twentieth-century ecologists—pushed urban intellectuals to recognize that the breadth and depth of the interdependencies that connected city dwellers to one another were even more extensive than city journalists, tenement novelists, and others had realized. Midcentury urbanists who took up the ecological habits of thinking on display in the AMNH and the *New Yorker* saw new kinds of interrelations among urbanites, especially among those who did not socially or physically interact with one another in the city's public spaces. These ecological paradigms allowed urbanists to highlight the significance of interrelationships among city dwellers who operated within very different urban spheres. Urban intellectuals used the language and logic of what scientific historians describe as "community" ecology to both solidify and expand the urbanist discourse of sociability.[5]

Urbanists turned to community ecology at a time when the city's physical and social landscapes were being radically transformed. The decentralization of U.S. cities picked up significant speed in the postwar years as the federal government's taxation, transportation, and mortgage policies underwrote a seismic shift of people and industry from central cities to the suburbs. As white middle-class city dwellers migrated to the suburbs—a migration made possible by federally underwritten loans—black migrants rode the wave of the Second Great Migration into the centers of Northern, Midwestern, and Western cities where they once again found themselves looking for inadequate housing and increasingly scarce job opportunities in the face of social and political hostilities. In an attempt to help cities weather the significant loss of white middle-class residents and businesses to the suburbs and simultaneously to manage the growing number of black residents within the central city's borders, a wide variety of urban professionals set out to remake the industrial city. They hoped to lure white shoppers, workers, and residents back to the central city by removing black and poor city dwellers from locations that would be redeveloped to accommodate the emerging postindustrial economy and the lifestyles that accompanied this new economic order. Financed with funds made available by the Housing Acts of 1949 and 1954, as well as additional federal and state legislation, cities pursued a course of urban renewal by razing slums, paving new highways, constructing new housing for the urban elite, building attractive cultural institutions, and ghettoizing the urban poor in subsidized housing projects. The decentralization of the metropolis and the rise of the urban renewal order in the postwar years created not only a more complex urban ecosystem but also a more fragile one. As urban professionals physically remade cities for a postindustrial economy, they substantially reconfigured the communities and relationships that had sustained and been sustained by the prewar city. The changing postwar city demanded new ways of thinking and talking about how urbanites were connected to one another.[6]

Community ecology gave postwar urbanists a language with which they could identify and articulate the value of the complex and sometimes imperceptible interconnections among urbanites that the processes of decentralization and urban renewal had disrupted. Urban intellectuals found in community ecology a cache of facts, values, and metaphors that allowed them to describe in new ways the configurations and dynamics of the relationships that constituted the city's increasingly brittle social landscape. Community ecologists not only illuminated the various ways organisms within an ecosystem depended on one another, but they also characterized those intra- and interspecies associations as cooperative. That is to say, community ecologists described relationships among organisms in the natural world as sociable ones. The affiliations that tied organisms to one another within an ecosystem were not grounded in deep intersubjective emotions or even physical familiarity but were instead rooted in physiological interdependencies and gregarious instincts. As community ecologists developed the terminology with which they might describe the proto-cooperative nature of ecological relationships, they built up a vocabulary that resonated with the sensibility of sociability. Urbanists drew on this vocabulary to expose and legitimate the wide variety of sociable affiliations that held urban communities together at a time in U.S. urban history when those communities were being dramatically transformed. Community ecology expanded the urbanist discourse of sociability by enabling it to account for associations that had been overlooked or ignored by those who forwarded the urban renewal order—including associations among city dwellers who may not have directly interacted with one another but who nevertheless depended on one another. This more expansive vision of urban sociability, in turn, enabled urbanists to imagine additional forms of fellow-feeling that might connect city dwellers to one another across lines of class, race, and geography.

The ecological urbanism that emerged at midcentury offered urban intellectuals very different ways of talking about relationships than those provided by the kind of urban ecology developed by the Chicago school of sociology during the interwar period. Robert Park and other sociologists from the Chicago school were among the first to tap into ecology's glossary in an effort to make sense of the city. They borrowed metaphors of competition, dominance, and succession from nineteenth- and early twentieth-century plant and animal ecology to explain the evolution of Chicago's neighborhoods—what Park referred to as the city's "mosaic of little worlds which touch but do not interpenetrate."[7] This first wave of ecological urbanists saw the city as a place where "secondary" (or informal) relationships trumped "primary" (or intimate) ones. Because the Chicago school's particular fusion of urbanism and ecology resonated with dominant depictions of the city as a place where alienation displaced intimacy as the emotion that city dwellers felt for one another, it retained a remarkable staying power.[8] But the appearance of ecology in venues such as the *New Yorker* and the AMNH signaled the formation of a very different strain of ecological urbanism. Unlike the Chicago school's variety, the ecological urbanism that began to materialize at midcentury was rooted in theories of interdependence and cooperation. These concepts had trumped notions of social Darwinism to become ecology's trademark paradigms. During the interwar years, a broad coalition of scientists began conducting research in an effort to replace early ecology's social Darwinian principles with evidence of cooperation as a fundamental biological impulse. Community ecologists and urban intellectuals drew on this new set of ecological principles to make sense of and explain to others what was happening in the postwar metropolis. In the postwar period, the city again became fertile ground for planting and nurturing ecology's habits of thinking.[9]

This chapter unearths the particular discourse of sociability embedded in the community ecology developed and disseminated by midcentury scientists, educators, writers, and institutions. It examines the efforts of community ecologists self-consciously to position their branch of ecology as a discourse that could be used to explain the social world. These community ecologists not only sought to discover the biological interdependencies among the organisms living together in an ecological community but also to show that these physiological interdependencies produced cooperative social ties. In the 1950s, urban institutions such as the *New Yorker* and the AMNH made it their business to teach city dwellers the principles of community ecology and expose the forms of sociability found in the natural world. Although the postwar period would produce many different formulations of ecological urbanism, this chapter focuses on those curated by J. B. Jackson in his quirky but influential *Landscape* magazine. During the 1950s and 1960s, Jackson published the work of several urbanists who used ecology to both redefine the parameters and explain the affective nature of urban relationships. These ecological urbanists understood the city to be a space that facilitated an infinite number of affiliations and interdependencies among city dwellers, as well as among all the organisms with whom these city dwellers shared the urban ecosystem. Viewing urban relationships in ecological terms allowed urbanists to perceive interconnections among city dwellers who shared few geographic, ethnic, or class obligations, as well as among urbanites and the city's nonhuman elements. These midcentury ecological urbanists began to imagine alternatives to the redevelopment strategies pursued by those committed to the urban renewal order. They recognized that the viability of urban sociability required a particular type of built environment. Ecological urbanists argued that the urban environment ought to replicate as closely as possible the natural world's diversity of forms.

Community Ecology's Sociable Impulse

In *Principles of Animal Ecology* (1949)—the theoretical and experimental consummation of the work community ecologists had been carrying out for the previous two decades—W. C. Allee, Alfred E. Emerson, Orlando Park, Thomas Park, and Karl P. Schmidt defined *ecology* as the "science of the interrelation between living organisms and their environment, including both the physical and the biotic environments, and emphasizing interspecies as well as intraspecies relations."[10] Although this definition of the relatively young discipline was not necessarily innovative, the authors' particular understanding of the interrelations formed between organisms and their environments, as well as within and among species, set them apart from their ecological predecessors. Unlike early twentieth-century ecologists such as Frederic Clements, who saw competition as the primary mode of interrelations among organisms, community ecologists argued that the cooperative relationships present in the natural world had been undeservedly ignored. While community ecologists did not deny the presence of competitive interactions among organisms, they set out to prove that these organisms collaborated in order to survive in their shared environments more often than scientists had acknowledged. Allee, perhaps the most vocal advocate of community ecology, claimed nearly twenty years prior to the publication of *Principles of Animal Ecology* that the "principle of co-operation should rank as one of the major biological principles comparable with the better recognized Darwinian principle of the struggle for existence." By the time his seminal textbook was published, Allee was less reserved in stating the significance of the role that cooperation played in the natural world. "After much consideration," he decreed, "it is my mature conclusion, contrary to Herbert Spencer, that the cooperative forces are biologically ... more important and vital" than the "disoperative and egoistic" tendencies.[11]

Because the cooperative behavior among organisms was primarily instigated by instinct, many community ecologists referred to the relational behavior activated by these impulses as proto-cooperation. Community ecologists filled pages of scientific studies with examples of the many different configurations that proto-cooperation assumed on multiple biological levels in the natural world. Summarizing these studies, the authors of *Principles of Animal Ecology* listed thirteen general forms that this "natural cooperation" might take, among which were the following: "plants and animals are able to modify an unfavorable environment to such an extent that, though some or all of the pioneers may be killed, others following and some associated with them can survive and even thrive when they could not do so in a raw environment"; many "biological processes are beneficially accelerated in the presence of populations of optimal size and density"; and "evolution proceeds more rapidly and certainly in populations of interbreeding animals that are not too small."[12] Proto-cooperation, in short, characterizes any type of physiological interaction that enables organisms and the ecosystems to which they belong to move toward and then maintain a state of equilibrium.

This proto-cooperative behavior connected every organism to a larger biotic community, a population unit that community ecologists most often referred to as an aggregation. Allee reasoned that the existence of these proto-cooperative aggregations proved that the interrelations among organisms in the natural world transcended the boundaries of kinship. The family, he reminded readers, was "merely one type of aggregation."[13] In addition to belonging to population groupings structured by sexual reproduction, all living organisms were also "necessarily members of loosely integrated racial and interracial communities, in part woven together by environmental factors and in part by mutual attraction between the individual members of the different communities."[14] Because the aggregations that community ecologists studied were solidified through socially positive rather than combative interactions, their work amplified the scope and social significance of the natural world's interconnectivity, which had been one of ecology's original calling cards. Through their exhaustive descriptions of proto-cooperative interactions in the animal world, community ecologists enhanced the ability of the public to intellectually conceptualize and emotionally tap into what it meant to live in a thoroughly interconnected environment. Community ecologists reinforced the public's ability to comprehend and embrace their particular ecological worldview by suggesting that the more visible and emotionally legible forms of cooperation among humans, mammals, and insects were the tip of a very deep biological order held together by proto-cooperative behavior. Allee's claim that "no animal is solitary throughout its life history" might come off as analogous to John Donne's well-known poetic claim that "No man is an island," but community ecologists were speaking literally rather than poetically. For them, it was cooperation all the way down.[15]

In an effort to legitimate their cooperative narrative about the natural world, community ecologists cobbled together an intellectual history for their particular branch of ecology.[16] The authors of *Principles of Animal Ecology* located the "germ of the idea of natural cooperation" in the "biologically absurd poetry" of fifth-century B.C.E. Greek philosopher Empedocles. This conceptual germ was "kept somewhat alive, often in barely recognizable form, by the succession of thinkers . . . who saw human society as a natural outgrowth from the life of other animals." But, according to the disciplinary genealogy assembled by Allee and his colleagues, the more ecologically recognizable notion of natural cooperation did not begin to emerge until the turn of the eighteenth century when Anthony Cooper, third earl of Shaftesbury, expounded a "positive philosophical emphasis on the nonegocentric interpretation of nature." Allee and his coauthors next inserted Adam Smith into their intellectual genealogy. In his *Theory of Moral Sentiments* (1759), Smith had, they claimed, "emphasized the same qualities" of natural cooperation articulated by Lord Shaftesbury "under the heading of 'sympathy' or 'fellow feeling'."[17] The intellectual genealogy of community ecology then passed through a much more likely cast of nineteenth- and twentieth-century characters: Charles Darwin (nature was not all about competition for the father of evolution), Alfred Espinas, Peter Kropotkin, Patrick Geddes, Sir John Arthur Thompson, William Patten, and William Morton Wheeler.

The intellectual history worked up by community ecologists says a lot about the kind of social order that they felt their science supported. By grafting ecology onto moral philosophy and naming Lord Shaftesbury and Smith as the field's intellectual ancestors, the authors of *Principles of Animal Ecology* implicitly assigned their science the task of updating their readership's understanding of the types of fellow-feelings about which Lord Shaftesbury and Smith had written two hundred years earlier. In setting out to help the public better understand the physiological workings of the natural world, community ecologists aspired to alter their readers' understanding of their own relationships. No community ecologist spelled out the social implications of the discipline more directly than Allee. In a 1943 *Science* magazine article that reads as if it were community ecology's manifesto, Allee forcefully made the case that, because science was the "most recently revitalized force in civilization," scientists shouldered the burden of developing new "methods for the education of the emotions." As Allee saw it, this emotional training required helping individuals discover the ways in which their emotional ties to others, both human and nonhuman, could be grounded in the biological realm. He insisted that the "data of biology, if properly understood," would enable man to "focus on his innate drives toward cooperation and attempt to set up a new order based primarily on some altruistic pattern."[18] Although Allee and his fellow community ecologists supposed that their research would engender the kind of sympathetic fellow-feelings that Smith, Shaftesbury, and other moral philosophers had described, their ecological findings and arguments were actually more likely to give rise to sociable fellow-feelings. The proto-cooperative interactions among organisms that community ecologists documented so extensively during the interwar period were more likely to inspire sociable than intimate relationships.

Displaying Ecological Sociability

When the AMNH board of directors hired Albert E. Parr away from his post as director of Yale's Peabody Museum in 1942, the New York institution had been failing in its self-appointed mission to educate the intellect and emotions of the public. Parr attributed the museum's struggles to its longstanding commitment to collecting and displaying a mind-boggling variety of exotic specimens. By focusing "their eyes on the great distances of time and space," Parr explained in his first annual report as director of the AMNH, natural history museums had "lost their most vital contacts with the real concerns of man" and, as a result, had been "reduced to functioning mainly as sources of sound and polite intellectual entertainment."[19] Natural history museums were, he fretted, becoming endangered species. The Akeley Hall of African Mammals, which opened in 1936, monumentalized the model of natural history museums from which Parr hoped to distance the AMNH. Consisting of twenty-eight dioramas featuring African animals grouped together in a recognizably domestic arrangement, Akeley Hall perfected the house-exhibition style through which the museum had been telling its story about communities found in the natural world.[20] Parr, a practicing and published community ecologist, hoped to replace the domestic narrative that the AMNH had been selling the public with an ecological story about nature's more important and vital form of sociality. He planned to create exhibits that would teach visitors about the web of biological and environmental relationships in which all species were enmeshed. Parr wanted to inform patrons that proto-cooperative aggregations of organisms, rather than individual family units, fueled the natural world.[21]

When it opened on May 15, 1951, the Felix M. Warburg Memorial Hall represented what Parr described as the "first major result in public exhibition" of the ecological "trend in the Museum's activities . . . and in the overall concept of the Museum's purposes."[22] Upon entering Warburg Hall from the Seventy-Seventh Street lobby, visitors would not have walked into an expansive room with dioramas lining the walls but would have instead been greeted by one large display case that featured a painted backdrop of Stissing Mountain in vibrant fall foliage and a foreground of three-dimensional casts of several small sumac trees, a large canoe birch tree, and other indigenous plants. From afar, "An October Afternoon Near Stissing Mountain" appeared to be nothing but a blown-up snapshot taken by a leaf-peeping tourist. The trunk of the large canoe birch tree, rather than an animal grouping, visually anchored the diorama, while the stunning foliage on the mountain seized the viewer's attention. Only as visitors neared the display would they begin to see tucked into and around the replicated landscape the diorama's habitat group: a red fox, monarch butterfly, blue jay, woolly caterpillar, praying mantis, dragonfly, black duck, and red-tailed hawk. The diorama's animal specimens were not only relatively inconspicuous and physically dispersed but also represented a variety of species. Because the fox, butterfly, blue jay, caterpillar, and other specimens were clearly not held together by familial obligations, "An October Afternoon" invited visitors to discover alternative relational patterns. Dr. Earl Martin, a biologist at Brooklyn College, reported to Parr that he and his students spent "as much as an hour" figuring out how the "detailed features" of "An October Afternoon" constituted "authentic parts of the whole picture." Even if the diorama did not spell out for visitors the precise nature of the associations among the organisms on display, it encouraged them to spend time contemplating the physiological and social dynamics of the habitat group.[23]

As visitors wound their way through Warburg Hall's S-shaped floor plan, they were taught from a variety of spatial, temporal, and biological points of view about the proto-cooperative relationships that confronted them in "An October Afternoon" and that were at work on multiple levels in an ecological system such as Stissing Mountain. An exhibit around the corner from "An October Afternoon" helped patrons understand exactly how proto-cooperation operated, by depicting the biological activity within a single environment over the course of a year. "Life in the Soil," one of the most popular and startling exhibits in Warburg Hall, consisted of four contiguous vitrines—two that contained vertical cutaways of the soil strata beneath a farmer's lawn and two that exposed the soil beneath the edge of a forest.[24] In the "Edge of Woodland" dyad, the winter soil profile revealed the nest of a white-footed mouse near the surface, an ant nest slightly beneath it, and a chipmunk nest near the bottom of the display. The spring version, a structural replica of its winter counterpart, disclosed a yellow jacket nest in the space formerly occupied by the white-footed mouse, and a small litter of baby chipmunks hunkering down in the nest previously inhabited by a single chipmunk. In the "Farmer's Lawn" dyad, the winter soil profile exposed three sections of a mole tunnel that had been dug since spring, inhabited in turn by a pine mouse, toad, and mole. Nothing in the display suggested that the mole was aware of the pine mouse and toad lodging in its tunnels; nor was there any indication that the white-footed mouse had volunteered his winter nest to the yellow jacket. The exhibit's plaques made it clear that the pine mouse simply took "advantage of mole tunnels to reach bulbs and roots for its winter food," while the "nest of the white-footed mouse, no longer needed by the owner, was taken over by a queen yellow jacket." In responding to

Figure 9. The Farmer's Lawn (Spring) vitrine from the "Life in the Soil" exhibit in the Felix M. Warburg Memorial Hall. Image #321876, American Museum of Natural History Library.

Figure 10. The Farmer's Lawn (Winter) vitrine from the "Life in the Soil" exhibit in the Felix M. Warburg Memorial Hall. Image #321876, American Museum of Natural History Library.

their shared environment, the mole, toad, mice, and yellow jacket unwittingly worked together to ensure one another's survival. Although Warburg Hall never used *proto-cooperation* to describe the activities of its habitat groups, "Life in the Soil" and the dioramas surrounding it effectively dramatized the core concept of community ecology for AMNH patrons.

In exhibiting proto-cooperative relationships, Warburg Hall did more than simply pass along a few scientific tidbits to museumgoers—it instructed them how to think ecologically. Parr and his colleagues had hoped that the museum would give visitors "pleasures that do not end with the museum visit, but repeat themselves a million times in everyday life beyond its walls."[25] At least some of the pleasures that patrons experienced beyond the museum were rooted in Warburg Hall's success in helping them recognize interrelationships in the natural world about which they had not known. An early visitor's enthusiastic response to Warburg Hall called attention to at least one of the forms that this pleasure might take: "Here is true art, the representation of reality, and an important lesson on Life showing the similarity and interdependence of all living things."[26] This patron's recognition of the interdependencies of the exhibited organisms prompted her to project onto the relationships among them an emotional connection strong enough to be able to bring dissimilar specimens onto a common social plane. She did not detect in the relationship between the mole and toad the type of familial love anthropomorphized by the African mammals in Akeley Hall. Rather, she and the millions of others who visited the AMNH's newest exhibit during the early 1950s were prodded to perceive in Warburg Hall's animal aggregations a fellow-feeling among the organisms that appeared to be grounded in their physical reliance on one another. Because these specimens clearly had not experienced any kind of emotional intersubjectivity, the fellow-feelings that patrons projected onto the interdependencies among them belonged not to an affective economy of intimacy but to one of sociability. Those who made their way through Warburg Hall perceived in the interrelations on display what Georg Simmel had described as sociability's "pure essence of association, of the associative process as a value and a satisfaction." In helping patrons comprehend the ecological value of the purely physical associations among organisms, Warburg Hall encouraged its visitors to imagine that a type of public amiability held the animal aggregations together.[27]

In the story about ecosystems that Warburg Hall shared with visitors, ecological sociability was capacious enough to hold together wide varieties of specimens. Parr and his colleagues almost exclusively displayed animal aggregations comprised of organisms from different species. Although community ecologists talked as much about the ways that proto-cooperation functioned within a single-species community as they did about its occurrence in multispecies aggregations, Parr only exhibited interrelationships within what Allee had described as interracial communities. By creating habitat groups populated by a biologically diverse range of animals, dioramas such as "An October Afternoon" and "Life in the Soil" portrayed a structure of sociability capable of connecting organisms across not just the biological borders that separated them but also the spatial and temporal boundaries imposed by biological differences. According to the visual logic of "An October Afternoon," the red fox and blue jay forged a sociable association that surmounted their biological differences through brief glances, coincidental contact, and physical proximity. "Life in the Soil" encouraged museum patrons to imagine a sociable association between the white-footed mouse and yellow jacket that overcame the spatial and temporal distances that separated them by implying an agreement between them to share the same subterraneous space. These interracial communities did not appear to demand that individual specimens support the inner lives of one another, but instead seemed to require of them an impersonal obligation to do what it took to maintain the ecological order.

Warburg Hall suggested to visitors that the biodiversity of an ecological community intensified rather than diminished the value of the interdependencies that connected organisms to one another. Parr went out of his way in designing exhibits to demonstrate that the stability of a single specimen in a habitat group depended on the presence and precise placement of a range of biologically distinct specimens around it. Several displays illuminated the significance of each ecological affiliation by positioning specimens at various points along the arc of a circle. Sometimes that cyclical pattern would be pointed out to onlookers. In "Cycle of Nutrition and Decay in the Water," arched arrows leading from one specimen to another communicated visually the message verbalized in the display's explanatory plaque: "Plants are fed upon by some animals which, in turn, are eaten by predators. Dead or decaying matter is further broken down by scavenging organisms. And thus is formed the complete cycle from nutrition to decay and back again to nutrition." The arrows and text in a display like "Cycle of Nutrition and Decay" legitimated and heightened the significance of every interconnection in the cycle by showing precisely how each participant was absolutely necessary to the others. Were the scavenging organisms to disappear, for example, the plants, herbivores, and predators would have been thrown off balance. It was not enough just to have the right number of specimens in an aggregation; the physiological functions each specimen contributed to its community were critical in maintaining that community's equilibrium. Warburg Hall offered visitors endless illustrations of Allee's assertion that no member of an animal aggregation "can be affected without changing some or even all the rest, at least to some slight extent."[28]

The community ecology that Carson shared with *New Yorker* readers in the 1950s would have been familiar to anyone who had visited Warburg Hall.[29] Her Profile of the Sea (1951) and Profile of the Edge of the Sea (1955) rehearsed for readers many of the same ecological principles on display in the AMNH. But where the social implications of ecology remained implicit in Warburg Hall, Carson's accounts of marine life explicitly articulated the explanatory possibilities that ecology offered to those interested in making sense not just of human communities but also of urban communities. Carson's ecological discourse of sociability resonated with and extended the urbanist discourse of sociability that the magazine had been developing for over two decades. Robert Lamond intuited this resonance when he declared that Carson's was the "best Profile since that of the Jollity Building some time ago."[30] As Carson wrote about the "delicately adjusted interlocking relationships" that made life in the sea possible, she mapped out for readers in scientific terms the nature of the social interconnections among urbanites that had been the focus of many of the *New Yorker*'s previous profiles. Given the venue in which they were reading Carson's new brand of nature writing, it would have been easy for readers to draw on her ecological wisdom to make sense of the city's social landscape—to realize that "what happens" to one member of the city's "odd community of creatures" "may well determine what happens" to another member of that urban community.[31]

Carson increased the likelihood that readers would perceive the applicability of an ecological discourse of sociability to the interrelationships that crisscrossed the city's social landscape by directly comparing the life of and interdependencies among seashore organisms to the life of and interdependencies among city dwellers. In her Profiles of the Edge of the Sea, published in the last two issues of August 1955, Carson attempted to help her cosmopolitan readers understand the nature of the proto-cooperative relationships that arose among the seashore's "many-layered community of animals" by frequently describing these aquatic aggregations as if they were urban communities.[32] She informed readers about the "cities of mole crabs" that lived where waves broke on sandy shores, the "shrimp city" that could be found just beneath the surface of the tidal flats, and the "underground city" of invisible "inhabitants" that brought "little heaps of refuse . . . up to the surface as if in an attempt at some sort of civic sanitation," and whose "chimneys and stacks and ventilating pipes of underground dwellings" might be seen protruding slightly above the surface of the beach. Examining these intertidal cities more closely revealed an "intricate interdependence of one species upon another."[33] In the low-water area of many rocky shores, Carson reported that she often found "cities of mussels" living in close "association" with "one of the red seaweeds—Gigartina." The Gigartina's stems and branches were, in turn, "thickly overgrown with the bryozoan sea lace, Membranipora, and with another bryozoan of coarser growth, Flustrella," which formed a "crust in which there are hundreds of small adjacent compartments, and from these the betentacled heads of resident creatures are thrust out." According to Carson, these and many of the other sea creatures that took up residence in the cities along the shoreline exhibited a "strong instinct of gregariousness," clearly preferring to live "neighbor against neighbor."[34]

In her Profiles of the Edge of the Sea, Carson constructed a conceptual bridge between natural and urban communities that encouraged readers to understand the type of fellow-feelings they had for their urban neighbors as the product of the kind of proto-cooperative relationships that connected sea creatures to one another. As they read about the "betentacled heads of resident creatures" sticking out of the "small adjacent compartments" formed by the sea's interwoven plant life, readers might imagine that these marine animals were held together by the same type of connection that bound together individuals occupying dense urban neighborhoods. According to Carson, sea creatures were gregarious—a term that community ecologists often used to describe the social traits of proto-cooperative animals—in the same way that urbanites were gregarious in a city's public spaces. Unlike many physiological traits, gregariousness is a biological instinct whose fulfillment requires the presence of and engagement with other organisms. Gregariousness implies a distinctly public and casual sociability. In characterizing the mussels and betentacled sea creatures as gregarious, Carson suggested that the physiological dependencies among these creatures produced both biological and affective interdependencies that propped up a public social order that enabled each organism to go about the business of surviving the "difficult world of the shore."[35]

Midcentury Ecological Urbanisms

Carson's metaphorical use of the city to help her readers grasp the sociability of ecological communities was deeply embedded in the rhetoric of community ecology. Community ecologists had been using analogies between natural and urban communities for many years in their efforts to help adherents understand the social nature of animal aggregations. But community ecologists had also insisted that their scientific studies could and should be used to make sense of human communities. Allee was particularly invested in deploying the findings of community ecologists to facilitate more peaceful international relations in the aftermath of World War II.[36] But many others put the principles of community ecology to use in their efforts to make sense of the city's social landscape. These comparative socioecologists were particularly drawn to the ways in which an ecological discourse of sociability might aid them in explaining the nature of the ties that connect city dwellers to one another and thus in assigning social value to urban communities that were too often seen as disconnected or socially impoverished. Of course, there was no single way to go about explicating an ecological understanding of the city's social orders. From the 1940s through the 1960s, when the intense physical and demographic transformation of the postwar city dramatically rearranged its social orders, both ecologists and urban intellectuals fabricated a variety of ecological urbanisms to show that the interdependencies that connected city dwellers to one another were far more expansive and socially significant than many urbanists had previously assumed.

One need look no farther than Allee's wife, Marjorie Hill Allee, to detect the beginnings of a new wave of ecological urbanisms. In 1944, Marjorie, a prolific and award-winning author of children's and young adult fiction, published *The House*, a novel about thirteen individuals who had come together from various walks of life to establish a cooperative house in Chicago's Woodlawn neighborhood. When Merritt Lane, the closest character the novel has to a protagonist, moves into the co-op at the beginning of the story, she draws on her recent experiences studying fish in the Caribbean and living among the archipelago's heterogeneous population in order to make sense of Chicago's social landscape—a landscape that was in demographic and physical flux during the 1940s. Not only was Chicago's black population growing at an unprecedented rate, becoming home to the second largest black community in the country by 1950, but an increasing number of Mexican, Puerto Rican, and Japanese migrants were settling in Chicago during this period. As white residents left the city in large numbers, Chicago became an even more racially and ethnically diverse city during the postwar period than it already had been.[37] When she returns to Chicago, Merritt draws on her scientific appreciation for ecological variety to move past the social barriers of race and class that prevented her housemates and neighbors from forming sociable attachments to many of the city's new inhabitants. When she discerns that one of the members of the co-op has "not quite adjusted to the city yet," Merritt explains to her that she'll "see a lot of queer specimens in the city." Although Hyde Park may not have sheltered the same "variety in races and costumes" that Merritt had "lived alongside" during her two years in the Caribbean, she suggests to her new roommate that imagining other city dwellers as specimens would enable her to coexist comfortably with the "odd people" that she would inevitably encounter in Chicago's public spaces.[38]

Merritt's enthusiastic admiration for the island's and the city's "queer specimens" offers her friends a slightly different way to think about and relate to other urbanites. After Merritt declares to the other members of the co-op, "I *like* variety!" the novel works hard to demonstrate how an appreciation of variety leads to a more satisfying way of urban life. When Merritt's housemates decide to accept Alice Chen's application to the co-op, knowing that it will cause their anti-Asian neighbors to kick them out of the neighborhood, they begin a search for a house and neighborhood that will better serve their cooperative enterprise. After moving north of Fifty-Fifth Street and realizing that the new house "suits us so much better in every way," Susie observes that Alice did them "a great favor."[39] Susie is not trying to claim that Alice intentionally helped her new housemates relocate and that she therefore deserves their deepest affections. Rather, Susie seems to be suggesting that, when urbanites embrace the diversity the city offers, they submit themselves to an ecological economy that ultimately leads to greater physical and social stability. By recognizing that Alice did them a favor in a proto-cooperative kind of way, Susie perceives the benefits of living alongside other "odd people" and begins to feel an appreciation for Alice that operates in conjunction with, but does not necessarily duplicate, the friendship that emerges as the two accumulate private experiences with one another. The ecological habit of mind that Merritt encourages her roommates to adopt leads not just to sociable relationships among members of the co-op but also to sociable interactions with those they encounter in Chicago's public realm.

Although Marjorie Allee did not seriously pursue *The House*'s ecological line of thinking about urban life in her later novels, other ecologically minded intellectuals developed more nuanced and sustained ecological approaches to the city in the postwar years. J. B. Jackson was perhaps the most ambitious curator of these midcentury ecological urbanisms, many of which he published in his experimental journal *Landscape*. When he circulated the first issue of *Landscape* in the spring of 1951, the journal aspired primarily to explore the "human geography"—a term Jackson defined as the "study of the relation between Man and his environment"—of the predominantly rural American Southwest.[40] Over the course of its first two decades, though, *Landscape* featured an increasing number of articles about the cultural landscape of the city—a trend precipitated, in part, by Jackson's call in 1957 for a "wider and more human understanding of the city and its problems." Jackson was particularly concerned about the transformation of the urban environment in the 1950s. He worried that the postwar city planner's "emphasis on convenience, cleanliness, and safety" had produced a "lopsided view of urban culture" that privileged the needs of the city's "white-collar workers" and marginalized "everything vulgar and small and poor" in the city.[41] Jackson heeded his own call by dedicating the magazine's Winter 1958–59 issue to an exploration of "The Urban Scene" and subsequently publishing the work of important midcentury urbanists such as Kevin Lynch, Jean Gottmann, Herbert J. Gans, Lewis Mumford, Grady Clay, and Reyner Banham. Many of the magazine's articles that examined the human geography of the city drew, to some degree, on the scientific principles and social ideals of community ecology. *Landscape*, as Hubert B. Owens noted, kept readers "abreast with the thinking of the world's leading experts in fields dealing with ecology and man's needs in the planning and control of outdoor space." Jackson's quirky but influential quarterly clearly suggested to readers that one of the most humane ways to respond to postwar urban problems was to approach the city and its inhabitants as an ecosystem.[42]

Unlike Marjorie Allee and many others who used community ecology as an analogy through which they might make sense of the city's social landscape, the ecological urbanists that appeared in *Landscape* saw the city, quite literally, as an ecological community—a "distinct environment," as Jackson put it, "where certain relationships evolve not only between men and men, but between men and the forces of nature." By viewing the city dweller as a "biological organism" rather than as a purely "social economic being," ecological urbanists dramatically expanded the range of the interrelationships into which the urbanite could be said to enter. As biological organisms, city dwellers depended not just on those who shared their own geographic, ethnic, or class affiliations in order to carry out their lives but on all the organisms with whom they inhabited the urban ecosystem. Every type of person and living entity within the city, not just those with whom one was familiar, played a hard-to-quantify role in one's ability to maintain one's lifestyle. As biological organisms, urbanites were also dependent for their well-being on the vast variety of nonliving, material elements that constituted the urban environment. The way city dwellers interacted with the city's material and natural infrastructure shaped their lives in subtle but significant ways. Ecological urbanists, then, understood the city to be a space that facilitated countless instances of "symbiosis: a living together of two dissimilar organisms in a close association which is advantageous to both."[43] Viewing urban relationships as symbiotic allowed urbanists to identify interconnections among city dwellers who had little in common, as well as among urbanites and the city's nonhuman elements.

This more expansive and inclusive view of the nearly infinite number of relationships in which every city dweller is inevitably situated required a reconsideration of the nature of the fellow-feelings that arose within those relationships. Viewing urban relationships as symbiotic pushed ecological urbanists to account for what Grady Clay described as the "new feeling" that emerged among dissimilar urban organisms as they operated in close association with one another.[44] As these urban intellectuals searched for ways to describe these distinct fellow-feelings, they enlarged the urbanist discourse of sociability that had been initially formulated by city journalists, tenement novelists, and others during the interwar period. Edgar Anderson, a professor of botany and the director of the Missouri Botanical Garden in St. Louis during the mid-1950s, was particularly invested in the project of verbalizing an ecologically inflected discourse of urban sociability. His earliest essays in *Landscape* primarily explored the affective nuances of the interspecies relationships into which individuals entered in the city. Anderson lamented society's fundamental belief "that the harmonious interaction of man and other organisms can only be achieved out in the country, that the average man is too noisy, too ugly, and too vile to be accepted as a close neighbor."

Contrary to popular opinion, Anderson insisted that city dwellers could experience harmony with nonhuman urban organisms by developing a "real interest in the ecology of our cities and the fascinating plants and animals which live there with us."[45] As Anderson walked the streets and alleys of St. Louis, he paid attention to the plants and animals with which he spent "so much of his life: trees of heaven, squirrels, sunflowers, dogs, dandelions, cats, crab grass, English sparrows, gingkoes, weeds of all sorts." Paying attention to the "dynamics" of his interactions with species so unlike himself enabled Anderson to experience what he described as a "fellow feeling for these organisms" with which he lived.[46]

Anderson and other ecological urbanists frequently tried to explain the quality of this interspecies fellow-feeling through the concept of harmony. In using *harmony* to characterize the sociable affects that bound dissimilar urban organisms to one another, ecological urbanists seemed less interested in the term's connotations of complete agreement and like-mindedness than in its musical undertones. For them, *harmony* captured the sensibility that could only be produced when a diverse arrangement of individual organisms contributed their individual sounds to the larger whole. To have harmonious interactions with squirrels, sunflowers, sparrows, and gingkoes was to sense the ways in which all these organisms worked together to create a biologically balanced and socially congruent chord. The fellow-feeling that Anderson claimed to have for other urban organisms rested on his awareness of the physiological function of each one and, therefore, of the dynamics of interdependency that held together the ecological community as a harmonious whole. His interest in the ecology of St. Louis pushed him to see how his own direct and indirect interactions with other urban organisms contributed to a biological and social state of harmony. This is not to say that Anderson was entirely unaware of the precarious nature of the urban ecosystem's balance. His ecological structure of sociable feeling was tinged with a consciousness that "*homo sapiens* is the most overwhelming of all the organisms in his primary and secondary effects" on the urban ecosystem.[47] Yet, rather than undercut the harmonious affect Anderson experienced as he situated himself in his city's larger ecological context, his self-awareness of his capabilities of disrupting the urban ecosystem's balance only intensified his fellow-feelings for the organisms with whom he shared the city.

The ecological urbanists who contributed to *Landscape* were eager to demonstrate that not only could city dwellers experience harmony with other organisms within the boundaries of the city, they might also have similarly harmonious interactions with other humans. They proposed that the same structure of sociability that generated fellow-feelings for nonhuman organisms was capable of instigating fellow-feelings for the average person in the city. In his contribution to "The Urban Scene" issue of *Landscape*, Anderson explained how the ecological habit of thinking and feeling that he had outlined in his previous essays put him in a position to acquire fellow-feelings for other urbanites. Writing about his experience while observing worshippers enter and leave a small colonial church in Washington, D.C., during breaks from his meetings at the National Science Foundation headquarters, Anderson recalled finding "Episcopalians and their visitors and friends quite as suitable and interesting objects for nature study as are ... chipping sparrows and bluebirds." Observing these urbanites with a "trained eye"—that is to say, an eye disciplined by an ecological habit of mind—Anderson sensed his interconnections with them despite the fact that he was not from their city and had never interacted with any of them. Because he had "accept[ed] Man as a part of Nature," Anderson found his own species to be the most "effective guide" to a "deeper understanding of natural history." By situating himself in relation to other city dwellers within the context of natural history's deep time, Anderson was able to appreciate the "colorful and apparently purposeful and satisfying folkways" of other city dwellers. He could confidently characterize himself as a "*sympathetic* observer" not because he felt intimately connected to the capital's Episcopalians but because his ecologically guided observations stimulated an "increasingly understanding mind" that was capable of sensing the harmony of his own species' diverse social customs and practices as they had been brought together within and orchestrated by the city.[48] His sociable fellow-feelings for Washington's churchgoers, with whom he did not directly interact, grew out of his acknowledgment that he depended on them to maintain the social harmonies produced by his own species' biological and cultural variety.

The ecological discourse of urban sociability that emerged within the pages of *Landscape* was perfectly poised to help urbanists find ways to talk about the increasingly complex interracial relations that urbanites inevitably formed as they moved through the postwar city's social landscape, but the journal's contributors failed to fully pursue this promising line of thinking. Anderson may have implied that the "colorful" Episcopalians toward whom he felt sociable were among the district's roughly 800,000 black residents, but he did not make racial identity a significant element of the ecological calculations that he executed as he processed his relationship with them. Although community ecologists had developed a scientific vocabulary for talking about what Allee had called "loosely integrated racial and interracial communities," midcentury ecological urbanists appeared unable or unwilling to transpose explicitly this scientific understanding of race to their accounts of the city's racial and interracial communities.[49] In the pages of *Landscape*, Jean Gottmann expressed his belief that "urban studies must reckon as much as any other regional analysis with the world's astounding variety," but he only managed to enumerate the type of variety that urbanists should consider in the relatively generic terms of "past cultures, vested interests, [and] proud traditions." While Gottmann and other ecological urbanists worked hard to develop an urbanist discourse that called on city dwellers to "respect the endless variety of the world we live in and to endeavor to let it develop in harmony," their inability to address more explicitly the particular arrangements of racial and ethnic variety, as well as the structures of power that shaped these arrangements, compromised that discourse's capacity to make sense of the midcentury city's social landscape.[50]

Urbanology and the Problems of the Expanding Metropolis

The ecological urbanisms that Jackson showcased in *Landscape* were particularly helpful to urbanists as they attempted to make sense of the significant transformations in the postwar city's built environment and intervene in conversations about the redevelopment of the city. Ecological urbanists were especially attuned to what Jackson called the "Problems of the Expanding Metropolis," and they hoped to address those problems by helping others perceive the ways in which the physical decentralization of the metropolis and urban renewal affected the extensive interdependencies among city dwellers and their urban environment. In the postwar period, ecological urbanists argued that, in order to facilitate sociable connections among urbanites, those who designed and redeveloped cities had to be responsible for creating an environment that would put urbanites in a position to recognize their biological and social interdependencies with other urban organisms. Jackson demanded that those who planned, built, and governed the city recognize that "every time we heap up a mass of masonry or cut through a hill or drain a swamp or plant a row of trees or fill the air with smoke or pave an open area," we are to some extent changing built and natural environments that mediate all the interrelations that take place within the city. Because the urban environment played such a vital role in facilitating "harmonious social relationships," as well as our "physical wellbeing," Jackson and others encouraged city planners, architects, and developers to be extremely cautious in altering the physical landscape. To modify the forms, spaces, lights, and sounds in which city dwellers carried out their activities and affiliations was to alter the structure of urban sociability.[51]

None of the ecological urbanists who contributed to *Landscape* made the link between the condition of the urban environment and the social quality of urban relationships more clear than the longtime director of the AMNH. Near the end of his tenure at the museum, Parr leveraged his credentials as a scientist and museum educator to establish himself in the increasingly contested field of city planning and design. He developed and promoted what he called, in work he published in *Landscape* and other venues in the 1960s, the science of "urbanology."[52] Parr's particular brand of ecological urbanism grew out of his conviction that the urban environment suffered increasingly from the "creeping blight of monotony."[53] Speaking at the 1955 International Design Conference in Aspen, Colorado, while still directing the AMNH, Parr lamented the "dreadful harmony of uniformity that had characterized so many city and suburban attempts to improve the accommodations rather than the life of man." Deploying the vocabulary and values of community ecology on display in Warburg Hall, Parr proposed an alternative approach to urban design that would embrace a "harmony of diversity." "We always hear of the beautiful harmony of nature," he reminded his audience, "but usually tend to forget that it is based on a far greater diversity of forms" than typically found in the city's built environment.[54]

Because Parr believed that the urban environment ought to aspire to replicate the "diversity of forms" that made possible the "harmony of nature," he was particularly disgusted by the bland design of most modernist architecture. Although he spoke and wrote about diverse cityscapes and varied skylines as abstract objects, he no doubt formulated his ecological arguments about urban design as he responded over time to the particular processes of physical and institutional transformation experienced by the AMNH during his time as its director. In 1941, a year before Parr's arrival at the AMNH, Robert Moses, New York City's leading proponent of urban renewal, had accused the city's museums of being too "musty." Singling out the AMNH and several other museums, Moses claimed that these institutions—much like the slums—needed to be physically and administratively "revitalized."[55]

Responding to Moses's demands, Parr and the museum's board of trustees announced in January 1943 that they and the city would extensively remodel the AMNH following the war. With the AMNH's approval, the city assigned the Park Department's consulting architect, Aymar Embury II, to modernize the museum's outdated structure. A longtime collaborator with Moses, Embury called for a radical scaling back and streamlining of the AMNH's intricate romanesque exterior, including the removal of the corner towers that jutted into the skyline. Despite widespread public opposition, Parr originally backed Embury's modern architectural redesign for the AMNH. He felt that the architect had "achieved a simple and dignified treatment giving interest to all facades and a harmonious background for the New York State Roosevelt Memorial." After the war, however, Parr remodeled his ideas about what exactly made for a harmonious urban environment. He revoked his support for the harmony of uniformity advocated by Embury in favor of the harmony of diversity advocated by Warburg Hall's ecological exhibits. Lacking sufficient funds and institutional support, the AMNH opted to shelve Embury's blueprints permanently and preserve the museum's original romanesque façade.[56]

Through his particular expressions of an urbanist discourse of sociability, Parr pushed urban designers, architects, and developers to cultivate a biologically, aesthetically, and texturally diverse urban environment primarily because he felt strongly that this was the most effective environment for advancing harmonious social relationships. In his efforts to convince the public that a city's architectural "diversity is actually good for us, perhaps even essential," Parr fashioned ecologically informed arguments about how the "relationship between the human mind and its inanimate milieu" influenced the relationships among city dwellers.[57] Urban design mattered to Parr because it had social consequences. Like many midcentury urbanists, Parr tried to prove the credibility of his theories by using them to explain the origins of juvenile delinquency. Parr attributed the escalation of the period's signature social ill to the "denial of opportunities for emotional attachments to the environs of the personal habitat, brought about by the increasing blandness and homogenization of urban surroundings."[58] And, according to Parr, the city dweller that was not emotionally attached to the urban environment would struggle to develop emotional attachments to those who lived in that environment. Bland architecture and level skylines set off a chain reaction that ultimately resulted in the period's frequently cited scenario in which crimes were "committed in the street in full view of many witnesses who watched the incidents without doing anything to prevent the misdeeds from running their course." Although Parr admitted that there were "undoubtedly many factors operating together to produce such apparently callous and cowardly indifference"—such as the "acute condition of slums and racial strife"—he insisted that an increasingly homogeneous urban environment played a crucial role in bringing about these social catastrophes.[59] As he explained to *Landscape*'s readers in an article published in the Winter 1964–65 issue, the "loud delinquency of the juvenile" is a response to the "sensory famine" of the city. Those who did not feel attached to their neighborhood could not feel attached to their neighbors, even when those neighbors' lives were endangered. The blandness and homogenization of their urban surroundings had made it difficult for these onlookers to recognize and feel their interdependency with those being mugged.[60]

The "fine grained diversity of the cityscape" that Parr and other ecological urbanists advocated would, they promised, replace social tension with harmony. As Parr put it in his second *Landscape* essay, the kind of urban environment that gave city dwellers the opportunity to meet their biological cravings would "not permit the degree of withdrawal into the circle of the like-minded which now seems to have become so desirable." Instead, as Parr later explained, an ecologically diverse urban environment produced "unforeseen encounters" with other urban organisms that "you did not know existed and therefore could never have included in your planned relationships, ephemeral or enduring."[61] These unplanned encounters "spun the warp of our social fabric." Even when these spontaneous social exchanges did not involve an "exchange of words," they made it impossible to think of the others with whom one inhabited the city as "alien devils in the dark" and to feel toward these strangers "all the vicious feelings that complete ignorance between antagonists is likely to encourage."[62] Preserving and promoting the "city's pluralism of forms, people, and institutions" would, as Parr and other ecological urbanists contended, go a long way toward helping city dwellers replace whatever "vicious feelings" they might have for their neighbors with fellow-feelings. For them, the vitality of an urban sociability ultimately depended on the maintenance of an ecologically diverse urban environment.[63]

CHAPTER 5

Jane Jacobs and the Consolidation of Urban Sociability

In 1955, William H. Kirk—the head worker at East Harlem's Union Settlement from 1949 to 1971—approached the staff of *Architectural Forum* hoping to convince them to investigate the dramatic transformations that had been changing the face and feel of his neighborhood. By the mid-1950s, East Harlem and many other New York neighborhoods had begun to witness and deal with the effects of Title I of the U.S. Housing Act of 1949, the most transformative domestic element of President Harry S. Truman's Fair Deal, and the Housing Act of 1954. With millions of dollars in funds earmarked by the federal government for slum clearance projects that would pave the way for private developments and public works, New York's municipal leaders had stepped up the urban redevelopment game that they had begun to play a dozen years earlier when the U.S. Housing Act of 1937 was passed. By the end of the 1950s, the city had built or nearly completed sixteen Title I projects that had displaced a total of 100,000 low-income people. New York had become the primary site for the nation's urban renewal experiment. No other neighborhood had experienced the cataclysmic physical and social disruptions brought about by urban renewal to the extent that East Harlem had. By 1965, 164 acres of this section of the city had been razed to accommodate fifteen new residential projects that housed 62,400 residents—more than a quarter of the neighborhood's total population. East Harlem had become the most substantial materialization of the urban renewal ethic that sociologists, planners, elected officials, and others had been championing since the New Deal period.[1]

When Kirk walked into the offices of *Architectural Forum*, East Harlem and many other urban neighborhoods throughout the United States had been traumatized by society's continued investment in a social model that privileged primary, intimate relationships. The rise of the urban renewal order in cities across the nation uprooted, to a degree that had not been seen in the history of U.S. urbanism, relationships that had flourished within the city's physical spaces. Although a wide range of social, political, and economic desires propelled urban renewal projects forward, its existence as both a policy and a practice rested on the culture's fundamental assumption that casual, public affiliations among city dwellers had little, if any, emotional substance and social value. The urban renewal order was the culmination of the public's longstanding belief that real relationships did not exist in the city—especially in certain parts of the city.[2]

As urban renewal gained momentum during the 1950s, those who hoped to call attention to its extensive consequences had to find ways to convince the public that the social affiliations and networks that it broke up were, in fact, valid. The dramatic transformation of cities during the postwar period presented urbanists with a wide range of problems, but one of the most pressing of these was figuring out how to write and talk about the relationships that were being disrupted by urban renewal in a way that made a persuasive case for their preservation. The threat that urban renewal posed to city communities compelled those who wanted to keep them intact to find convincing ways to describe the social interdependencies that held communities together as socially legitimate ones. Although ecological urbanists, social workers, tenants of soon-to-be-demolished buildings, and others had begun to raise concerns about the effects of urban renewal on city communities in the early 1950s, an increasing number of urban intellectuals and city dwellers in the latter half of the decade fought to wrest the right to represent the city's physical and social landscape away from urban renewal's proponents. Urbanites competed with city planners, architects, and politicians not only for the right to live and work in the city but also for the right to represent the nature of their interactions with one another and to determine the value of the social orders that gave their lives meaning.[3]

When Kirk invited the staff of *Architectural Forum* to visit East Harlem to see what urban renewal had done to his neighborhood and to help his neighbors develop strategies to counteract the powerful vision that was continuing to remake its landscape, Jane Jacobs, one of the magazine's associate editors, became particularly interested and took him up on his offer. With Kirk as her guide, Jacobs discovered what she later described as the "social poverty" of East Harlem's new housing-project terrain.[4] On their long walks through East Harlem in the mid-1950s, Kirk helped Jacobs develop a "way of seeing" and "understanding the intricate social and economic order under the seeming disorder of cities." Jacobs would become one of the most outspoken opponents of the urban renewal order and most influential proponents of a new "way of seeing" the city and its social orders. Her paradigm-shifting book, *The Death and Life of Great American Cities* (1961), may have billed itself in its opening lines as an "attack" on "modern, orthodox city planning and rebuilding," but it might just as well be described as an attack on her culture's refusal to acknowledge the social and emotional validity of the informal affiliations and casual interactions among urbanites in public spaces.[5] In a letter she wrote to Chadbourne Gilpatric of the Rockefeller Foundation—the institution that supplied her with two grants to write *Death and Life*—Jacobs expressed her hope that the book she was then writing would enable readers to see that "within the seeming chaos and jumble of the city is a remarkable degree of order, in the form of relationships of all kinds that people have evolved and that are absolutely fundamental to city life." At least initially, then, Jacobs did not see her project exclusively in terms of its contributions to the city planning profession, but also intended it to be a significant intervention in a broad conversation about what she called "big-city communities." Jacobs emphasized the centrality of the "very intimately interlocked (although often casually so)" relationships that sprung up in the city's public spaces. The bulk of the city's "social capital," she claimed, was not minted in the parlor but on its streets and in its stores.[6]

While many credit Jacobs with developing a radically new way of thinking about city life and its relation to urban form, she drew on and extended the urbanist discourse of sociability that had begun to emerge several decades prior to the publication of *Death and Life* in her efforts to legitimize casual interactions among urbanites.[7] Jacobs, in fact, was quick to acknowledge her indebtedness to other urban intellectuals, admitting that there are "quite a number of people today looking at the city in the same way I am doing, and I intend to draw on the observations of many of them."[8] However, Jacobs may not have recognized the extent to which those on whose observations she drew were the products of institutions and intellectual channels that harbored urbanist discourses that sought to illuminate the wide range of fellow-feelings that connected urbanites to one another. As the previous chapters demonstrate, urban intellectuals had been searching for some time for ways to understand and represent the value of the various types of interdependencies that connect city dwellers to each other. Jacobs pursued and amplified their insights throughout *Death and Life*. That is to say, she may have, as Herbert Gans observed, formulated a "badly needed urban myth for our now almost entirely urbanized society" in a way it had not been formulated before, but she cobbled together this urban myth by reaching back into an intellectual past.[9]

In an attempt to position Jacobs as one who codified and extended, rather than originated, an urbanist discourse of sociability, this chapter excavates the discursive threads that Jacobs brought together in her efforts to challenge the urban renewal order's dismissive approach to city relationships. In the process of making it her business to write about urbanism—a process that began in the 1930s—Jacobs picked up habits of thinking and writing about urban relationships while working as a city journalist, collaborating with settlement workers, and studying ecology and the life sciences. Reading *Death and Life* as a site through which these multiple conversations about urban sociality flow not only helps clarify Jacobs's social ideals, but also lifts the intellectual and material legacy of the urbanist discourse of sociability out of obscurity. Jacobs was not the only urbanist to recognize and call attention to the devastation that urban renewal brought to the city's social orders, but she was unique in her ability to respond to this devastation by weaving together the efforts of previous urbanists, who sought in different ways to legitimize urban relationships, into a coherent vision of the city's social landscape. Jacobs understood that the social problems generated by urban renewal policies and projects could be addressed, at least in part, by drawing on the intellectual resources that had been built up by urbanists over the course of the first half of the twentieth century. Mobilized by the seriousness and scope of urban renewal's threat to the city's social structure, Jacobs synthesized the intellectual traditions of urban sociability. She took what had been relatively discrete attempts to characterize urban affiliations as emotionally significant and gave those expressions the weight and sensibility of a cultural formation. The publication of *Death and Life* signaled the consolidation and popularization of the urbanist discourse of sociability.

Jacobs solidified the urbanist discourse of sociability by giving it definition in the city's built environment. She both called attention to the existing urban forms that facilitated sociable connections among urbanites and developed planning principles that would call into being cityscapes that encouraged city dwellers to cultivate fellow-feelings for one another in the public realm. More intentionally than the urban intellectuals who preceded her, Jacobs attempted to transcribe the urbanist discourse of sociability into the city's built environment. Given the increasing power of the urban renewal order to materialize within the city's hardscape its ideas about what kind of relationships mattered, Jacobs understood how important it was to delineate and prescribe urban forms capable of instigating sociability. She knew that these sociable urban forms would transmit the discourse of sociability to the public more effectively than any other medium.

Jane Jacobs and Urban Journalism

Shortly after the publication of *Death and Life*, the important midcentury urbanist Charles Abrams remarked somewhat offhandedly that Jacobs had "come to the big city's defense with an exposition that would make E. B. White, O. Henry, and Meyer Berger forever sing her praises."[10] Abrams perceived a connection between Jacobs's urban reportage and her message. He intuited that Jacobs's distinct style of exposition—a style aligned with the kind of city journalism that White and Berger had helped develop in venues such as the *New Yorker*—was closely connected to her defense of the city's social orders then being broken up by urban renewal projects. Although she was not as prolific in her journalistic output as White and Berger, Jacobs was their peer. Her writing career spanned the same decades as the *New Yorker*'s first wave of city journalists; she published her first city sketch in *Vogue* in November 1935 and continued writing about the city for various magazines and newspapers up until and through the publication of *Death and Life*. Jacobs may have been a talented journalist in part because of her technical abilities, but her use of journalism to defend the city's social orders from urban renewal's disruptive forces depended less on her organizational and grammatical fastidiousness than on her familiarity with and investment in the genre of urban journalism that White, Berger, and others had developed in their attempts to capture the kind of sociability practiced by urbanites. Jacobs's experience as a city journalist initiated her into the habits of thinking and writing that helped her perceive what she would later describe as the "art of urbanity."[11]

In the mid-1930s, Jacobs got her start in city journalism and her introduction to the urbanist discourse of sociability embedded in this medium when she published a series of four sketches in *Vogue* magazine. Each of these short articles focuses on one of the city's working districts: the fur, leather, diamond, and flower districts. In writing about these quirky nooks in the city's economic landscape, Jacobs had to find ways to help her readers

Figure 11. Jacobs at her typewriter, ca. 1961. Jane Jacobs Papers (MS.1995.029), John J. Burns Library, Boston College. When Leticia Kent described Jacobs as an "urbanologist" during an interview she conducted with the controversial urbanist for *Vogue*, Jacobs responded, "Please don't describe me as an urbanologist." Asked for a more suitable label, Jacobs responded matter-of-factly, "An author." See Jane Jacobs, "More Babies Needed, Not Fewer," interview by Leticia Kent, *Vogue* (August 15, 1970): 86.

make sense of geographies and communities that might have initially struck them as chaotic and unorganized. In writing about the frequent auctions that were a central feature of the diamond district's economic infrastructure, she admitted that they initially appeared to be "baffling" and "haphazard, a mix between hocus-pocus and mind-reading."[12] But like White, Berger, and other *New Yorker* journalists, Jacobs worked hard to help her readers move beyond these initial impressions and to put them in a position to recognize the order beneath the apparent disorder of the diamond district. The ability to write about the complex order of the city's economically and demographically diverse communities would be critical to Jacobs's success in constructing a new urban myth. One of her most important assertions in *Death and Life* is that "under the seeming disorder of the old city, wherever the old city is working successfully, is a marvelous order for maintaining the safety of the streets and the freedom of the city." Because the perpetuation of the urban renewal order ultimately depended on convincing urbanites that certain city communities lacked social coherence and could therefore be dismantled without consequence, Jacobs's early efforts to write about the "complex order" of various city communities would put her in a position to later challenge the assumptions of those who backed redevelopment projects.[13]

Although Jacobs first began to write about the "marvelous order" of urban communities in articles about New York's peculiar working districts, the nature of that order for her was distinctly social. Much like her contemporaries at the *New Yorker*, Jacobs was interested in the ways in which the city's economic infrastructure created opportunities for urbanites to interact with one another in emotionally meaningful ways. In her *Vogue* sketches about the fur, leather, diamond, and flower districts, Jacobs spent time describing the financial mechanisms that made these distinct economies tick. But she paid as much attention to the affective textures of the social orders created by merchants, shoppers, and others who engaged with one another in these sections of the city. Describing the interactions among those who populated the fur district, Jacobs observed: "At every hour of the day, the sidewalks and gutters of the district are crowded with groups of cigar-puffing fur merchants, dapper buyers, and salesmen from the adjoining garment district, who engage in loud and unrestrained dickering, as though they were anxious to advertise all the details of every transaction." In Jacobs's early urban reportage, she frequently characterized the interactions among these city dwellers as "dickering"—a term that appeared in three of her four *Vogue* pieces.[14] While dickering denotes an exchange shaped by the objectives of a commercial transaction, it also suggests an interaction whose communication patterns and affective qualities exceed the commercial purposes that bring the participants together. The merchants, buyers, and salesmen crowding together on the sidewalks and gutters of the fur district were participating in a form of sociability that brought them not only financial benefits but also emotional satisfaction. Through their "loud and unrestrained dickering," they hoped to "advertise" their public identities to those directly involved in the business transaction, as well as other urbanites within earshot. They wanted to establish a sense of fellow-feeling with other fur-district denizens by having their public identities acknowledged and recognized.

Jacobs's investment in dickering as an indispensable form of urban sociability deepened as the rise of the urban renewal order began to undermine the ability of city dwellers to enact this particular art of urbanity. As her career's brief entrance into the orbit of the *Village Voice* in the late 1950s suggests, the rhetoric of Jacobs's well-known anti-urban renewal activism grew out of her continued commitment to the social practice of dickering. Started by Dan Wolf, Ed Fancher, and Norman Mailer in October 1955, the *Village Voice* was born out of the desire of its founders to extend and defend the city's public realm. The *Village Voice* saw Greenwich Village as a "crystallization and intensification of almost every variety of urban life," and it crafted editorial policies and literary practices that would "give voice to all the many divergent factors, pressure groups, attitudes, and conflicting personalities of the Village." In both its feature articles and regular columns, the *Village Voice* endorsed its version of urban sociality in large part through its opposition to local urban renewal projects. Its editors, staff writers, guest contributors, and vocal neighbors repeatedly positioned their understandings of urban relationships in direct opposition to what one editorial described as the "attitudes of Mr. Robert Moses toward the public and its supposed realm (*Asphalt Is Good for You* Division)."[15] More specifically, the *Village Voice* articulated its social ideals in its sustained campaign against the city's plans to construct a four-lane highway through Greenwich Village's Washington Square Park. In just its third issue, the startup newspaper devoted its primary editorial column to publicizing its "view that any serious tampering with Washington Square Park will mark the true beginning of the end of Greenwich Village as a *community*." Because the park helped its users "appreciate the wonderful complexity of New York" while simultaneously reminding them of the "distance they have to cover in their relations with other people," Washington Square provided a vital public space in which "Villagers of enormously varied interests and backgrounds" could aspire toward and achieve a sense of fellow-feeling with one another. In short, the *Village Voice* was what happened when the tradition of urban journalism that Jacobs and *New Yorker* reporters pioneered in the 1930s confronted urban renewal's assumptions about the meaninglessness of urban relationships.[16]

Jacobs never wrote feature articles for the *Village Voice*, but she made several cameo appearances in its pages, where she defended the value of relationships forged in public spaces like Washington Square—relationships built on a sort of dickering that did not necessarily revolve around commercial transactions. Several of Jacobs's speeches about the Washington Square crisis were either transcribed in full or excerpted for the *Village Voice*'s readers. Her advocacy of urban sociability in the *Village Voice* calls attention to the substantive and stylistic qualities that her work shared with the type of city journalism embraced by the fledgling newspaper. In its November 20,

1957, issue, a front-page article reprinted large sections of a speech Jacobs had delivered at the Cooper Union during the previous week. As head of the Greenwich Village Study housing committee, Jacobs had assumed the responsibility of updating the community on the committee's findings. She reasoned with her audience that the "mass displacement of present Villagers from the community" that would inevitably accompany the housing projects being built by the New York City Housing Authority (NYCHA) and private developers was "too high a price—in both individual and community terms—to pay for improved housing." Even if retaining the neighborhood's residents meant allowing some of them to continue living in cold water flats, Jacobs contended that many would prefer maintaining their low rents and social networks to acquiring the "new amenities of housing." Jacobs channeled for her listeners at Cooper Union the logic of urban sociability that both journalists and novelists had developed in the 1930s and 1940s; it is as if Jacobs were invoking and then amplifying the rationale of Betty Smith's condemnation of public housing in *A Tree Grows in Brooklyn* (1943) as "a place of living where sunlight and air were to be trapped, measured and weighed, and doled out so much per resident."[17] While Jacobs might rightly be accused of romanticizing life in cold-water flats, her point was that the affective currency generated among urbanites as they dickered in places like Washington Square was as essential to the vitality of urban life as improved housing.

Jacobs's journalistic valorization of dickering and the type of sociability it embodied climaxed in an important article she published in the April 1958 issue of *Fortune* magazine—an article that acted as a bridge between her apprenticeship in city journalism and her writing of *Death and Life*. In "Downtown Is for People," Jacobs pushed the urbanist discourse of sociability cultivated by interwar journalists and novelists beyond where her predecessors had taken it. She did not just celebrate the relationships that naturally arose on the city's sidewalks and in its shops but encouraged city dwellers actively to preserve and create spaces capable of facilitating the kind of public interactions that she found so valuable. Because the city's pedestrian spaces served as the "major point of transaction and communication" among urbanites, Jacobs suggested that the "street, not the block," was, contrary to what Clarence Perry and others had argued for decades, "the significant unit" of city life. Given the vital functions that it performed, Jacobs insisted that, rather than "banish the street," cities ought to push their streets to "work harder" by making them "more surprising, more compact, more variegated, and busier than before—not less so." The city would also benefit from constructing the kind of space that Jacobs described as a "trading post"—open spaces (but not too open) where urbanites such as "lawyers, officeholders, office seekers, various types of insiders and would-be insiders" could "cluster" together and dicker. In "Downtown Is for People," Jacobs began to translate the observations about urban relationships that she had made as a city journalist into planning principles. More forcefully than her forerunners, she encouraged city dwellers to "get into the thick of the planning job" and "adapt the rebuilding machinery" to bring about the "end results" that they and she wanted: a city that possessed the kinds of public spaces in which urbanites could forge sociable fellow-feelings for one another.[18]

In *Death and Life*, Jacobs not only further enumerated planning principles that would facilitate fellow-feelings among city dwellers, but she also continued to clarify the urbanist discourse of sociability that she had refined in her journalism. Like many urban intellectuals in whose footsteps she followed and who would follow her, she recognized the problem of using intimacy as a standard with which to evaluate and engineer urban relationships. Jacobs understood what Richard Sennett would articulate about a decade after *Death and Life*'s publication—that "intimacy is a tyranny" that has "distorted our understanding of the purposes of the city."[19] Given her awareness of intimacy's tyranny among urban professionals, Jacobs explicitly called attention to the distinction between intimacy and sociability throughout *Death and Life*. She observed that those who embraced intimacy as a social ideal assumed that "if anything is shared among people, much should be shared" and that individuals should therefore "enlarge their private lives" as much as necessary in order to connect in emotionally intimate ways with others. The problem with expecting urbanites to achieve what Jacobs referred to as "togetherness" was that the spatial dimensions of the postwar city undermined the social conditions through which these types of close relationships could be widely achieved. Jacobs admitted that togetherness might be desirable and plausible in a village or town where the "connections among its people keep crossing and recrossing," thus giving residents enough shared private experiences with which to fashion personal relationships. But in a large city, even a village-sized population lacked the "innate degree of natural cross-connections within itself" necessary to achieve cohesion through repeated private exchanges. Given the spatial disparities between the village and the city neighborhood, urban planners who used the "ideal of supposedly cozy, inward-turned city neighborhoods" as the "point of departure for nearly all neighborhood renewal plans" would inevitably fail because cities simply lack the raw spatial and social material through which city residents might attain intimate relationships with one another. "Togetherness," Jacobs quipped, is a "fittingly nauseating name for an old ideal."[20]

Rather than try to stimulate togetherness among city dwellers, Jacobs proposed that those responsible for shaping the city's built environment ought to create spaces that enabled urbanites to develop a "feeling for the public identity of people" (56). As Jacobs knew well from her nearly twenty-five years of writing about the city as a journalist, the spaces where city dwellers could display their own public identities and acquire a fellow-feeling for the public identities of others were the city's streets. Contrary to the wisdom passed down by urban intellectuals such as Jacob Riis, who construed a crowd gathered on a sidewalk or in an alley as a sign of social poverty, Jacobs suggested that the ability of urbanites to form healthy public relationships depended almost entirely on the soundness of the city's "social structure of sidewalk life" (68). The "casual, public contact" with other urbanites that city dwellers experience on the city's sidewalks "*implies no private commitments*" and therefore does not lead to the kinds of affections that hold together "*ties of kinship or close friendship or formal responsibility*" (56, 82; italics original). Instead, the sum of an urbanite's "little sidewalk contacts" produces what Jacobs described as a "web of public respect and trust" (56). One of the most striking features of Jacobs's explanation of how urban sociability works is that the fellow-feelings that connect city dwellers to one another are not necessarily tethered between specific individuals. The "feeling for the public identity of people" that an urbanite might acquire in the city's public realm is capable of helping that individual feel connected to a people (any individual who might occupy a specific place in the city) as well as to a particular person. The structure of urban sociability about which Jacobs theorized in *Death and Life* is expansive enough to enable city dwellers to feel respect for and to trust anyone who might enter the web of public spaces that they frequently inhabit.

Unlike relationships that operate on the affective logic of togetherness, in which both parties must share everything with one another, those built on the kind of urban sociability that Jacobs described could better accommodate the wide range of social differences possessed by those who occupied and moved through the postwar city. Because cities are full of people "who do not know each other in an intimate, private social fashion and in most cases do not care to know each other in that fashion" (55), Jacobs argued that cities that failed to provide individuals with spaces in which they could experience and maintain emotionally satisfying "sidewalk contacts" often cultivated residents that were "exceedingly choosy as to who their neighbors are, or with whom they associate at all" (63). According to Jacobs, urbanites tend to avoid those with different racial, ethnic, and class backgrounds when there are no public spaces in which they might interact. Only when city dwellers have the option of interacting with others within the public realm of sidewalks, stores, and parks could they practice what Jacobs described in a different context as the "art of taking interest and pleasure in people different from oneself and in ways of life different from one's own, rather than being automatically fearful, incurious or disapproving."[21] When city dwellers do not have to take on the "paraphernalia of obligations" that accompany private relationships, they tend to be on "excellent sidewalk terms" with all sorts of people (62). Jacobs was not suggesting that these sidewalk affiliations lack emotional commitment, but instead that they generate different types of interpersonal connection. The affects of "interest and pleasure" that initiate and sustain sociable relationships can give rise to a type of fellow-feeling that Jacobs characterized as a "modicum of public responsibility" (82). Acquiring a feeling for the public identity of people enabled urbanites to feel that they had something to do with one another, but not everything. Contrary to the many urban intellectuals who had fretted about the emotional legitimacy of urban relationships, Jacobs insisted in *Death and Life* that these sociable relationships are just as authentic as private relationships—they "can and do endure for many years, for decades" (62).

A Way of Seeing the City:
Jane Jacobs and the Settlement Movement

If Jacobs found her way to an urbanist discourse of sociability through city journalism and relied heavily on this medium to articulate the value of sidewalk relationships, she significantly deepened her understanding of urban sociability through her involvement with the mid-twentieth-century settlement movement. Jacobs picked up a settlement way of seeing the city not just as she walked around East Harlem with Kirk but also as she served on Union Settlement's Board of Directors and contributed to several of the institution's ad hoc committees. It is true, as the second chapter demonstrates, that the urbanist discourse of sympathy developed by Progressive Era settlement intellectuals helped pave the paths on which bulldozers and cranes had traveled into neighborhoods like East Harlem. Having exposed the many ways in which economic, political, and cultural forces had degraded the urban home, interwar settlement leaders lead a chorus of voices demanding slum clearance and affordable housing in the hope that the redevelopment of the city's domestic spaces would enable urbanites to maintain their most intimate relationships. But settlement writers had also, from the movement's turn-of-the-century beginnings, attended to and championed the kind of public life they encountered on the streets of the working-class and immigrant neighborhoods in which they lived. Although interwar settlement leaders had almost entirely abandoned this element of the movement's urbanist discourse, postwar settlement intellectuals revived the narratives through which Progressive Era workers had legitimized the public associations into which city dwellers entered as they worked out their lives in the city. When the U.S. Housing Act of 1949 accelerated the pace of slum clearance and public housing construction, settlement workers in places such as East Harlem were among the first to blow the whistle on the damage that urban renewal initiatives were inflicting on the city's social orders. As postwar settlement workers responded to the dramatic disruption of the social networks and affiliations that city dwellers had established in the public sphere, they modified the Progressive Era movement's urbanist discourse of sympathy in order better to represent the sociable nature of these relationships. Consequently, urban intellectuals operating within the postwar settlement movement made significant contributions to the development of an urbanist discourse of sociability.[22]

Because East Harlem had served as the nation's premier testing ground for the construction of public housing during the postwar period, Kirk and others at Union Settlement led the charge in updating the settlement movement's urban narratives in order to better identify and defend the forms of sociability threatened by the urban renewal order. To remain relevant to the neighborhood of which they had been a part since 1895, Union Settlement recognized the pressing need to "find out what the coming of a modern housing project meant to the community." If Kirk and his fellow settlement workers discovered that the community's social and economic problems "had not disappeared, but had altered or had taken on new forms," then they and their institution would need to develop new strategies for addressing the evolving needs of their neighbors.[23] Jacobs both learned from and contributed to the efforts of Union Settlement residents and other postwar settlement leaders to translate the movement's discourse of sympathy into a discourse of sociability that would better help the communities to which they belonged make sense of and respond to the physical and social transformations of their neighborhoods. Her apprenticeship at Union Settlement and her association with other postwar settlement leaders pushed her to think in more nuanced terms about the subtle and sometimes counterintuitive ways structures of urban sociability were shaped by the city's built environment.[24]

Jacobs's experiences at Union Settlement played a particularly important role in pushing her to attend to the ways that racial, ethnic, and class identity shaped the affective possibilities of urban sociability. By midcentury, large numbers of Puerto Ricans and African Americans had joined a shrinking Italian population in East Harlem. The construction of multiple public housing projects in the neighborhood during the 1950s only further tilted the neighborhood's demographic balance toward its black and Boricua populaces. Although Jacobs has taken some heat for overlooking the specific material inequities and social biases facing urban minorities and the urban poor—an oversight that is often attributed to what some readers feel is an disproportionate emphasis in *Death and Life* on her experiences in her West Village neighborhood—recognizing the significant degree to which her urban vision was shaped by her experiences in East Harlem might help us perceive the ways she stretched the discourse of sociability to account for the social experiences of the postwar city's marginalized inhabitants.[25]

As influential as Jacobs's walks around East Harlem with Kirk were to the development of her understanding of urban relationships, her familiarity with Union Settlement's "A Study of George Washington Houses" may have been even more critical to her apprehension of the postwar settlement movement's discourse of sociability. In the tradition of Jane Addams's *Hull-House Maps and Papers* (1895) and W. E. B. Du Bois's *The Philadelphia Negro* (1899), Union Settlement conducted a formal sociological study of the George Washington Houses, one of East Harlem's many postwar subsidized housing projects. Led and written primarily by Ellen Lurie and based on "first-hand material gathered directly from the project tenants" by settlement workers and trained volunteers, "A Study of George Washington Houses" revealed that previous settlement workers and public housing advocates had been wrong in many ways about the positive changes that public housing projects would bring to working-class urban communities. Composed of "building after building" of "identical tall red brick rectangles," the study noted that East Harlem's new housing projects tended to attract a homogenous segment of the population. As a result, these newly formed urban communities lacked the variety of residents that would enable them to attend to one another's physical and emotional needs—they all had similar sets of wants and expertise. Because the housing projects were inhabited almost exclusively by young families with small children, for instance, even those programs designed to socialize the housing project community were hard-pressed to do so because the community lacked a sufficiently large pool of teenage and elderly babysitters that would enable young parents to attend social events: "many grandchildren; few grandparents."[26] This urban monoculture demanded a type of self-sufficiency that project residents had difficulty achieving. Rather than produce the kind of close-knit urban communities for which public housing advocates had yearned, George Washington Houses and other East Harlem housing projects created what some characterized as a "civic and social wasteland." Whatever "feeling and mutual identity a community had before the bulldozer came in," one settlement worker explained, was left "shattered" in wake of the bulldozer.[27]

The discourse of sociability that Lurie and her fellow settlement workers developed in "A Study of George Washington Houses" was particularly invested in helping urbanites think hard about what she characterized as "project design and its influence on tenant relationships."[28] When she teamed up with Kirk, Lurie, and Mildred Zucker, a social worker at East Harlem's James Weldon Johnson Community Center, to spearhead the Housing Committee of the East Harlem Council for Community Planning (EHCCP) in 1958, Jacobs sharpened her understanding of the ways in which urban design could facilitate the casual relationships and affiliations that she had learned to see as central to city life while writing about the city as a journalist. The EHCCP's Housing Committee petitioned the NYCHA for time to generate alternative blueprints for the soon-to-be-built DeWitt Clinton Houses. Having received approval and some funding from the NYCHA, the committee met with Perkins & Will Architects in January 1959 to discuss innovative ways to reassess what had become standard public housing architectural and design practices. During its initial consultation meeting, the committee informed the architects that the Clinton Houses would ideally "duplicate and not change the manner of living" East Harlem residents had been practicing for years in their old neighborhood. To this end, it suggested that the project

Figure 12. Ellen Lurie's study of East Harlem's George Washington Houses played a critical role in the development of Jacobs's understanding of the relationship between the built environment and the quality of the city's social landscape. New York City Housing Authority Records, La Guardia and Wagner Archives.

use "streets as focal points" and create other spaces in which residents could maintain public relationships. The committee encouraged the architects to include "niches and irregularities in building lines to accomplish 'door step living'"—the type of social practice that had earned the neighborhood its reputation as a slum but that postwar settlement workers such as Kirk, Lurie, and Zucker placed at the center of their urbanism. Rather than build the kind of self-contained neighborhoods that public housing advocates had been championing since the New Deal Era, the committee wanted "outside life to penetrate into project" life. Hoping that Perkins & Will would help them translate the findings of "A Study of George Washington Houses" into East Harlem's built environment, the EHCCP Housing Committee begged the architecture and design firm to "bleed street life into our project."[29]

In her presentation of the Housing Committee's proposals for the Clinton Houses to the NYCHA at a hearing on February 3, 1959, Jacobs packaged the postwar settlement discourse of sociability for a public audience. She opened the meeting by acknowledging what many have accused her of ignoring—that "poverty" and "discrimination," among other factors, had contributed in significant ways to East Harlem's "troubles." But Jacobs and her committee were also "convinced that a great part of the poor social showing of East Harlem's projects is owing to the physical design of the buildings themselves and their grounds." Because the NYCHA privileged "open space" and "distance between buildings" at the expense of street life, East Harlem's postwar housing projects typically consisted of high-rise apartment buildings that had been set apart not only from one another but also from the surrounding neighborhood. The problem with these groupings of relatively isolated residential structures, Jacobs explained, was that they ignored the "social structure of city neighborhoods, particularly poor neighborhoods." Rather than accommodate the "highly communal and cooperative society among families in the old slums," housing projects tended to "sacrifice the constant, casual and varied human contacts which provided not only the controls, but also the interests and the avenues to most opportunity and mutual assistance in the old slum." Jacobs accused the NYCHA of imposing on East Harlem a built environment that had been designed to support "a kind of sophisticated family individualism" rather than the real "social structure of city neighborhoods"—social structures that had been developed by the neighborhood's minority communities to allow individuals access to social and economic opportunities.[30] Jacobs, in short, accused the NYCHA and other proponents of urban renewal not only of discriminating against the urban poor by displacing them in disproportionate numbers and breaking up their social and economic networks but also by embracing architectural styles and design principles oriented primarily toward white middle-class families and the social structures that best suited them.

Jacobs's commitment to the postwar settlement movement's understanding of urban sociability underwrote not only her critiques of postwar housing project design but also the specific architectural and design recommendations she hoped the NYCHA would embrace. Jacobs begged the NYCHA to develop urban spaces that would support sociable interactions among city dwellers. Rather than repeat the standard project design of high-rise buildings clustered around open space, she recommended that the Clinton Houses mix low-rise, walk-up buildings with the more typical high-rise structures. These smaller walk-ups would contain about thirty family-sized apartments built around an open courtyard. By eliminating "elevators, enclosed corridors and enclosed stairwells," the large families occupying these smaller buildings would be better able to supervise children at play below "from the windows of apartments above"; the committee wanted "mothers of all good-sized families to be within easy calling distance to the ground." The open corridors and courtyards of these walk-ups would also provide families with the kinds of public spaces that would "foster acquaintance and interdependence" without making them feel that they had been "unnaturally imposed on each other and all privacy or sense of choice lost."[31] The committee's design proposals for Clinton Houses would attempt to stimulate interactions capable of generating the sociable fellow-feelings that residents had felt for one another as they interacted in the streets, delicatessens, coffee shops, and hardware stores that had been torn down to make way for the housing project. Rather than try to cultivate a sense of togetherness among individuals within the project, Jacobs argued instead that the NYCHA ought to do its best to create the conditions under which tenants might experience the alternative emotional register of urban sociability: acquaintanceship and interdependence.

Jacobs and her committee forwarded architectural and design recommendations that sought not only to facilitate sociable interactions within the built environment of the project but also to catalyze acquaintanceships among tenants and those living beyond the project's boundaries in the old neighborhood. Given its location on Lexington Avenue—one of East Harlem's busiest and most socially active streets—Jacobs insisted that the project "enhance the surrounding streets" rather than turn its back on them. "Busy streets, filled with people," she philosophized, are "safe upon which to walk, are interesting for standing or strolling, and as can be seen in East Harlem are greatly used as casual meeting places and adult recreation grounds where dominoes are played, music enjoyed, television watched outdoors, snacks vended and the like." A street-oriented project would also better support the neighborhood's commercial establishments, which would in turn strengthen the "vital community role" that they and their proprietors played. Jacobs suggested that the popular Spanish motion picture house nearby on Lexington Avenue ought to be embraced by the Clinton Houses because it would provide a casual meeting place for the Puerto Ricans and other Spanish speaking residents who lived in the project and those who did not. Ensuring the survival of the neighborhood's existing commercial establishments and the human networks of which they were important nodes would require what Jacobs called "community planning."[32] For Jacobs, community planning involved more than just soliciting input from the community—though

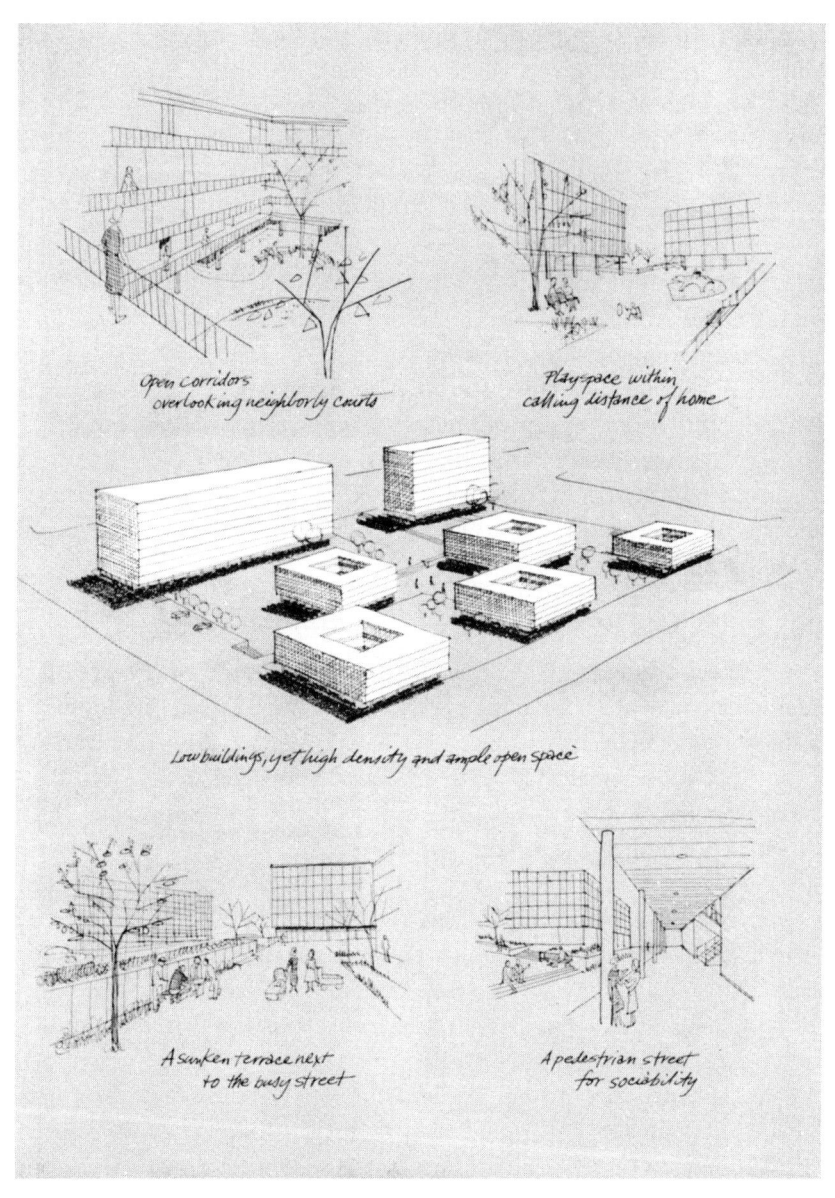

Figure 13. Kirk, Lurie, Zucker, and Jacobs teamed up with architects from Perkins & Will to develop a proposed redesign of East Harlem's DeWitt Clinton Homes. Jacobs helped present their proposal to the NYCHA in 1959. This sketch was published in *Architectural Forum* in April 1959.

she certainly embraced a planning process that drew on voices from everyday city dwellers—but, perhaps more important, entailed preserving and developing spaces that would enable city dwellers to witness and acknowledge the interdependencies that propped up their communities. She wanted the NYCHA to develop plans that would support urban communities, but to do so with a better understanding of what kinds of relationships really held those communities together.

While it did not take long for the NYCHA to decide that it could not afford to materialize the EHCCP Housing Committee's specific architectural and design recommendations, Jacobs preserved in *Death and Life* the postwar settlement movement's discourse of sociability that animated the committee's Clinton Houses proposal.[33] She most explicitly translated the lessons she had learned from East Harlem's settlement intellectuals in her discussion about "salvaging projects" near the end of her seminal work—a section of the book that is too often overlooked by readers but that serves in many ways as the culmination of Jacobs's theories about the influence of design and architecture on urban relationships. In an attempt to salvage urban relationships by salvaging public housing, Jacobs formulated several specific "design strategies and tactics" that might help weave postwar housing projects back into the "living city" (372). Although not much could be done to alter a project's basic physical dimensions (doing so would be too expensive), Jacobs recommended manageable ways to modify a public housing project's hardscape in order to facilitate sociable interactions among city dwellers who lived in or near these structures. Most important, she argued, "new streets must be designed" to run through the project (394). These streets should both "tie into the few fixed features within the project" and connect "with streets beyond the project borders" (395). These new streets, which might pave over a project's underutilized green spaces, were critical in reconnecting city dwellers to one another through casual contact. Additional street space within a project might, for instance, be utilized by street vendors; these vendors would not only act as a "partial economic substitute for the missing old, low-overhead store space" but would also stimulate "cross-use" of the project's previously underused spaces by enticing pedestrians to walk through the project to buy their goods or simply observe the commercial and social activity generated by the vendors (396). As Jacobs saw it, the bottom line of any scheme for salvaging public housing must entail getting city dwellers both within and beyond the project "circulating around and spreading themselves through time in all public spaces" (397–98). Only as urbanites affiliated with one another in public spaces could they reconstruct the structure of sociability that had been demolished by the federal bulldozer.

Jacobs channeled the postwar settlement movement's discourse of sociability in *Death and Life* in order to undermine what a long line of urban intellectuals had been telling the public about the social insignificance of urban relationships. When we recognize the deep connections between the planning principles that Jacobs forwarded and the way of seeing the city's social landscape that Kirk, Lurie, and other midcentury settlement workers championed, we can better perceive the ways in which *Death and Life* grew out of and perpetuated this particular strand of the urbanist discourse of sociability. *Death and Life*, in fact, might be viewed as a settlement study that grew out of Jacobs's experiences at Union Settlement and her interactions with settlement workers in East Harlem. In many ways, it reads as an expanded and more accessible version of Lurie's "A Study of George Washington Houses." In both content and form, *Death and Life* reflects the postwar settlement movement's fundamental belief that the heart of a city neighborhood lies in its public rather than its domestic spaces.

Jane Jacobs and the Nature of Diversity

Like other midcentury urbanists who sought out intellectual and rhetorical strategies to call attention to the social consequences of urban renewal, Jacobs took up the language and logic of ecology. She drew on ecology's growing scientific authority to give her settlement-inspired vision and journalistic account of urban relationships the kind of conceptual coherence and cultural credibility necessary to debunk what she described as the "pseudoscience of city planning" (13). Jacobs deployed ecological concepts and terms to validate and reiterate an understanding of urban sociability that she had developed through her immersion in city journalism and postwar settlement work. The "life sciences," she suggested in the concluding chapter of *Death and Life*, could provide urbanists with invaluable "strategies for thinking" about and defending the interconnections that were, as she had demonstrated throughout the book, essential to the viability of city life (438, 428). Because cities pose the same kinds of "problems in organized complexity" that the life sciences attempted to apprehend, Jacobs claimed that taking up ecological "habits of thought" would enable urbanists to better understand the postwar city's shifting physical and social landscapes (439, 440). Jacobs's particular brand of ecological urbanism both solidified and amplified the urbanist discourses of sociability that she had brought together in *Death and Life*.[34]

Jacobs's ecological urbanism rested on a fundamental assumption that she shared with many other midcentury ecological urbanists—that cities were extensions of, rather than separate from, the natural world. Her assertion that "cities of human beings are as natural . . . as are the colonies of prairie dogs or the beds of oysters" sounds as if it could have been lifted from any number of articles published in J. B. Jackson's *Landscape* during the 1950s. In fact, she quoted directly in *Death and Life* from Edgar A. Anderson's "The City Watcher"—his contribution to "The Urban Scene" issue of *Landscape* (1958–59)—to support her claims about the naturalness of the city. For Jacobs, as for many of the *Landscape* writers, viewing cities as part of the natural world meant that they ought to be treated as living organisms. While Jacobs was quick to admit that the "organizations of living protoplasm and the organizations of living people and enterprises" are distinct entities, she insisted that cities, like aggregations of protoplasm, consist of "intricately interconnected, and surely understandable, relationships" (439). In other words, cities may contain different types of interconnections among their inhabitants from those that bound organisms to one another, but both human and natural communities were systems of organized complexity and could therefore be understood by tapping into the same "intellectual fund" set up by those who professionally pursued the life sciences (438). Jacobs's deep conviction that cities generated the same kinds of connections among their inhabitants as those that connected organisms in any ecosystem—that cities *were* ecosystems—meant that understanding a city required "learning its intricate relationships and interconnections with other factors or quantities" (440).

As Jacobs sought to better to understand the "intricate relationships and interconnections" among city dwellers and their built environment, she realized that urbanites provided one another with what she repeatedly described as "mutual support." In a speech she delivered at the New School on April 20, 1958, Jacobs noted that the city "consists of an intricate, living network of relationships—made up of an enormously rich variety of people and activities"—that ultimately depends on the "mutual support of every kind which must work, and work well, in a city."[35] Jacobs clarified the ways in which urbanites give, often unknowingly, one another mutual support in one of *Death and Life*'s best-known and misread passages. Often interpreted as a celebration of the intimacies the right kind of city neighborhood ought to engender among its residents, Jacobs's description of the daily sidewalk scene outside her West Village home more closely resembles a community ecologist's account of a habitat group. She compared the movement and exchanges that took place on Hudson Street to an "intricate ballet in which the individual dancers and ensembles all have distinctive parts which miraculously reinforce each other and compose an orderly whole" (50). As she would point out later in *Death and Life*, this urban dance was not performed exclusively by a cast of friends or even acquaintances; rather, it included a mix of residents, workers, and tourists who, for the most part, did not know one another. The ballet on Hudson Street did not grow out of a social order that had already achieved "harmonious consensus" but instead came together as "different people, bent on different purposes," appeared at "different times" but used the "*same* streets" (374, 183). The mere presence of different kinds of people on Hudson Street and its tributaries allowed each of them to provide one another with the kind of "intricate mutual support" that gave the individual dancers the "freedom . . . to make and carry out countless plans" (14, 391). Drawing directly from community ecology's glossary to characterize these interactions, Jacobs informed readers that these and other pedestrians were "unconsciously cooperating" (153).

While this type of cooperation among city dwellers may usually be unconscious, Jacobs insisted that participating in the processes that supported the lives of other city dwellers, even those one did not know, and being supported by them could produce satisfying relationships. Those who repeatedly use the same street at the same time may, even if their purposes for occupying the street are different, have enough sociable interaction with one another that they eventually develop a personal, though not necessarily intimate, relationship. Jacobs, for instance, became acquainted with Mr. Lofaro, the "white-aproned fruit man" on Hudson Street, after nodding and smiling at him "many a morning for more than ten years" in order to assure and be assured by him that "all is well" (51). But her long-standing relationships with individuals from her neighborhood are not the only type of associations made possible through the networks of mutual support that connect urbanites to one another. Jacobs recounted in *Death and Life* an experience she had while waiting for a bus on a street in Manhattan's Lower East Side. After she had stood at the bus stop for just a minute or two, a woman "opened a window on the third floor of a tenement across the street and vigorously yoo-hooed" at her. After getting Jacobs's attention, the woman "shouted down, 'The bus doesn't run here on Saturdays!'" She then directed Jacobs, through a "combination of shouts and pantomime," to a place where she could catch a bus (38). This interaction may not have produced the same interpersonal affection that Jacobs's repeated exchanges with Mr. Lofaro generated, but it did give her the sense that this third-floor kibitzer was part of a broader social structure that provided her with the mutual support she needed to carry out her plans. Jacobs's sociable interactions with this woman from the Lower East Side both contributed to and confirmed the "assumption of support" that underwrote her interactions with other strangers in the city. Her assumption that she would receive both direct and indirect support from other urbanites to carry out her business created what she described as a feeling of "trust" (56). The trust that grew out of her awareness of the networks of mutual support that bound her to other urbanites gave rise to fellow-feelings that connected her to them in meaningful ways. Despite the ephemerality of some of the relationships that grew out of unconscious cooperation, Jacobs confirmed their affective legitimacy by describing the binding emotion as one of trust.

Jacobs made it clear to readers that the systems of mutual support that fostered a wide range of emotionally rewarding public relationships ultimately depended on the ability and willingness of urbanites to share the same physical spaces in the city. Only as city dwellers' daily routines moved them through the same streets, stores, and other public arenas would they recognize the extent to which their ability to carry out their own plans ultimately depended on the mutual support of various other urbanites. And according to Jacobs, the quality of the city's built environment played a critical role in inspiring urbanites to get out onto the city's sidewalks, stores, and squares. Much like Anderson, Albert E. Parr, and other midcentury ecological urbanists, Jacobs suggested that the best way to motivate urbanites to use the city's public spaces was to ensure the existence of "useful or interesting or convenient differences fairly near by"; nobody, she observed, "travels willingly from sameness to sameness and repetition to repetition, even if the physical effort required is trivial" (129). Guided by ecology's strategies for thinking about the physiological and social purposes of variety, Jacobs operated on the assumption that an aesthetically, economically, and culturally diverse urban environment would most effectively draw city dwellers into the streets as frequently and extensively as would be necessary to create and sustain a social landscape that provided individuals with intricate mutual support. "Differences, *not duplication*," she explained, "make for cross-use and hence for a person's identification with an area greater than his immediate street network" (130). Jacobs felt that the urban environment ought to approximate the variety of forms and textures that any natural environment would possess.

Many of Jacobs's signature planning principles grew out of her ecologically informed way of thinking about the built environment's role in facilitating the cross-use of city spaces and the subsequent sociable interactions that such cross-use made possible. She argued that urban neighborhoods and districts "must serve more than one primary function" in order to "insure the presence of people who go outdoors on different schedules and are in the place for different purposes, but who are able to use many facilities in common." She felt strongly that city blocks "must be short" so that those moving through the city might have many "opportunities to turn corners" and thus encounter a wide variety of scenes and people. Jacobs encouraged cities to "mingle buildings that vary in age and condition" so that they might shelter a diverse range of inhabitants, enterprises, and aesthetic styles (150). And she advocated the need for a "dense concentration of people," for only when cities possessed a sufficiently dense population could they sustain all of the other kinds of diversity that are "natural to big cities" (151, 143). These and other tenets of Jacobs's approach to city planning were developed primarily to cultivate, sustain, and preserve as many layers of diversity within the urban ecosystem as possible. Diversity of all kinds—demographic, economic, cultural, and aesthetic—mattered to her because diversity is a vital precondition for the intricate mutual support that enables urbanites to trust one another. "City diversity," as she understood it, plays a critical role in setting in motion the processes of urban sociability (151).

By repeatedly characterizing the urban ecosystem and the interdependencies that it fostered as "intricate," Jacobs portrayed the city as a delicate organism. A "city ecosystem," she explained in her "Foreword" to the Modern Library's 1993 edition of *Death and Life*, consists of "complex interdependencies of components" that are "vulnerable and fragile, easily disrupted or destroyed."[36] Like the stability of the ecosystems found in upstate New York's Pine Plains or the shorelines of the Atlantic coast, the stability of the urban ecosystem was precarious. Any number of alterations to any part of the system might throw it irrevocably out of balance. As the opening lines of *Death and Life* made clear, the greatest threat to the city ecosystem in Jacobs's mind was the "current city planning and rebuilding" efforts that sought to renew the city by razing and redeveloping large swaths of it (3). When one recognizes that the city's "mutual supporting arrangements of various enterprises and people are living arrangements," Jacobs explained to city planner Samuel R. Mozes shortly after the publication of *Death and Life*, one understands how "absolutely immoral" it would be to interfere with those arrangements by extensively altering the habitats of residents, businesses, and other organizations.[37] Redeveloping big chunks of the city's built environment would not just displace individuals and enterprises but would, more significantly, break up the forms of mutual support that made living in the city manageable. Jacobs encouraged her readers to be sensitive to the fragility of the urban ecosystem. One of these readers explained that, prior to reading *Death and Life*, "I had always thought of [cities] as organisms, but until now, they were organisms of whose biology I knew almost nothing, and whose health I took to be beyond the power of mere mortals (including politicians and city planners) to affect."[38] After reading *Death and Life*, he grasped just how susceptible the city organism was to the disrupting influence of those who were integral components of it.

The moral imperative of Jacobs's ecological urbanism and the urbanist discourse of sociability that it supported was to preserve the city ecosystem—an imperative that stimulated a distinct type of fellow-feeling among urbanites. Jacobs understood better than most ecological urbanists that the preservationist impulse emanating from ecological paradigms could help urbanites feel emotionally attached to and ethically responsible for one another. This preservationist affect drove much of Jacobs's own activism. When, immediately after *Death and Life*'s release, New York City's Housing and Redevelopment Board recommended a traditional raze-and-reconstruct housing project for Jacobs's West Village neighborhood, she and her neighbors managed to shoot down the city's Title I redevelopment proposal and earn the right to design their own project. With the assistance of the Perkins & Will architectural firm with whom she had worked to design a plan for the De Witt Clinton Houses just a few years earlier, Jacobs and the West Village Committee developed the "West Village Plan for Housing" in 1963. The city's plan would have displaced many living in the community, leveled older structures, and wiped out local businesses. The West Village Plan, by contrast, was driven by the West Village Committee's "*main requirement that not a single resident ('not a single sparrow,' as one member put it) shall be displaced involuntarily from the neighborhood, and that no business depending upon site location shall be uprooted.*"[39] As the biblical reference to God's awareness of and concern for every sparrow suggests, the committee's commitment to preserve the right of every individual and enterprise to remain in the neighborhood both grew out of and solidified an emotional connection to them. While the members of the relatively small committee could not have known every one of their neighbors, their ecological strategies for thinking about the need to preserve as much of their neighborhood's diversity as possible enabled them to feel attached enough to their neighbors to defend their right to remain in a very particular place in the city. Knowing that each individual and enterprise constituted an irreplaceable part of the web of mutual support that made city life sustainable and satisfying, Jacobs and her allies experienced a sense of fellow-feeling for those who inhabited the urban ecosystem of which they were a part.

That ecologically informed fellow-feeling generated very specific city-building strategies. Jacobs and those who worked with her to design the West Village Houses insisted that their primary goal was to "devise, as a public example, a practical means of adding harmonious planned housing *into* an existing community without any sacrifice of the people already there." The West Village Committee proposed achieving this structural and social harmony by adhering to many of the design principles that Jacobs had laid out in *Death and Life*. *The West Village Plan for Housing* called for integrating "new and older structures" in a way that would enable the new structures to "conform to the existing scale of the neighborhood and harmonize with its texture." The plans also recommended that the housing structures include "apartments of varied size" so that the residential project would attract "variation in family size and family age," as well as "variation in incomes." Perhaps most important, recognizing that "street life is lively and traditional in the neighborhood," Jacobs and the West Village Committee developed a design that would maintain a "clear structural distinction between public street spaces and private courtyards or gardens." On the "street sides," for instance, "many small public plazas, sitting areas and irregularities of building line are provided, to make the public spaces more attractive and useful."[40] The West Village Committee hoped that its approach to design would preserve the structure of sociability that already existed in the West Village. In the end, political opposition, financial woes, and Jacobs's migration to Toronto in 1968 severely hampered the materialization of the socially sensitive design Jacobs and the West Village Committee had drawn up for the

West Village Houses. Despite the disappointing metamorphosis of the project, the West Village Houses, according to one perhaps overly optimistic resident, did not disrupt the social fabric of the neighborhood. Three years after the West Village Houses opened, this upbeat West Villager exclaimed that "old neighbors are busy absorbing new ones into neighborhood causes" and that, as a result, the neighborhood "is alive with people who nod and speak on the street."[41]

Jacobs's ecological "tactics for understanding" city life exposed the shortsightedness and even immorality of the proponents of urban renewal (439). Viewing the city as a complex organism that consists of a variety of interdependencies enabled Jacobs to argue that disrupting those intricate interconnections would compromise the ability of that organism to sustain life. She pointed out that the "supposed feasibility of [the] large-scale relocation of citizens" demanded by most renewal projects required planners and politicians to conceive of urbanites as "no longer components of any unit except the family" and to overlook the wide range of meaningful social interactions beyond the family unit that each individual experienced while living in the city. Ecology's growing street cred made it possible for Jacobs to argue convincingly that those who found it "intellectually easy and sane to contemplate the clearance of all slums and re-sorting of people" into housing projects were not only inhumane but also unscientific (437). They had, as Jacobs bluntly put it, fallen into the trap of "sentimentality" (447). Not only had urban renewal advocates acted sentimentally by privileging family relationships above all other types of relationships, but they had also behaved sentimentally in trying to simplify the organized complexity of the city. The strategies pursued by advocates of urban renewal—strategies that ignored the intricate interdependencies within the city—were sentimental because they were "inapplicable" to the city's complex reality (435). City planners and politicians who thought that they could clear a slum and rehouse some of its inhabitants in a housing project without significantly damaging the city's social fabric just did not make sense to Jacobs. "Sentimentality," as she succinctly put it, "plays with sweet intentions in place of good sense" (112). And "good sense," for Jacobs, entailed a process of thinking that attended to and respected the intricate interconnections that existed in any type of community. *Death and Life* taught readers that the habits of thinking found in life sciences such as ecology were capable of undermining the urban renewal order and the tyranny of intimacy on which that order had been built. By taking up the rhetoric of ecology, Jacobs persuasively accused the supposedly scientific and rational city planners of acting sentimentally—the very accusation that they had leveled against her and others who fought to protect urban neighborhoods and the relationships they sheltered from the bulldozer.

Death and Life and the Consolidation of Urban Sociability

Jacobs's thorough compilation of and important contributions to the urbanist discourse of sociability played a vital role in the success of her "attack" on "modern, orthodox city planning and rebuilding" (3). She was not the only urbanist to marshal the discourse of sociability in her efforts to push back against the logic of urban renewal, but *Death and Life* packaged and sold urban sociability to the public in a way that convinced it of the affective and social legitimacy of urban relationships to a degree that it had not been convinced before. By pushing these new habits of thinking about urban relationships into both professional and mainstream conversations about city life, Jacobs helped undermine the urban renewal order not only in New York but also throughout the United States and abroad.[42] Although there are many aspects of Jacobs's take on urban life and form in *Death and Life* that undercut urban renewal's core assumptions and aspirations, the dimension of her work that delivered the greatest blow to the urban renewal agenda was her ability to convince the public that the city was full of "relationships of all kinds that people have evolved and that are absolutely fundamental to city life."[43] Jacobs understood better than most of her contemporaries that, while "private investment" is ultimately what "shapes cities," it is our "social ideas (and laws)" that "shape private investment": "First comes the image of what we want, then the machinery is adapted to turn out that image" (313). By bundling together several different strands of a twentieth-century U.S. discourse of sociability, Jacobs reshaped her readers' social ideas about what kinds of relationships mattered and, consequently, helped redirect the investment of financial and social resources toward the type of city-building machinery that would facilitate a wide range of fellow-feelings among city dwellers.

Jacobs's synthesis of and contributions to an emerging discourse of urban sociability not only helped slow the physical and ideological forces of urban renewal but also fundamentally changed the way many came to think, talk, and write about cities. She intended from the early stages of writing

Death and Life not just to attack the urban renewal order but also to challenge what she described to Gilpatric as her culture's "two dominant and very compelling mental images of the city." Jacobs wanted to chip away at "the image of the city in trouble, an inhuman mass of masonry, a chaos of happenstance growth, a place starved of the simple decencies and amenities of life, beset with so many accumulated problems it makes your head swim." She also hoped to undercut the concept of the "rebuilt city, the antithesis of all that the unplanned city represents, a carefully planned panorama of projects and green spaces, a place where functions are sorted out instead of jumbled together, a place of light, air, sunshine, dignity and order for all."[44] Jacobs sought to replace these pervasive "mental images of the city" with an image that privileged the "marvelously intricate, constantly adjusting network of people" sheltered by cities.[45] In her efforts to bring visibility and social value to the city's vast interdependencies, Jacobs tapped into a rich, but somewhat dispersed, intellectual tradition established by urbanists who had made it their business to construct an urban imaginary that focused on the relationships and affiliations into which city dwellers entered in the public realm. Jacobs gave the discourse of urban sociability the kind of conceptual coherence and cultural legitimacy that it had not previously received, providing urbanites with distinct tactics for thinking about city life and creating urban form.

CONCLUSION

The Future of Urban Sociability

Joseph Mitchell, A. J. Liebling, Betty Smith, Albert E. Parr, J. B. Jackson, Edgar Anderson, William H. Kirk, Ellen Lurie, Jane Jacobs, and the many others who built up an urbanist discourse of sociability provided those who followed them with a much improved vocabulary for validating and evaluating the wide variety of interactions in which urbanites engage in the city's public and semi-public spaces. Although the standard of intimacy persists as an ideal by which urban encounters are sometimes measured, the structure of sociable fellow-feeling that emerged within U.S. urbanism during the first half of the twentieth century loosened the stranglehold that this standard once exerted on society's urban imaginary. The intellectual and material labor performed by the urbanists included in *The Sociable City*'s admittedly incomplete cultural history has significantly expanded the criteria that urban affiliations must meet to be considered socially and emotionally legitimate. As these urbanists have shown, the sympathetic process and the particular forms of fellow-feeling that it generates are not the only means by which individuals might experience meaningful relationships. Fellow-feelings are not limited to associations bound by the emotional intimacies of kinship and friendship but can instead take the form of a wry fondness for a street vendor, an ecological sense of harmony with both the human and non-human organisms with whom one co-occupies the city, and an appreciation for those one may never see but who nevertheless provide the mutual support that makes it possible to lead a satisfying life in the city.

The emergence of a sociable structure of fellow-feeling and the consequent legitimization of casual associations among city dwellers has altered, at least to some degree, the built environment of the U.S. city. The social ideal of togetherness against which Jacobs railed in *Death and Life* still operates at times as a guiding principle for urban professionals, but urban design has grown more and more attuned to the informal interdependencies urbanites develop as they live, work, and recreate in the city. City makers understand better than they have before their obligation to protect and facilitate sociable interactions among a city's inhabitants. If Frederick Law Olmsted's large urban parks materialized a sympathetic structure of fellow-feeling, New York City's High Line might be thought of as a sociable structure of fellow-feeling's material equivalent. Completed in 2014, the High Line is a 1.45-mile linear public park on the Lower West Side that sits atop what had been a disused elevated railroad line. Unlike Olmsted's parks, which were designed to shut out the city in order to allow urbanites to "keep alive the more tender sympathies" that would enable them to deepen their intimate relationships, the High Line embraces the social structure of sidewalk life.[1] Its narrow, linear spaces encourage users to glance at and casually acknowledge one another in passing. And while there are spaces in which one might engage in more intimate conversations with others, one must do so in full public view. The High Line lacks Central Park's open spaces and hidden nooks that were designed to accommodate the kinds of large and small group gatherings where urbanites could exercise their tender sympathies. The High Line instead provides a space in which city dwellers can practice being sociable. Its design promotes and validates the affective dynamics of the casual encounter among strangers.[2] The High Line serves as a convenient counterpoint to Olmsted's parks, but the growing strength of an urbanist discourse of sociability can perhaps be seen most clearly in the ways in which both large and small cities across the nation are changing city ordinances and zoning codes in an attempt to encourage designers, developers, and architects to create spaces that facilitate the sociable fellow-feelings that loosely bind people to one another.

While Jacobs may be largely responsible for popularizing the habits of mind and the design strategies that have given rise to discursive and material structures of sociability, we need to attend to the long tradition of urbanist inquiry that she consolidated, as well as to those traditions that fell outside her temporal and cultural purview. Preserving the range of disciplinary perspectives, cultural forms, narrative conventions, and glossaries that constituted the urbanist discourse of sociability that Jacobs brought together in *Death and Life* will make it easier for us to acknowledge and maintain the infinite variety of casual affiliations that make life in the city manageable for so many. But it is equally important to recognize that an urbanist discourse of sociability continued to evolve in the years after Jacobs packaged and sold a particular formulation of it in 1961. Since the publication of *Death and Life*, sociologists, city planners, architects, philosophers, political scientists, psychologists, novelists, visual artists, journalists, and others invested in making sense of U.S. urban experience have extended the conversation about the nature of urban sociality in productive ways. By no means a comprehensive list, a post-Jacobsian discourse of urban sociability has been enriched by works such as Harvey Cox's *The Secular City* (1965), William H. Whyte's *The Social Life of Small Urban Spaces* (1980), Richard Sennet's *The Conscience of the Eye* (1990), Karen Tei Yamashita's *Tropic of Orange* (1997), and Elijah Anderson's *The Cosmopolitan Canopy* (2011).[3]

The tradition of urbanist inquiry that *The Sociable City* traces becomes even more substantial and nuanced when one moves beyond U.S. urban history and culture. In looking to global urban history and culture, one discovers not only a significant prehistory to the urbanist discourse of sociability that took shape in the U.S. from the late nineteenth to the mid-twentieth century but also some of the most exciting contemporary conversations about the social and affective dynamics of urban sociality. Urban intellectuals such as Jan Gehl, Ash Amin, and AbdouMaliq Simone continue to push the urban imaginary to account for what Amin describes as the complex "geographies of affiliation" that give shape and texture to every city's social landscape.[4] As urbanists across the globe attend more carefully to the culturally specific structures of fellow-feeling that individuals bring to and develop within the cities they inhabit, the urbanist discourse of sociability will continue to evolve in healthy ways. We will become more adept at perceiving and protecting the countless "configurations of associational life," to borrow Simone's phrase, that city dwellers assemble in their efforts to deal with their particular urban conditions.[5] All of this is to say that there is still much work that needs to be done to grasp more fully the practices of affiliation and their corresponding structures of fellow-feeling that make it possible for urbanites to navigate the structural inequalities and social possibilities of the cities they inhabit. I hope this study will both inspire and act as a useful resource for such work.

As not only one of the most articulate proponents of urban sociability but also one of its greatest intellectual historians, Jacobs provided a useful model of what it might look like to turn toward urban histories and cultures beyond the twentieth-century United States in order to solidify an urbanist discourse capable of challenging society's inadequate understandings of urban sociality. Near the end of her career, Jacobs enjoyed a relatively brief stint as a literary reviewer. From 2001 to 2003, she reintroduced readers to the Modern Library editions of Charles Dickens's *Hard Times*, Upton Sinclair's *The Jungle*, and Mark Twain's *The Innocents Abroad or, The New Pilgrims' Progress*. In her introduction to *Hard Times*, Jacobs framed Dickens as a writer worth reading at the outset of the twenty-first century because he was a type of "seer" whose "themes vex us still": "environmental destruction, soul-destroying monotony of the built environment, the split between science and the humanities, [and] faith in narrow statistical analyses over other cogent considerations."[6] Reading *Hard Times* was a worthwhile endeavor, she suggested to her readers, because Dickens understood something about city life and communicated that understanding in a narrative form that enriched our collective urban imaginary.

Perhaps predictably, Jacobs spent a significant amount of time in her introduction to *Hard Times* highlighting Dickens's well-known description of what she described as Coketown's "monotony," one of the most pejorative terms in her vocabulary.[7] According to the novel's narrator, you "saw nothing in Coketown but what was severely workful. . . . The jail might have been the infirmary, the infirmary might have been the jail, the town-hall might have been either, or both, or anything else, for anything that appeared to the contrary in the graces of their construction. Fact, fact, fact, everywhere in the material aspect of the town; fact, fact, fact, everywhere in the immaterial." With its "several large streets all very like one another, and many small streets still more like one another, inhabited by people equally like one another, who all went in and out at the same hours, with the same sound upon the same pavements, to do the same work," Coketown is Jacobs's worst nightmare—the type of place that had borne the brunt of her pithy put-downs in *Death and Life*.[8] She pointed out that the character most comfortable in Coketown, Thomas Gradgrind, "had already made himself mentally and morally at home in a future where departments of planning would devote themselves to deliberately making the built environments of cities, towns, and suburbs monotonous in the name of virtue." Gradgrind's single-minded embrace of the "eminently practical," Jacobs suggested, anticipated the "pioneers and purists of modern architecture" she had skewered in *Death and Life*. Gradgrind, Jacobs speculated, "would have loved Le Corbusier's much later definition of a house as a machine for living."[9]

Coketown's physically monotonous landscape closely informs the paths that the novel's characters inevitably pursue. By setting its characters in motion in a city whose built environment cannot sustain an "intricate, living network of relationships," *Hard Times* exposes them to a variety of social misfortunes. As Jacobs noted, "private life in *Hard Times* fares as badly as public life," and no one is more affected by Coketown's weak social infrastructure than Stephen Blackpool. The center of the novel's most compelling and convoluted plotline, Blackpool spends his life working at the heart of Coketown's dark, industrial landscape as a factory hand. When he refuses to join the United Aggregate Tribunal in a show of proletarian solidarity with the rest of his coworkers, the local labor agitator, Slackbridge, punishes Blackpool with what Jacobs described as a "secular excommunication" that completely deprives him of "cooperation and other human contact." Blackpool's punishment, Jacobs implied, could only have been carried out in a place like Coketown that completely lacked public life on its streets and sidewalks.[10] Feigning an interest in assisting Blackpool during his social exile, Gradgrind's son Tom convinces the helpless factory hand to wait near a bank for further communication from him. Lingering in the deserted streets outside the bank as instructed, Blackpool "began to have an uncomfortable sensation upon him of being for the time a disreputable character." In a city where "some purpose or other is so natural to every one, that a mere loiterer always looks and feels remarkable," Blackpool becomes the sole suspect when a bank robbery—committed, of course, by Tom—is discovered the following day.[11]

The novel's most complex plot line hinges not only on Coketown's rigid class structure, but also on its nonexistent "social structure of sidewalk life," to borrow Jacobs's phrase.[12] In Jacobs's reading of *Hard Times*, the surface crime of the bank robbery points not only to the deeper crime of structural inequalities that uphold Coketown's social hierarchies but also to the deeper crime of Coketown's built environment. Blackpool's identity as an honest laborer could only be confused with that of a loitering bank robber in a place such as Coketown where, to use another of Jacobs's phrases, there is no "feeling for the public identity of people" because there simply aren't people who interact in the public sphere.[13] A city where all the pedestrians "went in and out at the same hours, with the same sound upon the same pavements, to do the same work" failed to generate the social infrastructure needed to sustain networks of intricate, mutual support among its inhabitants.[14] Dickens could not have transplanted the plots of *Hard Times* onto the London streetscapes that he describes in his other novels. The teeming sidewalks and multiple street contacts that we encounter, for instance, in *Our Mutual Friend* (1865) would have frustrated *Hard Times*'s narrative and cultural logic. Jacobs's reading of *Hard Times* is not an antiurban one, then, but one that instead draws attention to the social consequences of living in a city that embodies the wrong kind of urbanism.

Jacobs clearly had the late twentieth- and twenty-first-century city in mind when reintroducing readers to "Dickens the seer."[15] Like many other urbanists, Jacobs had grown increasingly concerned about the disappearance of public space and the loss of social, economic, and aesthetic diversity in the postindustrial city. The city of 2001 faced a very different set of challenges than did the city of 1961. Of course, the threat of the automobile and the construction of the highways it required, along with the erection of large-scale public works, persisted through the end of the twentieth century. But at the outset of the twenty-first century, urbanists confronted a different set of threats to the fragile interdependencies and affiliations into which city dwellers had entered in their efforts to survive in the city. The deregulation of the economy, reinvestment of capital (often foreign) in the capital cities of the service economy, gentrification of working-class neighborhoods, privatization of public and semi-public space, vigilant policing of social boundaries (often resulting in the incarceration of the urban poor), and the emergence of a socially hostile and aesthetically monotonous architecture worked together to undermine the diverse urban orders needed to maintain a stable structure of sociability. Facing this particular moment in urban history, Jacobs turned to Dickens as an urban thinker worth including in the tradition of urbanist inquiry she had consolidated forty years earlier. She sensed that Dickens infused an urbanist discourse of sociability with the strategies for thinking about urban sociality that were needed at that particular urban moment.

We would do well to follow Jacobs's lead in continually expanding and modifying the urbanist discourse of sociability described in *The Sociable City* in order to attend more carefully to the city's constantly evolving built environment and social landscape. Given the ongoing urbanization of the United States and, more importantly, the rapid urbanization of the planet, the task of developing more robust and nuanced strategies for thinking about the variety of urban affiliations into which city dwellers enter and the unlimited forms of fellow-feeling that those connections produce is an urgent one. In his efforts to understand urban life in the cities of Africa and Southeast Asia, for instance, Simone calls attention to the "combinations of generosity, ruthlessness, collaboration, competition, stillness, movement, flexibility, and defensiveness" practiced by city dwellers that exist on the city's peripheries. What these combinations of being together with others look like, Simone adds, also "depends on the particular histories of cities and their relationship to other combinations—that is, the combinations of economic policy, spatial organization, political culture and contestation, and how particular localities are situated in relationship to others, as well as other cities, regions, and economic poles."[16] Accounting for the variables that give shape to the associations that determine how successfully a city dweller navigates the periphery of Jakarta or Dakar will require, among other things, more sophisticated modes of recognizing and making sense of complex structures of fellow-feeling. Developing new patterns for talking about urban relationships and interpersonal affect will help move these often overlooked matters of sociality from the periphery to the center of our conversations about urban life. Taking urban sociality more seriously matters because, as this study has shown, a society's decisions about what kinds of relationships and interpersonal emotions matter determine the types of cities it builds and the kinds of opportunities those cities afford to those who live in them.

One of the keys to taking urban sociality more seriously, as *The Sociable City* has shown, is avoiding the temptation to dismiss the new configurations of affiliation that emerge in today's cities just because they are mediated by different technologies or take different relational forms than those in the past. As city dwellers develop new forms of communication, alter modes of transportation, experience shifting demographics, and inhabit different built environments, they will necessarily interact with and connect to one another in new ways. Rather than cynically conclude that the opportunities for urbanites to connect with one another in emotionally substantive ways have all but disappeared, this study suggests that the modes of sociability through which they acquire fellow-feelings for each other will continue to evolve and emerge over time. Consequently, the discourse of sociability that describes and validates these interconnections among city dwellers has and will continue to change. As urbanization accelerates across the globe and new forms of city life proliferate in the twenty-first century, those who pursue a study of the city's social landscape will need to continue to search for the language and mediums through which they might legitimize the affective value of the diverse relational forms into which city dwellers enter. Pursing the project to which the urbanists that appear in these pages have contributed will be critical to our efforts to create more just, sustainable, and satisfying cities.

NOTES

Introduction. Finding Fellow-Feeling in the City

1. Frederick Law Olmsted, "Public Parks and the Enlargement of Towns," in *The Papers of Frederick Law Olmsted, Supplementary Series: Writings on Public Parks, Parkways, and Park Systems*, vol. 1, ed. Charles E. Beveridge and Carolyn F. Hoffman (Baltimore: Johns Hopkins University Press, 1997), 179, 189.

2. Steven Conn, *Americans Against the City: Anti-Urbanism in the Twentieth Century* (New York: Oxford University Press, 2014), 6. For additional scholarship on antiurbanism in U.S. history and culture, see also Morton White and Lucia White, *The Intellectual Versus the City: From Thomas Jefferson to Frank Lloyd Wright* (Cambridge, Mass.: Harvard University Press and MIT Press, 1962); Leo Marx, "The Puzzle of Anti-Urbanism in Classic American Literature," in *Literature and the Urban Experience: Essays on the City and Literature*, ed. Michael Jaye and Ann Chalmers Watts (New Brunswick, N.J.: Rutgers University Press, 1981), 63–80; and Steve Macek, *Urban Nightmares: The Media, the Right, and the Moral Panic over the City* (Minneapolis: University of Minnesota Press, 2006).

3. Adam Smith, *The Theory of Moral Sentiments*, ed. Knud Haakonssen (1759; Cambridge: Cambridge University Press, 2002), 11–12, 27, 14. Providing a transatlantic genealogy of the concept of sympathy is beyond the scope of this study. Many other scholars have mapped some of sympathy's migrations from the Scottish Enlightenment to U.S. antebellum culture. See Terrence Martin, *The Instructed Vision: Scottish Common Sense Philosophy and the Origins of American Fiction* (1961; New York: Kraus Reprint, 1969); Gregg Camfield, *Sentimental Twain: Samuel Clemens in the Maze of Moral Philosophy* (Philadelphia: University of Pennsylvania Press, 1994); and Julie Ellison, *Cato's Tears and the Making of Anglo-American Emotion* (Chicago: University of Chicago Press, 1999).

4. According to Sam Bass Warner, Jr., Boston remained a "city which depended on people's walking for its means of transportation" through the 1870s. Sam Bass Warner, Jr., *Streetcar Suburbs: The Process of Growth in Boston (1870–1900)*, 2nd ed. (Cambridge, Mass.: Harvard University Press, 1978), 21.

5. Olmsted, "Public Parks," 179, 180.

6. Elizabeth Barnes, *States of Sympathy: Seduction and Democracy in the American Novel* (New York: Columbia University Press, 1997), 2. In recent years, scholars have called our attention to the fact that the experience of sympathy was not limited to "familial feeling." Cindy Weinstein has been particularly influential in her encouragement to break up the "monolithic and consistently pernicious account of sympathy" that has pervaded so much of the criticism of it. Cindy Weinstein, *Family, Kinship and Sympathy in Nineteenth-Century American Literature* (Cambridge: Cambridge University Press, 2005), 3. Some have moved beyond the "monolithic" analyses of sympathy by recovering distinct alternative modes of sympathy that operated at the heart of nineteenth-century sentimental culture. See Travis M. Foster, "Grotesque Sympathy: Lydia Maria Child, White Reform, and the Embodiment of Urban Space," *ESQ* 56, no. 1 (2010): 1–32; and Brigitte Nicole Fielder, "Affective Kinship in Nineteenth-Century Abolitionism," *American Quarterly* 65, no. 3 (2013): 487–514. Others, like Susan Lanzoni, attempt to illuminate the nuances of sympathy through careful archival work—work that reveals, for instance, that late Victorian thinkers "were simply not in agreement as to the definition of sympathy, or how it operated." Susan Lanzoni, "Sympathy in *Mind* (1876–1900)," *Journal of the History of Ideas* 70, no. 2 (2009): 265–87.

7. Olmsted, "Public Parks," 182–83.

8. Ibid., 189, 188.

9. Mary P. Ryan, *Civic Wars: Democracy and Public Life in the American City During the Nineteenth Century* (Berkeley: University of California Press, 1997), 14.

10. Olmsted, "Public Parks," 187.

11. Richard Sennett, *The Fall of Public Man: On the Social Psychology of Capitalism* (New York: Random House, 1974), 338

12. Raymond Williams, *Marxism and Literature* (New York: Oxford University Press, 1977), 133, 132. For an excellent explication of Williams's "structure of feeling" and its evolution within academic discourse since the 1970s, see Jonathan Flatley, *Affective Mapping: Melancholia and the Politics of Modernism* (Cambridge, Mass.: Harvard University Press, 2008), 24–27.

13. Jane Jacobs, *The Death and Life of Great American Cities* (New York: Random House, 1961), 313.

14. White and White, *Intellectual Versus the City*, 2.

15. Jane Addams, *Newer Ideals of Peace* (London: Macmillan, 1907), 29, 11.

16. Arthur Arent, *One-Third of a Nation*, in *Federal Theatre Plays: Prologue to Glory, One-Third of a Nation, Haiti*, ed. Pierre De Rohan (New York: Random House, 1938).

17. Iris Marion Young, *Justice and the Politics of Difference* (Princeton, N.J.: Princeton University Press, 1990), 237.

18. Betty Smith, *A Tree Grows in Brooklyn: A Novel* (New York: Harper, 1943).

19. For a particularly useful overview of the *flâneur*'s impact on American literature and culture, see Dana Brand, *The Spectator and the City in Nineteenth-Century American Literature* (Cambridge: Cambridge University Press, 1991).

20. See Lyn H. Lofland, *The Public Realm: Exploring the City's Quintessential Social Territory* (Hawthorne, N.Y.: Aldine De Gruyter, 1998).

21. Ash Amin, *Land of Strangers* (Cambridge: Polity, 2012), 6.

22. AbdouMaliq Simone, *City Life from Jakarta to Dakar: Movements at the Crossroads* (New York: Routledge, 2010), 5, 3, 58–59.

Chapter 1. The Settlement Movement's Push for Public Sympathy

1. Jane Addams, "Hull-House, Chicago: An Effort Toward Social Democracy," *Forum* 14 (October 1892): 227–28.

2. Jane Addams, "A New Impulse to an Old Gospel," *Forum* 14 (November 1892): 346. Addams originally delivered a version of this article in 1892 as a lecture at a summer school hosted by the Ethical Culture Societies in Plymouth, Massachusetts. She later included a significant portion of this article in the sixth chapter of her memoir, *Twenty Years at Hull-House* (New York: Macmillan, 1910).

3. See Ryan, *Civic Wars*, 202.

4. Addams, "New Impulse," 347.

5. Ibid., 350, 346.

6. W. E. B. Du Bois, *The Philadelphia Negro: A Social Study* (1899; Philadelphia: University of Pennsylvania Press, 1996), 3 (note: pagination is identical in all editions); W. E. B. Du Bois, *The Souls of Black Folk*, in *The Oxford W. E. B. Du Bois Reader*, ed. Eric J. Sundquist (1905; New York: Oxford University Press, 1996), 189. Du Bois had grown increasingly dissatisfied and preoccupied with the breakdown of interracial sympathy during the nation's post-Reconstruction period. While radical Republicans continued to try to facilitate affective alliances among blacks and whites, many white northerners and southerners became increasingly invested in forging an emotional reunion among themselves. See David W. Blight, *Race and Reunion: The Civil War in American Memory* (Cambridge, Mass.: Harvard University Press, 2001).

7. Addams, "New Impulse," 348.

8. Addams, *Newer Ideals of Peace*, 216, 214, 11.

9. Du Bois, *Philadelphia Negro*, 332, 388.

10. Addams, "New Impulse," 357.

11. Addams, "Hull-House, Chicago," 226.

12. Shannon Jackson provides a thorough and excellent account of the "spatial innovations" that settlement residents pioneered in their efforts to offer urbanites alternatives to the "larger time-space patterns of unregulated industrialism." Shannon Jackson, *Lines of Activity: Performance, Historiography, Hull-House Domesticity* (Ann Arbor: University of Michigan Press, 2000), 63, 69.

13. W. E. B. Du Bois, "The City Negro," 1910, W. E. B. Du Bois Papers, 1877–1963, W. E. B. Du Bois Library, University of Massachusetts Amherst, 19, 4 (hereafter Du Bois Papers).

14. Isabel Eaton, "The Theory and Ideals of the Settlement," *College Settlement News*, November 1896, 2; Clarence Meily, "The Stratification of Sympathy," *Charities and the Commons* 15, no. 13 (1905): 417.

15. "Report on the Questions Drawn Up by Present Residents in Our College Settlements and Submitted to Past Residents," *Publications of the Church Social Union* 29 (September 1896): 6. As Kristin Boudreau observes, the creation and preservation of the "fiction of shared blood," or "consanguinity," have always been one of sympathy's chief purposes and were seen by many eighteenth- and nineteenth-century U.S. politicians as critical to the operation of an egalitarian society. Kristin Boudreau, *Sympathy in American Literature: American Sentiments from Jefferson to the Jameses* (Gainesville: University Press of Florida, 2002), x.

16. Addams, "New Impulse," 353; for an account of the Social Gospel's relationship to urban life and culture, see Heath W. Carter, *Union Made: Working People and the Rise of Social Christianity in Chicago* (New York: Oxford University Press, 2015).

17. Vida Scudder, "Settlements Past and Future," *Eleventh Annual Report of the College Settlements Association, From October 1st, 1899, to October 1st, 1900* (Boston: A.T. Bliss, 1900), 6.

18. Jane Addams, "The Subtle Problems of Charity," *Atlantic Monthly*, February 1899, 163, 176; Addams, *Newer Ideals of Peace*, 11.

19. Du Bois, *Philadelphia Negro*, 332, 355, 390.

20. John P. Gavit, "Missions and Settlements," *The Commons* 2, no. 10 (1898): 3 (note: the name of the periodical changed over time).

21. "A Settlement Tribute," *Chicago Commons* 1, no. 8 (1896): 3, 4.

22. Samuel A. Barnett, "Education by Permeation," *Charities and the Commons* 16, no. 5 (1906): 187.

23. Jane Addams, *Democracy and Social Ethics* (New York: Macmillan, 1902), 154, 146.

24. W. E. B. Du Bois, *The Autobiography of W. E. B. Du Bois: A Soliloquy on Viewing My Life from the Last Decade of Its First Century* (New York: International, 1968), 198. For other descriptions of Du Bois's activities while living at the Philadelphia College Settlement, see Rosina McAvoy Ryan, "'A graduate school in life': The College Settlement of Philadelphia and Its Role in Providing Post-Baccalaureate Education for Women" (Ph.D. dissertation, Temple University, 2006), 261–62; and Samuel McCune Lindsay, Introduction to Du Bois, *The Philadelphia Negro* (1899 edition), viii.

25. Du Bois, *Philadelphia Negro*, 63.

26. Du Bois, *Autobiography*, 198.

27. Christopher Castiglia, "Abolition's Racial Interiors and the Making of White Civic Depth," *American Literary History* 14, no. 1 (2002): 37. For critiques of the forms of social control that emerged within the settlement movement, see Howard Jacob Karger, *The Sentinels of Order: A Study of Social Control and the Minneapolis Settlement House Movement, 1915–1950* (Lanham, Md.: University Press of America, 1987);

Rivka Shpak Lissak, *Pluralism and Progressives: Hull House and the New Immigrants, 1890–1919* (Chicago: University of Chicago Press, 1989); and Ruth Hutchinson Crocker, *Social Work and Social Order: The Settlement Movement in Two Industrial Cities, 1889–1930* (Urbana: University of Illinois Press, 1992). For a discussion of realism's reification and naturalization of social hierarchies, see Amy Kaplan, *The Social Construction of American Realism* (Chicago: University of Chicago Press, 1988). And for a history of slumming in the postbellum city, see Chad Heap, *Slumming: Sexual and Racial Encounters in American Nightlife, 1885–1940* (Chicago: University of Chicago Press, 2009).

28. Addams, *Democracy and Social Ethics*, 154, 38; Addams, "Subtle Problems of Charity," 176.

29. Herman F. Hegner, "Scientific Value of the Social Settlements," *American Journal of Sociology* 3, no. 2 (1897): 177.

30. For a thorough history of the relationship between the settlement movement and black communities during the first half of the twentieth century, see Elisabeth Lasch-Quinn, *Black Neighbors: Race and the Limits of Reform in the American Settlement House Movement, 1890–1945* (Chapel Hill: University of North Carolina Press, 1993).

31. W. E. B. Du Bois, "A Program for a Sociological Society," 1897, Du Bois Papers, 10, 8.

32. Du Bois, *Philadelphia Negro*, 6, 5. Although *The Philadelphia Negro* was marginalized as a sociological text for much of the twentieth century, scholars have recently begun to recognize the significance of its contributions to the discipline. See Michael B. Katz and Thomas J. Sugrue, eds., *W. E. B. Du Bois, Race, and the City: The Philadelphia Negro and Its Legacy* (Philadelphia: University of Pennsylvania Press, 1998); Reiland Rabaka, *Against Epistemic Apartheid: W. E. B. Du Bois and the Disciplinary Decadence of Sociology* (New York: Lexington, 2010); Marcus Anthony Hunter, *Black Citymakers: How* The Philadelphia Negro *Changed Urban America* (New York: Oxford University Press, 2013); Aldon Morris, *The Scholar Denied: W. E. B. Du Bois and the Birth of American Sociology* (Berkeley: University of California Press, 2015); and Kevin Loughran, "*The Philadelphia Negro* and the Canon of Classical Urban Theory," *Du Bois Review* 12, no. 2 (2015): 249–67. I am making the argument here that *The Philadelphia Negro* also deserves to be seen as a seminal text in the settlement movement's canon.

33. Du Bois, *Philadelphia Negro*, 209.

34. Ibid., 322.

35. "Family Schedule," in *Hull-House Maps and Papers*, by Residents of Hull-House (New York: Thomas Crowell, 1895), Questions 39–40.

36. Mary Jo Deegan claims that Du Bois "modeled his questionnaires and maps" on those used by Hull-House residents. Mary Jo Deegan, "W. E. B. Du Bois and the Women of Hull-House, 1895–1899," *American Sociologist* 19, no. 4 (1988): 306. For additional information about the schedules Du Bois used and their possible antecedents,

see Herbert Aptheker, Introduction to W. E. B. Du Bois, *The Philadelphia Negro* (Millwood, N.Y.: Kraus-Thomson, 1973), 15–17.

37. Du Bois, *Philadelphia Negro*, 326, n. 2.

38. Ibid., 329, 330.

39. Ibid., 394, 396.

40. Pennsylvania Society for Promoting the Abolition of Slavery, *The Present State and Condition of the Free People of Color, of the City of Philadelphia and Adjoining Districts, as Exhibited by the Report of a Committee of the Pennsylvania Society for Promoting the Abolition of Slavery, &c.* (Philadelphia: Merrihew and Gunn, 1838), Library Company of Philadelphia, 14, 3, 15, 9, 23. The PAS committee gathered statistics in five principal areas, four of which were intended to demonstrate the fiscal health of the Philadelphia Negro: "To the Number of the Colored Population"; "Real Estate and Personal Property"; "Taxes"; "House Rents, &c."; and "Of the Employment of the Colored Population and Views Connected with their Labor and Support." For a historical account of the Pennsylvania Abolition Society, see Richard S. Newman, *The Transformation of American Abolitionism: Fighting Slavery in the Early Republic* (Chapel Hill: University of North Carolina Press, 2002).

41. Pennsylvania Society for Promoting the Abolition of Slavery, *To the People of Color in the State of Pennsylvania* (Philadelphia: Merrihew and Gunn, 1838), Library Company of Philadelphia, 3.

42. "Report on the Questions," 21, 22, 23.

43. Addams, *Twenty Years at Hull-House*, 150. For additional studies of the roles settlement residents played in modifying the industrial city's built environment, see Jackson, *Lines of Activity*; Daphne Spain, *How Women Saved the City* (Minneapolis: University of Minnesota Press, 2001); Robin F. Bachin, *Building the South Side: Urban Space and Civic Culture in Chicago, 1890–1919* (Chicago: University of Chicago Press, 2004); Sharon Haar, *The City as Campus: Urbanism and Higher Education in Chicago* (Minneapolis: University of Minnesota Press, 2011); and Marta Gutman, *A City for Children: Women, Architecture, and the Charitable Landscapes of Oakland, 1850–1950* (Chicago: University of Chicago Press, 2014).

44. Dorothea Moore, "A Day at Hull House," *American Journal of Sociology* 2, no. 5 (1897): 640.

45. Olmsted, "Public Parks," 189.

46. Addams, "Hull-House, Chicago," 226.

47. As Shannon Jackson puts it, "settlement practices processually alternated and activated the private or public identity" of a single region within the settlement home. Jackson, *Lines of Activity*, 152.

48. Moore, "Day at Hull House," 636.

49. Addams, *Twenty Years at Hull-House*, 365–66.

50. Allen B. Pond, "The 'Settlement House'," part 3, *Brickbuilder* 11, no. 9 (1902): 178–83.

51. It is worth noting that, when Du Bois pitched his idea of a settlement house that catered to the city's black communities, such an institution would not have been a novelty. Harlem's White Rose Mission and the Tenderloin's New York Colored Mission had been operating on the settlement plan since the 1890s. As their names imply, these institutions were, at least initially, interested in performing social services that met their patrons' spiritual and moral needs. For fuller descriptions of the activities of these settlement houses, see Floris Barnett Cash, "Radicals and Realists: African American Women and the Settlement House Spirit in New York City," *Afro-Americans in New York Life and History* 15, no. 1 (January 1991): 7–17; and Ralph Luker, *The Social Gospel in Black and White: American Racial Reform, 1885–1912* (Chapel Hill: University of North Carolina Press, 1991), 167.

52. W. E. B. Du Bois, "First Meeting of Persons Interested in the Welfare of the Negroes of New York City," in *Against Racism: Unpublished Essays, Papers, Addresses, 1887–1961*, ed. Herbert Aptheker (Amherst: University of Massachusetts Press, 1985), 72, 73, 74. As Nancy Weiss reports, the meeting at which Du Bois proposed the creation of this New York settlement house was the first step in establishing the Committee for Improving the Industrial Condition of Negroes. See Nancy Weiss, *The National Urban League, 1910–1940* (New York: Oxford University Press, 1974), 20–21.

53. Mary White Ovington to W. E. B. Du Bois, October 7, 1904, Du Bois Papers, 1.

54. Ovington to Du Bois, January 25, 1905, Du Bois Papers, 3, 2. Ovington would eventually collect and publish much of her research in *Half a Man: The Status of the Negro in New York* (New York: Longmans, Green, 1911).

55. Ovington to Du Bois, January 25, 1905, 1. Du Bois expressed his approval of Ovington's approach in a personal letter, agreeing emphatically that having "white and colored management of your institutional work" is the "only sensible . . . method." Du Bois to Ovington, January 25, 1905, Du Bois Papers.

56. See Carolyn Wedin, *Inheritors of the Spirit: Mary White Ovington and the Founding of the NAACP* (New York: Wiley, 1998), 93.

Chapter 2. New Deal Urbanism and the Contraction of Sympathy

1. Helen Hall, "Community Studies," May 11, 1954, folder 89, Helen Hall Papers, Social Welfare History Archives, University of Minnesota, 12.

2. *A Dutchman's Farm: A Play, 1941*, folder 88, Helen Hall Papers, 32.

3. See Gail Radford, *Modern Housing for America: Policy Struggles in the New Deal Era* (Chicago: University of Chicago Press, 1996).

4. See Lizabeth Cohen, *Making a New Deal: Industrial Workers in Chicago, 1919–1939* (New York: Cambridge University Press, 1990), 249.

5. Catherine Bauer, *Modern Housing* (New York: Houghton Mifflin, 1934), 51, 37, 152, 44, 157, 213.

6. Lewis Mumford, *The Culture of Cities* (1938; New York: Harcourt Brace, 1970), 479, 482, 476, 481, 491, 484.

7. Robert E. Park, "The City: Suggestions for the Investigation of Human Behavior in the Urban Environment," *American Journal of Sociology* 20, no. 5 (1915): 593, 582, 597.

8. Louis Wirth, "Urbanism as a Way of Life," *American Journal of Sociology* 44, no. 1 (1938): 12–13, 17.

9. Cecil C. North, "The City as a Community: An Introduction to a Research Project," in *The Urban Community: Selected Papers from the Proceedings of the American Sociological Society, 1925*, ed. Ernest W. Burgess (Chicago: University of Chicago Press, 1926), 233, 234.

10. Albion Small, *Adam Smith and Modern Sociology: A Study in the Methodology of the Social Sciences* (Chicago: University of Chicago Press, 1907).

11. Robert E. Park and Ernest W. Burgess, *Introduction to the Science of Sociology* (1921; Chicago: University of Chicago Press, 1969), 397. In addition to citing Smith as the sociological authority on sympathy, Park and Burgess excerpted from Théodule-Armand Ribot's *The Psychology of the Emotions* (1897) and Nathaniel S. Shaler's *The Neighbor* (1904), both of which rehearse Smith's original description of sympathy. See Théodule-Arman Ribot, "The Three Levels of Sympathy," in Park and Burgess, *Introduction to the Science of Sociology*, 394–97; and Nathaniel S. Shaler, "Sympathetic Contacts Versus Categoric Contacts," in Park and Burgess, *Introduction to the Science of Sociology*, 294–98.

12. For a fuller exploration of the relationship between settlement workers at Hull-House and Chicago school sociologists, see Mary Jo Deegan, *Jane Addams and the Men of the Chicago School, 1892–1918* (New Brunswick, N.J.: Transaction, 1988); Mary Jo Deegan, *Race, Hull-House, and the University of Chicago: A New Conscience Against Ancient Evils* (Santa Barbara, Calif.: Praeger, 2002); and Haar, *The City as Campus*, chapter 2.

13. Charles Horton Cooley, *Social Organization: A Study of the Larger Mind* (1909; New York: Schocken, 1962), 23, 28. For an understanding of Cooley's contributions to the field of sociology, see Jeffrey Skalnsky, *The Soul's Economy: Market Society and Selfhood in American Thought, 1820–1920* (Chapel Hill: University of North Carolina Press, 2002).

14. Nicholas J. Spykman, "A Social Philosophy of the City," in *The Urban Community*, ed. Burgess, 58. Although Spykman was not a sociologist—he taught political science at Yale University—his discussion of primary and secondary contacts articulates succinctly the Chicago school's stance on these sociological categories.

15. Wirth, "Urbanism as a Way of Life," 11, 12, 15, 16.

16. Cooley, *Social Organization*, 25.

17. Park and Burgess, *Introduction to the Science of Sociology*, 284–85.

18. See, for instance, W. I. Thomas and Florian Znaniecki, *The Polish Peasant in Europe and America* (Chicago: University of Chicago Press, 1918–1920).

19. C. Wright Mills, "The Professional Ideology of Social Pathologists," *American Journal of Sociology* 49, no. 2 (1943): 174.

20. Park, "The City," 608.

21. Emory S. Bogardus, "Social Distance in the City," in *The Urban Community*, ed. Burgess, 48.

22. Park, "The City," 595.

23. Harvey Warren Zorbaugh, *The Gold Coast and the Slum* (Chicago: University of Chicago Press, 1929), 153–54.

24. Ibid., 266.

25. Ibid., 252.

26. Shelby M. Harrison, introduction to Clarence Perry, "The Neighborhood Unit: A Scheme of Arrangement for the Family-Life Community," in *Regional Survey of New York and Its Environs*, vol. 7, *Neighborhood and Community Planning* (1929; New York: Arno, 1974), 23. For a more detailed history of the relationship between urban sociology and city planning, see Howard Gillette, Jr., "The Evolution of Neighborhood Planning: From the Progressive Era to the 1949 Housing Act," *Journal of Urban History* 9, no. 4 (1983): 421–44; and John D. Fairfield, *The Mysteries of the Great City: The Politics of Urban Design, 1877–1937* (Columbus: Ohio State University Press, 1993), chap. 6

27. Charles S. Ascher, review of *The Rebuilding of Blighted Areas*, by Clarence Arthur Perry, *American Journal of Sociology* 40, 2 (1934): 267. For more recent assessments of the significance of Perry's writings on the neighborhood unit to the planning profession, see Lawrence J. Vale, *From the Puritans to the Projects: Public Housing and Public Neighbors* (Cambridge, Mass.: Harvard University Press, 2000), 142–50; Jason S. Brody, "Constructing Professional Knowledge: The Neighborhood Unit Concept in the Community Builders Handbook" (Ph.D. dissertation, University of Illinois at Urbana-Champaign, 2009; and Howard Gillette, Jr., *Civitas by Design: Building Better Communities from the Garden City to the New Urbanism* (Philadelphia: University of Pennsylvania Press, 2010), 60–76.

28. Perry, "The Neighborhood Unit," 34, 31, 126.

29. Ibid.," 126–27.

30. Clarence Perry, *Housing for the Machine Age* (New York: Russell Sage, 1939), 215.

31. Perry, "Neighborhood Unit," 100.

32. Olmsted, "Public Parks," 189. For a cultural history of Forest Hills Gardens, see Susan L. Klaus, *A Modern Arcadia: Frederick Law Olmsted Jr. and the Plan for Forest Hills Gardens* (Amherst: University of Massachusetts Press, 2002).

33. Perry, "Neighborhood Unit," 220; Clarence Arthur Perry, "The Tangible Aspects of Community Organization," *Social Forces* 8, no. 4 (1930): 563.

34. Clarence Arthur Perry, "City Planning for Neighborhood Life," *Social Forces* 8, no. 1 (1929): 99. In constructing a homogeneous urban environment, Perry insisted that planners and developers would simply be speeding along the natural processes

that Roderick McKenzie had observed at work in the city—namely, the "segregation of a city population 'along racial, economic, social and vocational lines'" (99).

35. Clarence Arthur Perry, "The Prevention of Slum Conditions Through City Planning: Preliminary Report of a Study," *Social Forces* 10, no. 3 (March 1932): 383, 384.

36. Perry, "Neighborhood Unit," 111. In the 1930s, Perry developed a few of these other plans. He advanced the most comprehensive of them in a detailed proposal for the development of a neighborhood unit on a forty-one-acre tract of land containing a hodgepodge of residential building types and commercial enterprises in the Winfield section of western Queens. See Clarence Arthur Perry, *The Rebuilding of Blighted Areas: A Study of the Neighborhood Unit in Replanning and Plot Assemblage* (New York: Regional Plan Association, 1933), 20.

37. Perry, "Prevention of Slum Conditions," 387.

38. Perry, *Rebuilding of Blighted Areas*, 49, 47.

39. For historical accounts of the U.S. Housing Act of 1937, see Terrence L. McDonald, *The Wagner Housing Act: A Case Study of the Legislative Process* (Chicago: Loyola University Press, 1957); Leonard M. Friedman, *Government and Slum Housing: A Century of Frustration* (Chicago: Rand McNally, 1968); Mark Gelfand, *A Nation of Cities* (New York: Oxford University Press, 1975); Rachel Bratt, *Rebuilding a Low-Income Housing Policy* (Philadelphia: Temple University Press, 1989); Radford, *Modern Housing*; D. Bradford Hunt, *Blueprint for Disaster: The Unraveling of Chicago Public Housing* (Chicago: University of Chicago Press, 2009); and Alexander von Hoffman, "The End of the Dream: The Political Struggle of America's Public Housers," *Journal of Planning History* 4, no. 3 (2005): 222–53.

40. *One-Third* was the most successful of the FTP's plays. Following its New York run, where it was seen by over 217,000 viewers, *One-Third* was picked up and performed by a number of FTP units, as well as civic and educational groups, in cities across the country: Detroit, Cincinnati, Philadelphia, Hartford, New Orleans, San Francisco, Seattle, and Portland. Because the FTP's mission to make its productions accessible to those who could not typically afford or did not usually want to attend the theater, *One-Third* was seen by hundreds of thousands of citizens from across the social spectrum. For a more detailed history of *One-Third*'s production history, see Hallie Flanagan, *Arena* (New York: Duell, Sloan and Pearce, 1940); Barry Witham, *The Federal Theatre Project: A Case Study* (Cambridge: Cambridge University Press, 2003); and Elizabeth A. Osborne, *Staging the People: Community and Identity in the Federal Theatre Project* (New York: Palgrave Macmillan, 2011).

41. As the name of this obscure dramatic form implies, Living Newspapers took their subject matter from the headlines of the day and hoped to present the everyday news to audiences in a way that would "turn the great natural and economic forces of our time toward a better life for more people." "Writing the Living Newspaper," Library of Congress, Federal Theatre Collection, 9. For a more detailed cultural history of the Living Newspaper's dramatic form and the Federal Theatre Project's production

of several Living Newspapers, see Douglas McDermott, "The Living Newspaper as a Dramatic Form," *Modern Drama* 8, no. 1 (1965): 82–94; Laura Browder, *Rousing the Nation: Radical Culture in Depression America* (Amherst: University of Massachusetts Press, 1998); and Ilka Saal, *New Deal Theater: The Vernacular Tradition in American Political Theater* (New York: Palgrave Macmillan, 2007).

42. Brooks Atkinson, "Saga of the Slums," *New York Times*, January 30, 1938; Edward Carberry, Review of Arthur Arent, *One-Third of a Nation, Cincinnati Post*, n.d., record group 69, box 153, Records of the Work Projects Administration, National Archives.

43. See Linda Williams, *Playing the Race Card: Melodramas of Black and White from Uncle Tom to O. J. Simpson* (Princeton, N.J.: Princeton University Press, 2001).

44. Burns Mantle, "'One-Third of a Nation' Reveals How Two-Thirds of Nation Cheats," *Daily News*, January 18, 1938.

45. Arent, *One-Third of a Nation*, in *Federal Theatre Plays*, 14; further references cited parenthetically.

46. Detroit Federal Theatre, "'one-third of a nation . . .' Production Report," Records of the Federal Theatre Project, record group 69, National Archives at College Park, College Park, Maryland.

47. Linda Williams might say that *One-Third* played the "race card" in its efforts to deepen the audience's emotional attachments to innocent tenement-house victims. Williams, *Playing the Race Card*, 4. In doing so, *One-Third* contributed to what Stephanie Leigh Batiste has described as the FTP's "race and class radicalism" by drawing upon the "experiences, histories, and futures" of black experience. Stephanie Leigh Batiste, *Darkening Mirrors: Imperial Representation in Depression-Era African American Performance* (Durham, N.C.: Duke University Press, 2011), 20, 3.

48. The villain plays an important role in bringing what Peter Brooks calls "moral legibility" to the social problem at the heart of any melodrama by clarifying and, often, simplifying the spectator's emotional obligations. Peter Brooks, *The Melodramatic Imagination: Balzac, Henry James, Melodrama, and the Mode of Excess* (1976; New Haven, Conn.: Yale University Press, 1995), 20.

49. Richard Watts, Jr., "The Living Newspaper's 'One Third of a Nation,'" *New York Herald Tribune*, January 30, 1938.

50. See Bauer, *Modern Housing*; and Edith Elmer Wood, *Recent Trends in American Housing* (New York: Macmillan, 1931).

51. According to Michael Szalay, the New Deal's "incursion into laissez-faire labor markets brought with it new socioeconomic functions for sentimental writing." Michael Szalay, *New Deal Modernism: American Literature and the Invention of the Welfare State* (Durham, N.C.: Duke University Press, 2000), 172. *One-Third*'s melodramatic attempt to work out the emotional rationale of the state's involvement in the free-market housing economy can be understood as one expression of sentimental writing's new function.

52. Howard H. Spellman, "After Seeing a Performance of '... One-Third of a Nation...,'" March 2, 1938, Records of the Federal Theatre Project, record group 69.

53. This is the moment in the play when, to use Ben Singer's description of melodramatic affect, the "process of emotional identification or, perhaps more accurately, of association, whereby spectators superimpose their own life (melo)dramas onto the ones being represented in the narrative," reaches its climax. Ben Singer, *Melodrama and Modernity: Early Sensational Cinema and Its Contexts* (New York: Columbia University Press, 2001), 45.

54. Helen Alfred, executive director of the National Public Housing Conference (NPHC), was particularly interested in inviting influential politicians to see *One-Third*. On March 2, 1938, she wrote Senator Sherman D. Minton of Indiana to invite him and the other "members of the United States Senate to be our guests, individually or collectively, at a performance of this socially important play." Fearful that funding for the programs for which she and the NPHC had fought might dry up, Alfred felt it would "be a good idea if the Senators at first hand could see for themselves how interesting [*One-Third*] is as an educational project and as a thrilling dramatic presentation." She hoped that the play would convince these influential politicians of the need for slum clearance and public housing more powerfully than had hundreds of hours of testimony during the legislative process. Helen Alfred to Sherman D. Minton, March 2, 1938, Records of the Federal Theatre Project, record group 69. And on the eve of New Orleans's construction of an $18 million Municipal Low-Cost Housing Project, Mayor Robert S. Maestri encouraged "all civic organizations and our entire citizenry to attend at least one performance of [*One-Third*] at Jerusalem Temple." Maestri trusted that the New Orleans FTP unit and the city's Group Theatre would ensure that the entire city get behind his decision to provide an "adequate living-environment for hundreds of our citizens." "WPA Federal Theatre of New Orleans Sponsored by The Group Theatre of New Orleans Presents '... one-third of a nation...' A Living Newspaper About Housing by Arthur Arent," Records of the Federal Theatre Project, Record Group 69.

55. "Model PWA Homes Opened to Public," *New York Times*, July 27, 1937; "19,000 Seek Space in Flats Project," *New York Times*, July 23, 1937. For more information about the history of Williamsburg Houses, see Richard Plunz, *A History of Housing in New York City* (New York: Columbia University Press, 1992), 219–21; Nicholas Dagen Bloom, *Public Housing That Worked: New York in the Twentieth Century* (Philadelphia: University of Pennsylvania Press, 2008), 50–55; and Peter Laurence, *Becoming Jane Jacobs* (Philadelphia: University of Pennsylvania Press, 2016), 44–47.

56. Federal Administration of Public Works, *Williamsburg Houses: A Case History of Housing* (Washington, D.C.: U.S. Government Printing Office, 1937), 5–7.

57. Charles S. Bilker, "Friendly Neighbors One and All," *The Projector* 1, 2, January 1, 1938, box 53E8, folder 14, New York City Housing Authority Records (hereafter NYCHA) La Guardia and Wagner Archives, La Guardia Community College, 3. Tenants of Williamsburg Houses were aided in their efforts to establish their new com-

munity by the NYCHA significant investment of resources in new types of tenant and community programs.

58. Lillian Cicio, "A Friend in Deed," *The Projector*, March 31, 1938, box 53E8, folder 14, NYCHA Records, 3.

59. "Our First Anniversary," *The Projector*, November 11, 1938, box 53E8, folder 14, NYCHA Records, 2.

60. I borrow the term "modern housing planners" from D. Bradford Hunt. For excellent accounts of the arguments put forward by Bauer and other "modern housing planners," see Hunt, "Was the 1937 U.S. Housing Act a Pyrrhic Victory?" *Journal of Planning History* 4, no. 3 (2005): 195–221; and Von Hoffman, "The End of the Dream."

Chapter 3. Literary Urbanists and the Interwar Development of Urban Sociability

1. Betty Smith, *A Tree Grows in Brooklyn* (1943; New York: HarperPerennial, 2006), 487.

2. Ibid., 367–68.

3. Georg Simmel, "The Sociology of Sociability," trans. Everett C. Hughes, *American Journal of Sociology* 55, no. 3 (1949): 255, 256, 255, 259.

4. For a history of the changing landscape of urban downtowns during the twentieth century, see Robert M. Fogelson, *Downtown: Its Rise and Fall, 1880–1950* (New Haven, Conn.: Yale University Press, 2001); and Alison Isenberg, *Downtown America: A History of the Place and the People Who Made It* (Chicago: University of Chicago Press, 2004).

5. Harold Ross, "Prospectus," 1924, *New Yorker* Records, box 2, folder 3, Manuscripts and Archives Division, New York Public Library, 1; Constance Moremus to *New Yorker*, May 5, 1951, New Yorker Records, box 952, Letters to the Editor (Praise), 1950–1959, New York Public Library. For additional studies of the *New Yorker*'s sophisticated style, see Mary Corey, *The World Through a Monocle: The* New Yorker *at Midcentury* (Cambridge, Mass.: Harvard University Press, 2000); and Louis Menand, *American Studies* (New York: Farrar, Straus, and Giroux, 2002).

6. *New Yorker* editors and staff created several different rubrics for fact writing. The writing appearing in the magazine's "Talk of the Town" and "Notes and Comment" sections consisted primarily of short pieces of reportage. The magazine's lengthier fact-writing rubrics included "Profiles," "A Reporter at Large," "Onward and Upward with the Arts," "Annals of Crime," "Our Footloose Correspondents," and "Letters"— all of which were vehicles for delivering facts, often about some aspect of city life, to readers, with as little editorializing as possible. For additional information about *New Yorker* fact writing, see Brendan Gill, *Here at* The New Yorker (New York: Random House, 1975); Thomas Kunkel, *Genius in Disguise: Harold Ross of the* New Yorker (New York: Random House, 1995); and Ben Yagoda, *About Town: The* New Yorker *and the World It Made* (New York: Da Capo, 2001).

7. E. B. White, "A Reporter at Large: News Outside the Door," *New Yorker*, October 28, 1933, 54, 58.

8. Alva Johnston, "A Reporter at Large: A Tour of Minskyville," *New Yorker*, August 6, 1932, 34, 37.

9. Sherwood Anderson, "A Reporter at Large: Stewart's, on the Square," *New Yorker*, June 9, 1934, 78, 77, 79.

10. Margaret Case Harriman, introduction to *Take Them Up Tenderly: A Collection of Profiles* (New York: Knopf, 1944), xi.

11. Alva Johnston, "Profiles: Cauliflower King—II," *New Yorker*, April 15, 1933, 18.

12. Joseph Mitchell, "Profiles: Mazie," *New Yorker*, December 21, 1940, 22, 23, 28.

13. Ibid., 22, 28.

14. A. J. Liebling, "Profiles: The Jollity Building I: Indians, Heels, and Tenants," *New Yorker*, April 26, 1941, 22, 23.

15. Ibid., 29, 30–31, 23.

16. Ibid., 26.

17. A. J. Liebling, "Profiles: The Jollity Building II: From Hunger," *New Yorker*, May 3, 1941, 24, 22, 29.

18. Meyer Berger, "Green Sunless Weed: *A Tree Grows in Brooklyn*," review of *A Tree Grows in Brooklyn*, by Betty Smith, *New York Times*, August 22, 1943.

19. Florence Haxton Bullock, "Growing Up Beside the Williamsburg Bridge," review of *A Tree Grows in Brooklyn*, by Betty Smith, *New York Herald Tribune*, August 22, 1943.

20. Orville Prescott, review of *A Tree Grows in Brooklyn*, by Betty Smith, *New York Times*, August 18, 1943.

21. For a thorough account of *A Tree Grows in Brooklyn*'s popular appeal, see Judith E. Smith, *Visions of Belonging: Family Stories, Popular Culture, and Postwar Democracy, 1940–1960* (New York: Columbia University Press, 2004). Smith explains that the novel "became part of a broad public conversation: Parent Teacher Associations, neighborhood groups, and women's clubs sponsored discussions of it; libraries reported that *Tree* was their most frequently requested book; ministers made reference to it in sermons.... By 1945 the book had sold three million copies" (41).

22. Smith, *A Tree Grows in Brooklyn*, 487, 6; further references to be cited parenthetically. The building at 227 Stagg Street, where Smith and her family lived for a time, was demolished during the construction of Williamsburg Houses. For a thorough account of Smith's experiences with the Federal Theatre Project, see Valerie Raleigh Yow, *Betty Smith: Life of the Author of* A Tree Grows in Brooklyn (Chapel Hill, N.C.: Wolf's Pond Press, 2008). According to Yow, Smith began acting on the FTP's "subway circuit" in New York City early in 1936 (82). After securing a FTP position at the University of North Carolina-Chapel Hill in May 1936, Smith and three other playwrights began writing the script for a Living Newspaper production about the cotton industry called *King Cotton* (97–98).

23. Betty Smith to Murry Godwin, November 16, 1928, quoted in Carol Siri Johnson, "The Life and Work of Betty Smith, Author of *A Tree Grows in Brooklyn*," Ph.D. dissertation, City University of New York, 1995, 51.

24. See Edward Said, *Orientalism* (New York: Pantheon, 1978).

25. Liebling, "Profiles: The Jollity Building II," 22.

26. See Arnold L. Hirsch, *Making the Second Ghetto: Race and Housing in Chicago, 1940–1960* (Chicago: University of Chicago Press, 1983); James R. Grossman, *Land of Hope: Chicago, Black Southerners, and the Great Migration* (Chicago: University of Chicago Press, 1989); Douglas S. Massey and Nancy Denton, *American Apartheid: Segregation and the Making of the Underclass* (Cambridge, Mass.: Harvard University Press, 1993); Farrah Jasmine Griffin, *"Who Set You Flowin'"? The African-American Migration Narrative* (New York: Oxford University Press, 1995); Thomas Sugrue, *The Origins of the Urban Crisis: Race and Inequality in Postwar Detroit* (Princeton, N.J.: Princeton University Press, 1996); Davison Douglas, *Jim Crow Moves North: The Battle over Northern School Segregation, 1865–1954* (New York: Cambridge University Press, 2005); and Khalil Gibran Muhammad, *The Condemnation of Blackness: Race, Crime, and the Making of Modern Urban America* (Cambridge, Mass.: Harvard University Press, 2010).

27. Richard Wright, *Native Son* (1940; New York: HarperPerennial, 1993), 20, 72.

28. St. Clair Drake and Horace R. Cayton, *Black Metropolis: A Study of Negro Life in a Northern City* (New York: Harcourt, Brace, 1945).

29. See Davarian L. Baldwin, *Chicago's New Negroes: Modernity, the Great Migration, and Black Urban Life* (Chapel Hill: University of North Carolina Press, 2007); Adam Green, *Selling the Race: Culture, Community, and Black Chicago, 1940–1955* (Chicago: University of Chicago Press, 2009); Jeffrey Helgeson, *Crucibles of Black Empowerment: Chicago's Neighborhood Politics from the New Deal to Harold Washington* (Chicago: University of Chicago Press, 2014); Lionel Kimble, Jr., *A New Deal for Bronzeville: Housing, Employment, and Civil Rights in Black Chicago, 1935–1955* (Carbondale: Southern Illinois University Press, 2015).

30. Nella Larsen, *Quicksand*, in *The Complete Fiction of Nella Larsen*, ed. Charles R. Larson (1928; New York: Anchor, 2001), 77, 125, 78.

Chapter 4. The Ecology of Sociability in the Postwar City

1. Edith Oliver, a staff editor at the *New Yorker*, had recommended Carson's manuscript for *The Sea Around Us* in 1950 to editor-in-chief William Shawn. Shawn had been even more enthusiastic about this relatively unknown naturalist and offered to buy nine of the book's fourteen chapters. He then condensed these chapters and published them, rather unusually, as a three-part series in June 1951 under the magazine's "Profiles" rubric.

2. Harold Ross, "Announcing a New Weekly Magazine: *The New Yorker*," reprinted in Kunkel, *Genius in Disguise*, 440.

3. Harrison Smith, "The Best Sellers," *Saturday Review of Literature*, October 27, 1951, 22; Dr. T. McKean Downs to *New Yorker*, July 2, 1951, Rachel Carson Papers, box 13, folder 229, Yale Collection of American Literature, Beinecke Rare Book and Manuscript Library, Yale University (hereafter Rachel Carson Papers); Miriam Teichner to Harold Ross, June 12, 1951, Rachel Carson Papers, box 13, folder 236.

4. Talk of the Town, "Ecological Exhibit," *New Yorker*, June 9, 1951, 22.

5. Community ecology was primarily concerned with describing individual organisms as members of larger intraspecies and interspecies aggregates. See Robert McIntosh, *The Background of Ecology: Concept and Theory* (New York: Cambridge University Press, 1985); Greg Mitman, *The State of Nature: Ecology, Community, and American Social Thought, 1900–1950* (Chicago: University of Chicago Press, 1992); and Michael Barbour, "Ecological Fragmentation in the Fifties," in *Uncommon Ground: Toward Reinventing Nature*, ed. William Cronon (New York: Norton, 1995).

6. The literature on the history of postwar urban history is extensive. For a good, but by no means exhaustive, introduction to this literature, see Martin Anderson, *The Federal Bulldozer: A Critical Analysis of Urban Renewal, 1949–1962* (Cambridge, Mass.: MIT Press, 1964); James Q. Wilson, ed., *Urban Renewal: The Record and the Controversy* (Cambridge, Mass.: MIT Press, 1966); Mark I. Gelfand, *A Nation of Cities: The Federal Government and Urban America, 1933–1965* (New York: Oxford University Press, 1975); Arnold Hirsch, *Making the Second Ghetto: Race and Housing in Chicago, 1940–1960* (New York: Cambridge University Press, 1983); Jon C. Teaford, *The Rough Road to Urban Renaissance: Urban Revitalization in America, 1940–1985* (Baltimore: Johns Hopkins University Press, 1990); Sugrue, *The Origins of the Urban Crisis*; Carlo Rotella, *October Cities: The Redevelopment of Urban Literature* (Berkeley: University of California Press, 1998); Robert O. Self, *American Babylon: Race and the Struggle for Postwar Oakland* (Princeton, N.J.: Princeton University Press, 2003); Samuel Zipp, *Manhattan Projects: The Rise and Fall of Urban Renewal in Cold War New York* (New York: Oxford University Press, 2010); Roger Biles, *The Fate of Cities: Urban America and the Federal Government, 1945–2000* (Lawrence: University Press of Kansas, 2011); and Christopher Klemek, *The Transatlantic Collapse of Urban Renewal: Postwar Urbanism from New York to Berlin* (Chicago: University of Chicago Press, 2011).

7. Robert E. Park, "The City: Suggestions for the Investigation of Human Behavior in the Urban Environment," *American Journal of Sociology* 20, no. 5 (1915): 577–612. The work of ecologist Frederic Clements perhaps best exemplifies the scientific principles through which the Chicago school sociologists explained the distribution of different ethnic groups and commercial enterprises throughout the city. For more detailed accounts of the Chicago school of sociology's Darwinian approach to ecology, see Brian Berry and John D. Kasarda, *Contemporary Urban Ecology* (New York: Macmillan, 1977), 4–7; and Larry Lyon, *The Community in Urban Society* (Philadelphia: Temple University Press, 1987), 32–40.

8. See Jennifer Light, *The Nature of Cities: Ecological Visions and the American Urban Professions, 1920–1960* (Baltimore: Johns Hopkins University Press, 2009). Light offers a thorough and convincing account of the ways this first iteration of urban ecology shaped the approach that a wide range of urbanists took to the city from the 1920s through the 1950s.

9. Sharon Kingsland describes the city as a "'new frontier' of ecology" during the mid-twentieth century. Sharon Kingsland, *The Evolution of American Ecology, 1890–2000* (Baltimore: Johns Hopkins University Press, 2005), 232.

10. W. C. Allee, Alfred E. Emerson, Orlando Park, Thomas Park, and Karl P. Schmidt, *Principles of Animal Ecology* (Philadelphia: Saunders, 1949), 1.

11. W. C. Allee, *Animal Life and Social Growth* (Baltimore: Williams & Wilkins, 1932), 149; W. C. Allee, "Where Angels Fear to Tread: A Contribution from General Sociology to Human Ethics," *Science*, June 11, 1943, 521.

12. Allee et al., *Principles*, 418.

13. W. C. Allee, "Relatively Simple Animal Aggregations," in *A Handbook of Social Psychology*, ed. Carl Murchison (1935; New York: Russell & Russell, 1967), 942.

14. W. C. Allee, *Cooperation Among Animals: With Human Implications* (New York: Henry Schuman, 1951), 21. This monograph was a revised and enhanced edition of Allee's *The Social Life of Animals*, first published in 1938.

15. Allee, "Where Angels Fear," 519.

16. The intellectual history of community ecology featured in the *Principles of Animal Ecology* is an expanded version of passages that Allee appears to have first published in *The Social Life of Animals* (1938). He continued to include segments of this history in later publications such as "Where Angels Fear to Tread" (1943) and *Cooperation Among Animals* (1951).

17. Allee et al., *Principles*, 30.

18. Allee, "Where Angels Fear," 522, 523, 524, 525.

19. Albert E. Parr, "The Year's Work," in *Seventy-Fourth Annual Report for the Year 1942* (New York: American Museum of Natural History, 1943), 14, 15.

20. As Donna Haraway points out, Akeley Hall told a story about "communities and families" that were "peacefully and hierarchically ordered" along traditional gender lines. Donna Haraway, "Teddy Bear Patriarchy: Taxidermy in the Garden of Eden, New York City, 1908–1936," *Social Text* 11 (Winter 1984/1985): 24.

21. In an internal memo written around July 1942 (during the beginning stages of planning Warburg Hall), it was most likely Parr who explained to AMNH employees, "In planning a hall the first question should be—not what objects do we want to place in the hall—but what STORY DO WE WANT THE HALL TO TELL. The objects should be used to drive home the salient points of the story and should (exceptions of course) no longer, except for study purposes, be regarded as sufficient unto themselves." In Ann Reynolds, "Visual Stories," in *Visual Display: Culture Beyond Appearances*, ed. Lynne Cooke and Peter Wollen (Seattle: Bay Press, 1995), 93.

22. Albert E. Parr, "Purposes and Progress Report of the Director," in *Eighty-Second Annual Report July, 1950, through June, 1951* (New York: American Museum of Natural History, 1951), 8. For a broader history of the transformations that the AMNH and, more generally, natural history museums experienced in the postwar years, see Karen A. Radar and Victoria E. M. Cain, *Life on Display: Revolutionizing U.S. Museums of Science and Natural History in the Twentieth Century* (Chicago: University of Chicago Press, 2014).

23. Earl A. Martin to Albert E. Parr, May 7, 1952, American Museum of Natural History, Central Archives, 1289.

24. In a survey conducted by William Schwarting in June 1951, visitors to Warburg Hall listed "Life in the Soil" as a favorite exhibit more frequently than any other exhibit. See William Schwarting, "Report on Felix M. Warburg Memorial Hall," June 8, 1951, American Museum of Natural History, Central Archives, 1237, 2. In my own visits to Warburg Hall, I observed that "Life in the Soil" is one of the few displays in Warburg Hall that still has the ability to capture the contemporary visitor's interest.

25. Albert E. Parr, *Mostly About Museums* (New York: American Museum of Natural History, 1959), 13.

26. Schwarting, "Report," 1.

27. Simmel, "Sociology of Sociability," 255. The AMNH witnessed a dramatic increase in attendance during the 1950s—when it surged to between 1.6 and 2.1 million annual visits. While it is impossible to know exactly how many of those visitors passed through Warburg Hall, according to several accounts, it was one of the AMNH's principal attractions during the fifties. In his January 1952 report for the Meeting of the Board of Trustees, Clarence L. Hay, secretary of the AMNH, informed the board that the "opening of the Warburg Memorial Hall is largely responsible for the impressive attendance figure of over 1,018,000 people for the first half of the fiscal year." Clarence L. Hay, "Report of the Secretary: Meeting of the Board of Trustees," April 30, 1951, American Museum of Natural History, Central Archives, 1158.1.

28. Allee, *Cooperation Among Animals*, 21.

29. The AMNH and the ecologists that it employed served as important resources for Carson as she researched and wrote about the sea. Parr's ecological study of sargassum weed and other obscure marine species were part of what Carson referred to as that vast body of "dry and exceedingly technical papers of scientists" through which she had to slog in order to "weld together" her "profile of the sea." Rachel Carson, "Origins of the Book, *The Sea Around Us*," Rachel Carson Papers, box 9, folder 162, 4. Carson also relied on the ecological expertise of Parr's colleagues at the AMNH. She claimed to "know of no one" who could communicate the nature of "ecological relationships and concepts" more clearly than Robert C. Murphy, the AMNH's Lamont Curator of Birds; his "insight into the intricacies of ecological relationships" was, she informed him, the "thing I always get most clearly from your books." Rachel Carson to Robert C. Murphy, April 11, 1950; and Rachel Carson to Robert C. Murphy, Octo-

ber 19, 1950, Rachel Carson Papers, box 12, folder 209. Carson held an equal amount of admiration for Richard Pough, the curator of the AMNH's Department of Conservation and Use of Natural Resources and founder of the Nature Conservancy. Because Pough's "interests [were] so prominently identified with the general field of ecology," she sought his "appraisal" of her work. Rachel Carson to Richard Pough, November 3, 1950, Rachel Carson Papers, box 103, folder 1973.

30. Robert Lamond to the *New Yorker*, June 14, 1951, Rachel Carson Papers, box 13, folder 231. See Liebling, "Profiles: The Jollity Building I," 22–31; and Liebling, "Profiles: The Jollity Building II," 22–29.

31. Rachel Carson, "Profiles: The Sea: I—Unforgotten World," *New Yorker*, June 2, 1951, 38.

32. Rachel Carson, "Profiles: The Edge of the Sea II: The Rocky Shores," *New Yorker*, August 27, 1955, 59.

33. Rachel Carson, "Profiles: The Edge of the Sea I: The Rim of Sand," *New Yorker*, August 20, 1955, 51, 46, 45, 50.

34. Carson, "The Edge of the Sea II," 50, 55, 55, 46, 50.

35. Carson, "The Edge of the Sea I," 34.

36. Allee observed, for instance, that a "major biological contribution to the discussion of a post-war world is that, solidly as the peck-right system is grounded in animal behavior, it is not the only pattern for human action that biology has to offer. Other animals show a somewhat stronger tendency toward essential cooperations than they do toward struggles for egoistic power." We need, Allee insisted, to "help arrange so that the existing trend toward a workable world organization will be guided along practical lines which accord with sound biological theory" (Allee, "Where Angels Fear to Tread," 525).

37. See Charlotte Brooks, "In the Twilight Zone Between Black and White: Japanese American Resettlement and Community in Chicago, 1942–1945," *Journal of American History* 86, no. 4 (2000): 1655–87; Lilia Fernandez, *Brown in the Windy City: Mexicans and Puerto Ricans in Postwar Chicago* (Chicago: University of Chicago Press, 2012); and Michael Innis-Jiménez, *Steel Barrio: The Great Mexican Migration to South Chicago, 1915–1940* (New York: New York University Press, 2013).

38. Marjorie Hill Allee, *The House* (Boston: Houghton Mifflin, 1944), 180, 45–46.

39. Ibid., 36, 75.

40. J. B. Jackson, "Human, All Too Human, Geography," *Landscape* 2, no. 2 (1952): 3.

41. J. B. Jackson, "The Stranger's Path," *Landscape* 7, no. 1 (1957): 15, 14.

42. Hubert B. Owens, Letter to the Editor, *Landscape* 10, no. 1 (1960): 5. Although its circulation numbers were relatively modest, *Landscape* and its particular blend of ecological urbanisms influenced the thinking of many of the postwar period's most influential urban intellectuals. In its ten-year anniversary issue, Louis I. Kahn, Ian L. McHarg, Paul Sears, Christopher Tunnard, and Lewis Mumford praised *Landscape* for what the latter described as its understanding of the "essential inter-relationship of

place and work and people." Lewis Mumford, Letter to the Editor, ibid. For an assessment of the significance of Jackson's work on cultural landscape studies, see Chris Wilson and Paul Groth, eds., *Everyday America: Cultural Landscape Studies* (Berkeley: University of California Press, 2003).

43. J. B. Jackson, "The Imitation of Nature," *Landscape* 9, No. 1 (1959): 9.

44. Grady Clay, "Symbiosis and the City," *Landscape* 9, no. 2 (1959–60): 9.

45. Edgar Anderson, "The City Is a Garden," *Landscape* 7, no. 2 (1957–58): 3, 5.

46. Edgar Anderson, "The Country in the City," *Landscape* 5, no. 3 (1956): 34, 35.

47. Anderson, "The City Is a Garden," 5.

48. Edgar Anderson, "The City Watcher," *Landscape* 8, no. 2 (1958–59): 8.

49. Allee, *Cooperation Among Animals*, 21.

50. Jean Gottmann, "Revolution in Land Use," *Landscape* 8, no. 2 (1958–59): 19, 20.

51. Jackson, "Imitation of Nature," 9, 10, 11.

52. See Albert E. Parr, "Psychological Aspects of Urbanology," *Journal of Social Issues* 22, no. 4 (1966): 39–45; and Albert E. Parr, "The Five Ages of Urbanity," *Landscape* 17, no. 3 (1968): 7–10.

53. Albert E. Parr, "City and Psyche," *Yale Review* 55 (1965): 71.

54. Parr, *Mostly About Museums*, 102.

55. "Museums Too Musty for Moses; He Says They Intimidate Visitors," *New York Times*, March 3, 1941.d

56. "Museum of Natural History Here Will Be Modernized After the War," *New York Times*, January 12, 1943. See Robert Stern, Thomas Mellins, and David Fishman, *New York 1960: Architecture and Urbanism Between the Second World War and the Bicentennial* (New York: Monacelli Press, 1995), 664.

57. Parr, "City and Psyche," 72; Parr, "Psychological Aspects," 42.

58. Albert E. Parr, "City as Habitat," *Centennial Review* 14, no. 2 (1970): 185–86.

59. Ibid., 185, 187.

60. Albert E. Parr, "Environmental Design and Psychology," *Landscape* 14, no. 2 (1964–65): 17.

61. Albert E. Parr, "The Design of Cities," *Architectural Association Quarterly* 3, no. 3 (1971): 23; Albert E. Parr, "The Child in the City: Urbanity and the Urban Scene," *Landscape* 16, no. 3 (1967): 4; Parr, "Design of Cities," 24.

62. Parr, "Child in the City," 4.

63. Albert E. Parr, "The Happy Habitat," *Journal of Aesthetic Education* 6, no. 3 (1972): 30–31.

Chapter 5. Jane Jacobs and the Consolidation of Urban Sociability

1. For studies that examine the effects of the U.S. Housing Act of 1949 and urban redevelopment more broadly on New York City, see J. Clarence Davies, III, *Neighborhood Groups and Urban Renewal* (New York: Columbia University Press, 1966); Joel

Schwartz, *The New York Approach: Robert Moses, Urban Liberals, and Redevelopment of the Inner City* (Columbus: Ohio State University Press, 1993); Hillary Ballon and Kenneth T. Jackson, eds., *Robert Moses and the Modern City: The Transformation of New York* (New York: Norton, 2007); Nicholas Dagen Bloom, *Public Housing That Worked: New York in the Twentieth Century* (Philadelphia: University of Pennsylvania Press, 2008); and Zipp, *Manhattan Projects*.

2. Urban historians have recently pointed out the need to situate urban renewal in the context of a history of ideas and culture rather than exclusively in social and political histories. This chapter and book are an attempt to do just that. See Samuel Zipp and Michael Carriere, "Thinking Through Urban Renewal," *Journal of Urban History* 39, no. 3 (2013): 359–65.

3. Sandy Zipp, Carlo Rotella, Christopher Klemek, Mandi Isaacs Jackson, Michael Carriere, Jennifer Hock, and other urban historians have recently reminded us that this fight for the right to determine the imaginative shape that the city should take and the type of relationships that the city ought to shelter was taken up by a host of urbanists who used a variety of representational strategies and mediums. See Rotella, *October Cities*; Mandi Isaacs Jackson, *Model City Blues: Urban Space and Organized Resistance in New Haven* (Philadelphia: Temple University Press, 2008); Zipp, *Manhattan Projects*; Klemek, *Transatlantic Collapse of Urban Renewal*; Michael Carriere, "Fighting the War Against Blight: Columbia University, Morningside Heights, Inc., and Counterinsurgent Urban Renewal," *Journal of Planning History* 10, no. 1 (2011): 5–29; and Jennifer Hock, "Bulldozers, Busing, and Boycotts: Urban Renewal and the Integrationist Project," *Journal of Urban History* 39, no. 3 (2013): 433–53.

4. Jane Jacobs, "The Missing Link in City Redevelopment," *Architectural Forum* 104 (June 1956): 133. This article was adapted from Jacobs's talk at the 1956 Harvard Urban Design Conference.

5. Jacobs, *Death and Life of Great American Cities*, 16, 15, 3.

6. Jane Jacobs to Chadbourne Gilpatric, July 1, 1958, box 390, folder 3380, , series 200R, RG 1.2, Rockefeller Foundation Archives, Rockefeller Archive Center (hereafter Rockefeller Foundation Archives); Jane Jacobs to Chadbourne Gilpatric, June 14, 1958; Jacobs to Gilpatric, July 1, 1958; Jacobs, *Death and Life*, 138. Unfortunately, many readers have misread the nature of her intervention, mistakenly assuming with Lewis Mumford that, for Jacobs, urban communities consisted exclusively of "a cluster of warm personal sentiments, associated with the familiar faces of the doctor and the priest, the butcher and the baker and the candle-stick maker." But as Jacobs would repeatedly make clear, the relationships that were so fundamental to life in the city were not necessarily those among "warmhearted neighbors." Unlike Mumford, she did not locate the "communal nucleus of the city" in the " 'primary' association of families and neighbors." Lewis Mumford, "The Sky Line: Mother Jacobs' Home Remedies," *New Yorker*, December 1, 1962, 152, 168.

7. Urban historian Robert Fishman, for instance, claims to "know of no earlier and certainly no more eloquent and perceptive source" for the "discourse of public space"

than the "first six chapters of *Death and Life*." "The Mumford-Jacobs Debate," *Planning History Studies* 10, no. 1-2 (1996): 7.

8. Jacobs to Gilpatric, July 1, 1958.

9. Herbert Gans, "The Dream of Human Cities," *New Republic*, June 7, 1969, 30. For a much more thorough and extensive treatment of Jacobs's life and work prior to the publication of *Death and Life*, see Laurence, *Becoming Jane Jacobs*.

10. Charles Abrams, Henry S. Churchill, Leonard K. Eaton, Robert L. Geddes, Percival Goodman, Kevin Lynch, Eugene Raskin, and Catherine Bauer Wurster, review of Jane Jacobs, *The Death and Life of Great American Cities*, "Abattoir for Sacred Cows," *P/A* (April 1962): 196.

11. Jane Jacobs, "Public Life—At Sidewalk Scale," n.d., Jane Jacobs Papers, MS95-29, box 25, folder 8, Burns Library, Boston College, 2 (hereafter Jane Jacobs Papers).

12. Jane Butzner [Jacobs], "Diamonds in the Tough," *Vogue*, October 15, 1936, 156.

13. Jacobs, *Death and Life*, 50.

14. Jane Butzner [Jacobs], "Where the Fur Flies," *Vogue*, November 15, 1935, 103. For Jacobs's other uses of "dickering" in her *Vogue* articles, see Butzner [Jacobs], "Diamonds in the Tough," 154; and Jane Butzner [Jacobs], "Flowers Come to Town," *Vogue*, February 15, 1937, 113.

15. "Our Policy (?)," *Village Voice*, November 30, 1955, 4; "Those People Down There," *Village Voice*, May 30, 1956, 4. According to Robert Fishman, the *Voice* mounted the "*intellectual* opposition to Moses that would transform American urbanism." Robert Fishman, "Revolt of the Urbs: Robert Moses and His Critics," in *Robert Moses and the Modern City: The Transformation of New York*, ed. Hilary Ballon and Kenneth T. Jackson (New York: Norton, 2007), 125–26.

16. "The Park," *Village Voice*, November 9, 1955, 4. Many of the *Voice*'s early readers saw it as an attempt—often a failed one—to produce a neighborhood newspaper version of the *New Yorker*. Frances Beamis, for instance, complained that the first issue of the *Village Voice* was "too obvious an attempt to be original and entertaining" and tried to put its editors in their place by informing them that their fledgling weekly was "not a Village newspaper, nor is it a *Cue* or *New Yorker*." "Not Wanted," *Village Voice*, November 2, 1955, 4. Another reader warned the *Voice* of "forcing a pseudo-sophistication that your writers are not clever enough to carry through." "Pseudo-Sophisticated Imitators?" *Village Voice*, November 2, 1955, 4.

17. Smith, *A Tree Grows in Brooklyn*, 487.

18. Jane Jacobs, "Downtown Is for People," *Fortune*, April 1958, 139, 134, 137–38, 240.

19. Sennett, *The Fall of Public Man*, 338, 339.

20. Jacobs, *Death and Life*, 62, 115, 62; hereafter cited in parentheses in the text. In drawing such a stark contrast between the social landscapes of villages and cities, Jacobs (perhaps knowingly) oversimplified the distinction between the two. Herbert Gans's *The Urban Villagers* (1962) and Oscar Lewis's *La Vida* (1966) would articulate substantial challenges to the folk/urban-society binary on which Jacobs relied. See

Herbert Gans, *The Urban Villagers: Group and Class in the Life of Italian-Americans* (New York: Free Press, 1962); Oscar Lewis, *La Vida: A Puerto Rican Family in the Culture of Poverty—San Juan and New York* (New York: Random House, 1966); and Ulf Hannerz, *Exploring the City: Inquiries Toward an Urban Anthropology* (New York: Columbia University Press, 1980), Chapter 3.

21. Jacobs, "Public Life—At Sidewalk Scale," 2.

22. For a more thorough exploration of the settlement movement's complex relationship to urban renewal, see Jamin Rowan, "Sidewalk Narratives, Tenement Narratives: Seeing Urban Renewal through the Settlement Movement," *Journal of Urban History* 39, no. 3 (2013): 392–410.

23. Ellen Lurie, "A Study of George Washington Houses: The Effect of the Project on Its Tenants and the Surrounding Community," 1955–1956, Union Settlement Association Papers, box 11, bolder 13, Columbia University Rare Book and Manuscript Library, ii (hereafter Union Settlement Association Papers).

24. Although Jacobs singled out Kirk as the principal source of her urban vision, she cited various settlement workers throughout *Death and Life* as authoritative interpreters of city life. In *Death and Life*, Jacobs praised Mary Kingsbury Simkhovitch of New York City's Greenwich House for fusing the "neighborhood networks" through which Greenwich Village had acquired much of its "social capital" (138). She credited Frank Havey, settlement director of Boston's North End Union, for recognizing that the city sidewalk is the space where a healthy urban "community is at its strongest" (79). In addition to crediting these settlement leaders for teaching her particularly valuable lessons in how to see and think about urban relationships, Jacobs singled out Blake Hobbs and Ellen Lurie of East Harlem's Union Settlement, Helen Hall of the Lower East Side's Henry Street Settlement, and Dora Tannenbaum of the Lower East Side's Grand Street Settlement as key figures in her intellectual genealogy.

25. I. D. Robbins was one of the first to criticize Jacobs for not paying "attention to the matters of class, race, and intercultural relationships and their effect on where and how people live." I. D. Robbins, review of *The Death and Life of Great American Cities*, by Jane Jacobs, *Village Voice*, November 16, 1961, 16. More recently, William Saunders has worried that, by turning a blind eye to issues of race and class, Jacobs's urban vision has produced what he dubs the "comfortable passive pleasures of cappuccino urbanism." William Saunders, "Cappuccino Urbanism, and Beyond," *Harvard Design Magazine* 25 (2006/2007): 3.

26. Lurie, "A Study of George Washington Houses," Union Settlement Association Papers, box 11, folder 13, ii, II-24, II-23.

27. In Zipp, *Manhattan Projects*, 322, 323. Zipp suggests that "A Study of George Washington Houses" provided the facts that enabled social researchers from Union Settlement to "recognize the beginnings of an uprising against public housing and urban renewal-fed displacement on the part of public housing residents themselves." These discoveries put Union Settlement and its East Harlem collaborators in a position to turn the "East Harlem experience" into what Zipp claims was a "major source

of inspiration for an informal, but ultimately effective, movement to dislodge modernist urbanism from its reigning influence over the practice of architecture and planning, an effort that made up one part of the revolt against urban renewal" (303).

28. Lurie, "A Study of George Washington Houses," V:5.

29. Perkins & Will Architects, "DeWitt Clinton Housing Study," January 8, 1959, Union Settlement Association Papers, box 35, folder 8, , 1–2. Originally founded in 1921, the East Harlem Council for Community Planning had been a local civic and business group settlement workers and other social activists revived in the 1950s in an attempt to spark community development; see Zipp, *Manhattan Projects*, 320.

30. Jane Jacobs, untitled manuscript, February 3, 1959, Union Settlement Association Papers, box 35, folder 8, 2–4. Ellen Lurie describes this untitled manuscript in another document as "Jane Jacobs' Presentation to the Housing Authority on DeWitt Clinton."

31. Ibid., 7–8.

32. Ibid., 8–13, 16.

33. William Reid, the chairman of the NYCHA, informed Kirk that the Housing Committee's proposals were rejected because they "violated the Multiple Dwelling Law of New York State and the Building Code and the Zoning Resolution of New York City.... These legal and other defects went to the very heart of the proposals made by Perkins and Will, so that the adoption of their plan was impossible." William Reid to William Kirk, March 17, 1961, Union Settlement Association Papers, box 36, folder 10, 1–2. Kirk responded by reminding Reid that Jacobs had acknowledged the possibility that "their plan permitted modifications to achieve full compliance"—modifications the NYCHA apparently refused to consider. William Kirk to William Reid, April 4, 1961, Union Settlement Association Papers, box 36, folder 10, 1.

34. As Peter Laurence has shown, Jacobs's interest in ecology and the life sciences dates back at least as far as her studies at Columbia University in the late 1930s. While enrolled in the university's extension program, Jacobs took courses in biology, zoology, and geology. See Laurence, *Becoming Jane Jacobs*, 54. When she published *Death and Life*, it was, as David Kinkela demonstrates, "part of a larger ideological movement that embraced ecology as an alternative model for human development." David Kinkela, "The Ecological Landscapes of Jane Jacobs and Rachel Carson," *American Quarterly* 61, no. 4 (2009): 905. Alongside works such as Jean Gottman's *Megalopolis: The Urbanized Eastern Seaboard of the United States* (New York: Twentieth-Century Fund, 1961) and Lewis Mumford's *The City in History: Its Origins, Its Transformations, and Its Prospects* (New York: Harcourt, Brace and World, 1961), *Death and Life* "reinstated," as Michael Sorkin points out, the "conceptual centrality of ecology ... in the production of urban models." Michael Sorkin, "The End[s] of Urban Design," *Harvard Design Magazine* 25 (2006/07): 7.

35. Jane Jacobs, untitled manuscript, April 20, 1958, Jane Jacobs Papers, MS95-29, box 25, 2.

36. Jane Jacobs, Foreword to *The Death and Life of Great American Cities* (New York: Modern Library, 1993), xvii.

37. "Planning: Waste or Wisdom?" *National Observer*, April 22, 1962, 12.

38. Karl Fogel to Jane Jacobs, August, 1997, Jane Jacobs Papers, MS02-13, box 1, folder 1.

39. West Village Committee, *The West Village Plan for Housing* (New York: West Village Committee, 1963), Jane Jacobs Papers, box 3, folder 2.

40. Ibid.

41. In Mary Perot Nichols, "Inner City Infill: Build In, Don't Bulldoze," *Apartment Life, Liberty and the Pursuit of Happiness* (September 1977: 32). For a much more thorough account of Jacobs's involvement in the West Village Houses, see Christopher Klemek, "From Political Outsider to Power Broker in Two 'Great American Cities': Jane Jacobs and the Fall of the Urban Renewal Order in New York and Toronto," *Journal of Urban History* 34, no. 2 (2008): 309–32.

42. See Klemek, *Transatlantic Collapse*.

43. Jacobs to Gilpatric, July 1, 1958.

44. Ibid.

45. Jacobs to Gilpatric, June 14, 1958.

Conclusion. The Future of Urban Sociability

1. Olmsted, "Public Parks and the Enlargement of Towns," 187

2. For a more thorough history of and assessment of the High Line, see Joshua David and Robert Hammond, *High Line: The Inside Story of New York City's Park in the Sky* (New York: Farrar, Straus, and Giroux, 2011); and David Halle and Elisabeth Tiso, *New York's New Edge: Contemporary Art, the High Line, and Urban Megaprojects on the Far West Side* (Chicago: Chicago University Press, 2014).

3. Harvey Cox, *The Secular City: Secularization and Urbanization in Theological Perspective* (New York: Macmillan, 1965); William H. Whyte, *The Social Life of Small Urban Spaces* (Washington, D.C.: Conservation Preservation, 1980); Richard Sennet, *The Conscience of the Eye: The Design and Social Life of Cities* (New York: Knopf, 1990); Karen Tei Yamashita, *Tropic of Orange: A Novel* (Minneapolis: Coffee House Press, 1997); and Elijah Anderson, *The Cosmopolitan Canopy: Race and Civility in Everyday Life* (New York: Norton, 2011).

4. Amin, *Land of Strangers*, 33.

5. AbdouMaliq Simone, *For the City Yet to Come: Changing African Life in Four Cities* (Durham, N.C.: Duke University Press, 2004), 5.

6. Jane Jacobs, "Introduction: Dickens as Seer," in Charles Dickens, *Hard Times* (1854; New York: Modern Library, 2001), xiii, xii. Jacobs's introductory essay also appeared in the *New York Review*; see Jane Jacobs, "Charles Dickens, Seer," *New York Review*, July 19, 2001, 29–30.

7. Jacobs, "Dickens as Seer," xiv.
8. Charles Dickens, *Hard Times* (1854; New York: Modern Library, 2001), 27, 26–27.
9. Jacobs, "Dickens as Seer," xv.
10. Ibid., xix.
11. Dickens, *Hard Times*, 181.
12. Jacobs, *Death and Life*, 68.
13. Ibid., 56.
14. Dickens, *Hard Times*, 26.
15. Jacobs, "Dickens the Seer," xiii.
16. Simone, *City Life from Jakarta to Dakar*, 24.

INDEX

Abolitionism, 32–33, 65
Abrams, Charles, 128
Addams, Jane: "A New Impulse to an Old Gospel," 16; Nineteenth Ward, Chicago, 15–16; Settlement Movement, 9, 15–22, 33–34, 36–37; sociology, 27
Adelphi Theatre, 61, 68
Africa, 159
African Americans: Chicago, 15, 28, 115; displacement by urban renewal, 99–100; East Harlem, 137; Harlem, 63–65; New York, 28, 38–40; Philadelphia, 17, 25–33; and Settlement Movement, 19–20, 28, 38–40, 167 n.51; sociability, 95–97, 119–20; Washington, D.C., 119
Alison, Archibald, 2
Allee, Marjorie Hill, 114–16
Allee, W. C., 102–5, 114, 120, 179 n.36
American Museum of Natural History (AMNH): Akeley Hall of African Mammals, 106, 110; "Cycle of Nutrition and Decay," 111–12; and ecology, 12, 98–99, 101–2, 106–12; Felix M. Warburg Memorial Hall, 98, 106–12, 121, 177 n.21, 178 n.27; "Life in the Soil," 107–11; 178 n.24; "An October Afternoon Near Stissing Mountain," 106–7, 111; proposed redesign of, 121–22
Amin, Ash, 13, 156
Anderson, Edgar, 117–19, 145, 147, 154
Anderson, Elijah, 156
Anderson, Sherwood, 81
Architectural Forum, 124, 125
Arent, Arthur, 10, 47, 61–70, 76
Ascher, Charles S., 55
Atlanta University, 28
Atlantic Monthly, 22

Banham, Reyner, 116
Barnes, Elizabeth, 4
Barnett, Samuel A., 24
Bauer, Catherine, 10, 44, 55, 74
Bennett, Edward H., 34
Berger, Meyer, 11, 79, 85–86, 128–29
Bilker, Charles S., 71
Blair, Hugh, 2
Bogardus, Emory, 52, 56
Bohemians, 16
Brecht, Bertolt, 63
Brooklyn: 19, 71, 75–76, 85–94
Brotherhood, 20–21
Burgess, Ernest W., 46, 49, 56
Burnham, Daniel H., 34
Busch, Niven, Jr., 79

Carberry, Edward, 62
Carson, Rachel, 12, 98, 112–14, 175 n.1, 178 n.29
Castiglia, Christopher, 27
Cayton, Horace, 96
Charities and the Commons, 20
Chicago: African Americans, 15, 28, 115; Columbian Exposition of 1893, 34; Near North Side, 52–53; Nineteenth Ward, 15–16, 22; *Plan of Chicago*, 34; South Side, 95–96; Woodlawn, 114
Chicago Commons, 23, 27
Chicago School of Sociology, 47–57, 88, 101
Church Social Union, 33
Cicio, Lillian, 73
Cincinnati Post, 62
City Planning: emergence of, 54; and urban sociology, 54–55
Clay, Grady, 116, 117
Clements, Frederic, 103, 176 n.7

College Settlement News, 20
College Settlement of Philadelphia, 16–17, 25
Conn, Steven, 2
Cooley, Charles Horton, 50–51, 56
Cooper, Anthony (Third Earl of Shaftesbury), 104–5
Cox, Harvey, 156

Dakar, 160
Darwin, Charles, 105
Death and Life of Great American Cities, The. See Jacobs, Jane
Decentralization, 77, 99–100, 120
Denison House, 21
Detroit Federal Theatre, 63
DeWitt Clinton Houses, 138–43, 149
Dickens, Charles: *Hard Times*, 156–59; *Our Mutual Friend*, 158
Di Donato, Pietro, 76
Donne, John, 104
Down, T. McKean, 98
Drake, St. Clair, 96
Dreiser, Theodore, 26
Du Bois, W. E. B.: Lincoln Settlement, 19; *The Philadelphia Negro*, 22, 29–33, 137; Settlement Movement, 9, 17–18, 22–23, 28–33, 38–39; Sociology, 28–33, 165 n.32; *The Souls of Black Folk*, 17

East Harlem, 124, 125, 135–44
East Harlem Council for Community Planning, 138–39, 143
Eaton, Isabel, 20
Ecology: aggregation, 103–4; at American Museum of Natural History, 98–99, 101–2, 106–12; and Carson, Rachel, 112–14; and Chicago School of Sociology, 101; community ecology, 99–100, 103–5, 114, 176 n.5; cooperation, 103, 105; equilibrium, 103; harmony, 118; in *Landscape*, 102, 116–23; in *New Yorker*, 98–99, 101–2, 112–14; proto-cooperation, 100, 103–4, 109–10; and social Darwinism, 101; as urbanism, 12, 101, 114–23, 145–52
Embury, Aymar, II, 122
Emerson, Alfred E., 102
Empedocles, 104
Espinas, Alfred, 105

Fair Deal, 124
Fancher, Ed, 131
Farrell, James T., 76
Federal Administration of Public Works, 71–72
Federal Theatre Project (FTP), 10, 61–70, 87, 170 n.40
Flâneur, 13
Forest Hills Gardens, 57
Fortune. See Jacobs, Jane

Gans, Herbert J., 116, 127
Gavit, John P., 23
Geddes, Patrick, 105
Gehl, Jan, 156
George Washington Houses, 137–39
Germans, 16
Gilpatric, Chadbourne, 126, 153
Godwin, Murry, 90
Gold Coast and the Slum, The (Zorbaugh), 52–53
Gold, Mike, 76
Gottmann, Jean, 116, 120
Great Depression, 43, 77, 80
Great Migration, 64, 95
Greeks, 16

Hall, Helen, 42
Harlem, 63, 96
Harriman, Margaret Case, 81
Harrison, Shelby M., 54
Hegner, Herman F., 27
Henry, O., 128
Henry Street Settlement: *A Dutchman's Farm*, 42–43; Neighborhood Playhouse, 42
High Line, 155
Himes, Chester, 95
Holden, Arthur C., 60
House, The (Allee), 114–16
Housing for the Machine Age (Perry), 56
Howells, William Dean, 26
Hull-House Maps and Papers, 28, 31, 137
Hull-House Settlement: founding, 15; as "place of exchange," 34–38; spatial dynamics, 19; Woman's Club, 36; Working People's Social Science Club, 36

Industrial City, 3–4
International Design Council, 121

Interwar City: crisis of affect, 44; transformation of, 43–44
Introduction to the Science of Sociology (Park and Burgess), 49, 51
Italians: Chicago, 15, 16; East Harlem, 137; Philadelphia, 17

Jackson, J. B., 102, 116–17, 120–21, 154
Jacobs, Jane: city planning, 126, 133–34, 138–43, 144, 148–52; consolidation of discourse of sociability, 13, 126–28, 133–35, 139–40, 152–53, 155–57; Cooper Union, 132; *Death and Life of Great American Cities, The*, 8–9, 13, 126–27, 129, 133–35, 143–44, 145–50, 152–53, 154–55, 157; DeWitt Clinton Houses, 138–43; diversity, 148; "Downtown is for People," 132–33; East Harlem, 125–26, 137–44; East Harlem Council for Community Planning Housing Committee, 138–39, 143; ecological urbanism, 127, 145–52, 184 n.34; "feeling for the public identity of people," 134–35; *Fortune*, 132; intimacy, rejection of, 133–34, 181 n.6; journalism, 127, 128–35; life sciences, 144–45; New School, 145; post-industrial city, 159; review of *Hard Times* (Dickens), 157–59; settlement movement, 127, 135–44, 183 n.24; streets, value of, 132–35, 141–43, 146, 150; "togetherness," 133–34, 154; Toronto, 150; Union Settlement, 135, 137–38; urban renewal, opposition to, 126–27, 129–31, 138–43, 148–53; *Village-Voice*, 130–32; *Vogue* sketches, 128–30; West Village, 137, 146, 149–50; West Village Committee, 149–50; West Village Houses, 149–51
Jakarta, 160
James Johnson Community Center, 138
Japanese, 115
Jews: in Brooklyn, 92–93; in Chicago, 15; in Philadelphia, 17
Johnston, Alva, 79, 80, 82, 95
Jones, Verina Morton, 39
Journalism, 77–86, 128–35
Juvenile Delinquency, 122

Kirk, William H., 124–25, 135–37, 144, 154, 184 n.33

Kropotkin, Peter, 105

Landscape, 102, 116–23, 145, 179 n.42
Larsen, Nella, 95–97
Lescaze, William, 70–71
Liebling, A. J., 11, 79, 83–85, 94, 95, 154
Lincoln Settlement, 19, 39–40
Living Newspaper, 62, 170 n.41
London, Jack, 26
Lurie, Ellen, 137–39, 144, 154
Lynch, Kevin, 116

Mailer, Norman, 131
Mantle, Burns, 62
Martin, Earl, 107
Massachusetts Abolition Society, 32
McKelway, St. Clair, 79
McKenzie, Roderick D., 56
Meily, Clarence, 20
Melodrama, 62, 65–66, 69–70
Mexicans, 115
Miller, Herbert A., 56
Mills, C. Wright, 51
Missouri Botanical Garden, 117
Mitchel, Joseph, 11, 79, 82–83, 95, 154
Moore, Dorothea, 35
Moses, Robert, 121
Mozes, Samuel R., 149
Mumford, Lewis, 44, 55, 116, 181 n.6

National Industrial Recovery Act, 61
National Science Foundation, 119
Native Son (Wright), 95–96
Neighborhood Unit, 54–60
New Deal, 46, 61–62, 68–69, 86, 94, 124, 139
New York City: Bowery, 82–83; Greenwich Village, 131; Lower East Side, 42, 59, 146–47; Lower West Side, 155; Minskyville, 80; Mount Olivet Baptist Church, 38; Rockefeller Center, 85; Sheridan Square, 81; Tuskegee Apartments, 39; Upper West Side, 82; Washington Square Park, 131
New York City Housing and Redevelopment Board, 149
New York City Housing Authority (NYCHA), 70, 90, 132, 138–43, 184 n.33
New York City Tenement House Commission, 66
New York Times, 62

New Yorker: absence of diversity in, 95; Carson, Rachel, 112–14; city journalism, 128–31; fact writing, 79, 173 n.6; "Profiles," 81–85; Prospectus for, 78–79; "A Reporter at Large," 79–81; and sociability, 11, 79–85
North, Cecil C., 48
Nostalgia, 94–95

Oliver, Edith, 175 n.1
Olmsted, Frederick Law, 1–7, 15, 34, 46, 57, 155
Olmsted, Frederick Law, Jr., 57
One-Third of a Nation (Arent), 10, 47, 61–70, 170 n.40, 172 n.54
Ovington, Mary White, 38–40, 167 n.55
Owens, Hubert B., 116

Park, Orlando, 102
Park, Robert E., 47–51, 53, 56, 64, 76, 101
Park, Thomas, 102
Parr, Albert E., 105–12, 121–23, 147, 154
Patten, William, 105
Pennsylvania Abolition Society, 32–33, 166 n.40
Perkins & Will Architects, 138–39, 142, 149
Perry, Clarence Arthur, 47, 54–61, 70, 76, 132, 170 n.36
Philadelphia, 17, 25–26, 29–32, 96
Phipps, Henry, 39
Polish, 16
Pond, Allen B., 37
Post, Langdon W., 70, 76
Prescott, Orville, 86
Principles of Animal Ecology (Allee), 102–4
Progressive Era, 17, 34, 40, 136
Public Housing, 10, 45–46, 70–74, 87, 136–43
Public Works Administration Housing Division, 61, 70–71, 75
Puerto Ricans, 115, 137, 141

Queens, 57, 59
Quicksand (Larsen), 96–97

Realism, 26–27
Reconstruction, 65, 163 n.6
Regional Survey of New York and Its Environs, 54–55, 60
Riis, Jacob, 134

Rockefeller Foundation, 126
Ross, Harold, 78–79, 98
Roth, Henry, 76
Russell Sage Foundation, 57
Russians, in Chicago, 16
Ryan, Mary P., 5

Schmidt, Karl P., 102
Scudder, Vida, 21
Second Great Migration, 99
Segregation, 16–17, 95
Sennett, Richard, 7, 133, 156
Sentimental Culture, 2
Settlement Movement: and African-Americans, 28, 167 n.51; interwar, 136; postwar, 136–37; Progressive Era, 9–10, 15–41, 136; spatial strategies, 33–41
Seventh Ward. *See* Philadelphia
Simkhovitch, Mary Kingsbury, 9, 38
Simmel, Georg, 50–51, 76
Simone, AbdouMaliq, 14, 156, 159–60
Sinclair, Upton, 26, 157
Small, Albion, 49
Smith, Adam, 2–3, 49, 104–5
Smith, Betty, 11, 75–76, 85–94, 132, 154
Smith, Harrison, 98
Sociability: consolidation of discourse of, 126–28, 133–35, 139–40, 152–53, 154–55; as "dickering," 130–32; ecological discourse of, 99–102, 105, 110–14, 116, 117–20, 122–23, 146–52; emergence of structure of, 7–9, 11, 76–78; future of discourse of, 156, 159–60; as gregariousness, 113; interracial, 95–97, 97; and *New Yorker*, 79–85; post-Jacobsian discourse of, 156; postwar settlement discourse of, 137–44; prehistory of, 156; in *A Tree Grows in Brooklyn*, 87–94
Social Gospel, 20–21
Sociology: Chicago School of, 47–57, 88, 101; and city planning, 54–55; and Settlement Movement, 27–31
Southeast Asia, 159
Spellman, Howard H., 68
Spencer, Herbert, 103
Spykman, Nicholas, 50, 168 n.14
St. Louis, 117
Starr, Ellen Gates, 15
Stowe, Harriet Beecher, 63

"A Study of George Washington Houses," 137–39
Sympathy: and Adam Smith, 2–3, 49, 104–5; as affective process, 3; and Bauer, Catherine, 44; and city planning, 54–59; consanguinity, 164 n.15; as emotional product, 4; evolution of structure of, 7, 9–10; and Frederick Law Olmsted, 2–5; inadequacy of, 8, 41; as intimacy, 10–11, 41, 45; and Mumford, Lewis, 44; New Deal discourse of, 62–70, 73–74, 97; nineteenth-century discourse of, 21, 46, 57; "public sympathy," 17, 19, 22–24, 32; settlement discourse of, 9, 17–33, 40–41, 54, 136; sociological discourse of, 49–54

Teichner, Miriam, 98
Tenements, 11–12, 15, 29, 34, 39, 42–43, 45, 47, 52, 61–69, 73–74, 76, 86–88
The Theory of Moral Sentiments (Smith, Adam), 2–3, 49, 104
Thomas, William I., 56
Thompson, John Arthur, 105
Thrasher, Frederick M., 56
Toomer, Jean, 95
Toronto, 150
A Tree Grows in Brooklyn (Smith, Betty), 11–12, 75–76, 85–94, 132
Truman, Harry S., 124
Twain, Mark, 157

Uncle Tom's Cabin (Stowe), 63, 65
Union Settlement (House) Association, 124, 135–37. *See also* Jacobs, Jane
University of Chicago, 46–47
University of Michigan, 89
Urban Renewal, 12, 46, 100, 124–25, 127, 129–31, 136, 138–43, 148–53, 181 n.3
Urbanology, 121

U.S. Housing Act of 1937, 10, 46, 61, 68–69, 74, 75–76, 95, 124
U.S. Housing Act of 1949, 95, 100, 124, 136
U.S. Housing Act of 1954, 100, 124

Village Voice, 130–32, 182 n.16
Vogue. *See* Jacobs, Jane

Wagner-Steagall Act. *See* U.S. Housing Act of 1937
Washington, D.C., 119
Watts, Richard, Jr., 66
West, Dorothy, 95
West Village Committee. *See* Jacobs, Jane
West Village Houses. *See* Jacobs, Jane
The West Village Plan for Housing, 150–51
Wharton, Edith, 26
Wheeler, William Morton, 105
White, E. B., 11, 79–80, 95, 128–29
White Flight, 99–100
White, Morton and Lucia, 9
Whyte, William H., 156
Williams, Raymond, 7
Williamsburg, 70–73, 75–76, 85–94
Williamsburg Houses, 70–73, 75–76, 87, 90, 93, 94
Williamsburg Houses: A Case History of Housing, 71, 72
Winesburg, Ohio (Anderson), 81
Wirth, Louis, 48, 50–51
Wolf, Dan, 131
Wood, Edith Elmer, 68
Wright, Richard, 95–96

Yamashita, Karen Tei, 156
Young, Iris Marion, 11

Zorbaugh, Harvey, 52–54, 56
Zucker, Mildred, 138–39

ACKNOWLEDGMENTS

The Sociable City began its life at Boston College. It is hard to imagine a more intellectually stimulating and humane place to start down the path that has led to the publication of this book. Carlo Rotella's willingness to respond to both the small and large pieces of the project, while constantly underwriting my efforts with his mantra of "good work—keep going," pushed me past every stumbling block. I benefited enormously from Chris Wilson's ability to nurture the seeds of my ideas into full bloom. And David Quigley improved the quality my argument with his unique expertise as an urban historian and with his sheer enthusiasm. These fine scholars and human beings have continued to play an important role in the evolution of this project.

I am thankful to Bob Lockhart and Casey Blake for seeing potential in the earliest versions of *The Sociable City* and for helping me to reimagine the scope of this project. Along with the two incredibly perceptive readers of the manuscript secured by Penn Press, their feedback on and vision for the book pushed me to write a much more ambitious, nuanced, and, I hope, accessible book than I would have otherwise written. I cannot think of a more fitting home for *The Sociable City* than "The Arts and Intellectual Life in Modern America" series; I am grateful to Bob and Casey for inviting me to contribute to this exciting series.

For additional advice, encouragement, and support, I have more people to thank than I can be trusted to remember. I want to thank my teachers, classmates, and friends at Boston College, including Rosemarie Bodenheimer, Amy Boesky, Mary Crane, Trevor Dodman, Paul Doherty, Gene Gorman, Jason Kerr, Catherine Michna, Patrick Moran, Nick Parker, Min Song, Robert Stanton, Chad Stutz, Laura Tanner, and Nirmal Trivedi. Although I only taught for two years at Wake Forest University, I am thankful for the support and collegiality I received from Bruce Barnhart, Anne Boyle, Dean Franco, Susan Harlan, Melissa Jenkins, and Judith Madera. I have been at Brigham Young University for the past six years and have found it to be a more stimulating and compassionate home than I could have asked for. I have received invaluable intellectual and emotional support from Frank Christianson, Jesse Crisler, Dennis Cutchins, Ed Cutler, Emron Esplin, Mary Eyring, Trent Hickman, Zach Hutchins, Brian Jackson, Jason Kerr, Keith Lawrence, Daryl Lee, Peter Leman, Nick Mason, Kristin Matthews, Rob McFarland, Brian Roberts, Jill Rudy, Jacob Rugh, Leslee Thorne-Murphy, and Matt Wickman. I am particularly grateful to Phil Snyder for the encouragement and kindness he has extended to me as chair of the Department of English. Of course, those who have supported and shaped this project are not limited to the academic institutions with which I have been affiliated. *The Sociable City* is better because of fellow urbanists such as Mike Carriere, Stephen Goldsmith, Joseph Heathcott, Jennifer Hock, Peter Laurence, Ben Looker, Tim Mennel, Max Page, Daphne Spain, and Sandy Zipp.

Although I do not remember all their names, I am extremely grateful to the archivists and librarians at the American Museum of Natural History Library, Boston Athenaeum, Boston Public Library, Columbia University Rare Book and Manuscript Library, John J. Burns Library at Boston College, La Guardia and Wagner Archive, Library Company of Philadelphia, and Rockefeller Archive Center.

During the course of researching and writing *The Sociable City*, I received generous financial support from the School of Arts and Sciences at Boston College, the William C. Archie Fund for Faculty Excellence at Wake Forest University, and the Rockefeller Foundation's Archive Center Grant-in-Aid.

Finally, I am fortunate to have had a substantial fan club of family and friends cheering me on. Thanks to Chad and Christy Rowan, Rebecca and Derek Theurer, Rachael and Tyler Rushton, Spencer Rowan, Clark and Kathleen Hinckley, Holly and Rob Lesan, Spencer and Victoria Hinckley, Ada and Chris Bowler, Joseph and Jenni Hinckley, and Lizzie and J. T. Davis. Looking forward to seeing them in varying combinations at various times has motivated me to sprint when I needed to sprint, and being with them has allowed me to relax when I needed to relax. I'm particularly grateful to my parents, Creed and Ellen Rowan, for instilling in me the work habits and self-discipline that laid the practical foundations of this project. In a family that breeds dentists, it would have been easy for me to feel I was disappointing them by choosing an alternative profession. I have never once felt that I lacked their full and enthusiastic support. Thank you.

My greatest debts are to Ann and our children Eliza, Ashton, Benjamin, Kate, Alden, and Milo. They have given this project its necessary temporal and emotional boundaries and have happily sacrificed their own plans and needs so that I could finish this project. Ann has been my biggest fan and greatest support for sixteen years. We fell in love in and with the city together. Words cannot express how grateful I am to have her as a best friend and fellow lover of cities.